Pearl Dinan.

WITHDRAWN

ESSAYS OF TODAY
[1926-1927]

ESSAYS OF TODAY
[1926 - 1927]

Selected by
Odell Shepard
and
Robert Hillyer

Student's Edition

Published *by* **The Century Co.**
NEW YORK   LONDON

154897

N D S U LIBRARY
FARGO N D

Copyright, 1928, by
THE CENTURY CO.

First printing March 1928

238

PS
688
S45
1926-27

PRINTED IN U. S. A.

FOREWORD

The modern periodical has provided a swift medium for social commentary. In the form of essays or articles, this reaches a very much larger public than the pamphlets and volumes of our ancestors; furthermore, it reaches the public before the problem under consideration has become stale. These favorable conditions have stimulated the production of social criticism. The polite essay is a rarity, the travel sketch is by no means as popular as it was a while ago, but the article dealing with existing conditions is eagerly sought by editors and eagerly read.

Today America is in an extremely introspective mood. We delight in examining ourselves—possibly a late substitution for the old Puritan habit of examining one's conscience—and even in offering ourselves for examination by foreigners. I sometimes think we are the more pleased when the verdict is unfavorable. Moreover, we are interested, though not quite so much, in examining the events and figures of the past, setting them in a new light, generally an unheroic light, that we may see them as they were.

Is there not, perhaps, a subtle connection between our self-consciousness and our absorption with those who have gone before? I believe it quite probable that the popularity of realistic biography is another proof that misery loves company. Our world is sceptical of the tissue it has woven around itself. It is dissatisfied. After examination, it records a number of minor ills which, one way or another, go back to the basic ill of the century: the lack of adjustment to new industrial conditions. This difficulty involves our entire civilization; few would dare attempt its solution, even theoretically; and therefore we are likely to find more than a little pessimism in an analysis of the situation. How natural, indeed how inevitable, that we should exhume the past to find evidence of similar problems which shall make our own seem not so egregiously serious, so inhumanly insoluble! To romanticize the past is to condemn the present. Let us therefore show the dead as they really were in all their weakness as well as their glory, lest, by forever thinking them happier and grander than ourselves, we despair of betterment. We would not say that modern biography holds to any such program deliberately; rather, the program is implicit in the modern biographical method.

Certainly, whatever their underlying relationship, social criticism and realistic biography engross most of our essayists. National manners, speech, education, commercialism—these, together with the personages of other times, are the favorite topics.

Nearly everyone admits the presence of grievous faults in modern civilization. It has become the essayists' task, if not to suggest a remedy, at least to point them out that a remedy may be suggested. There are several disadvantages to this preoccupation with problems, similar to the disadvantages of the problem novel which flourished two decades ago. In the first place, we find a tendency toward purely destructive comment. Anyone who has come into contact with a part of our industrial society feels moved to point out the exact shortcomings of the whole. Secondly, although few will miss the vanishing travel sketch, the disappearance of the polite or moral essay many will deplore. And lastly, the consideration of so many problems which cannot be—or we hope they cannot be—

eternal, has removed from the typical essay the more lofty, thoughtful, or philosophical elements which made perdurable the writings of the older essayists.

We may balance against these disadvantages, several conspicuous virtues of the modern article. We have already remarked on the swiftness with which the reading public is informed of weaknesses in the social fabric—a process which becomes a mild propaganda toward improvement. Again, we are in a period of transition; we are "in stays," when a gust from the right quarter may put us on our proper course. It must also be said in favor of the modern essayist that, in contrast to his journalistic cousin, he is wonderfully unprejudiced in an era of violent feelings. We note that the disadvantages we pointed out as applying to this sort of writing in general, do not apply to the superior examples of it.

The new biography, too, shows general faults and virtues when compared to what has gone before. Our biographers do not romanticize their subjects, but they do sometimes set the facts in such emphases as distort or even falsify them. Yet at its best the new method is lively, human, and enthusiastic.

It has been the editors' aim to choose the best as well as the most representative articles which have recently appeared in the magazines. Through no deliberate intention, they soon discovered that their material was largely drawn from the kinds of writing we have so briefly discussed: social criticism, with much attention to education —admittedly one of the weakest props to our society— and biographical sketches. And from these articles they selected those which seemed neither destructive nor biased. Adjusting their criteria, they tried to include the essays which will have some lasting interest as a comment on our times. And, of course, they welcomed the occasional deviation from the general trend which added so much to the variety of the collection.

With these soft words we deftly lead up to the expression of our gratitude to authors and publishers who so generously have given their material. Such acknowledgment is a convention, but we give voice to it with heart-felt appreciation. The way of the anthologist is hard —and justly so. He seizes on what is not his and demands that the rightful owner confirm him in the possession of it. The inclusion of an essay in this book, therefore, is testimony not only to its own merits, but also to its author's excellent good nature. We rightly reserve this most telling passage for the expression of our thanks to the collaborators who, all unknown to each other, have written this book, of which its editors are proud.

Note.—In each essay included in this volume, the original spelling has been preserved.

CONTENTS

ESSAYS OF TODAY: 1926–1927

THE AMERICAN SCENE AND CHARACTER *

A Resident Alien to Alien Critics

BY JOHN COWPER POWYS

WHEN I read certain vindictive strictures on America, wherein one philosophic observer after another analyzes human life in this country to such disparaging result, I feel a longing to make some sort of a reply. Like all "strangers within the gates" I have had my shocks and my malicious reactions; but these experiences, granting them freely their due place, have left a margin, a border-land, of something else, about which it would seem ungrateful to hold my tongue. I think that the worst things in this country are emphatic and imposing, the best things imponderable and fluid; and for that reason any adequate answer to these old-world criticisms must go to work in a subtle indirect manner and deal in nuances and intimations rather than in downright indignant retorts.

And, after all, is not this in itself the best retort that could be made? Against these point-blank accusations that the American Scene exercises a sinister influence upon human civilization, is it not the most penetrating "apologia" we could make use of, to throw into relief just those intangible things that touch most intimately the life of the spirit, indicating them here, and again there, dispersed through the whole chaotic spectacle? Yes, and

* Reprinted from *The Century Magazine* by permission of the author and of the editors.

3

not only indicating them; showing the effect of these finer fragilities, these aspects of American life that are less solid than bricks and mortar, less obvious than bridges and railroads, upon at least one old-world mind.

A "resident alien" like myself whose profession carries him into every part of the country feels as he reads books such as the recent ones by Joad and Siegfried that these attacks are much easier to make than to answer. It does not suffice to enumerate certain outstanding advantages which America possesses over all other quarters of the globe; advantages that no indictments can shake. Over these the more intangible felicities ebb and flow and waver, like clouds of midges above a powerful life-giving stream.

The solid advantages can be quickly summed up. Such is the indulgence women enjoy and their unrestricted self-expansion; such are the economic opportunities for the masses of the unprivileged; such are the endless labor-saving and health-preserving scientific inventions; such is the thinning out of those "armies of the homeless and the unfed" that poison the wells of life for all; such is the airy buoyancy and gaiety—in spite of all its devastating extremes of heat and cold—of the atmospheric climate of this continent.

Commenting upon the most obvious of these solid advantages, let me say at once that while we foreigners detect plenty of limitations to *democracy* along political and economic lines we are compelled to do unstinted honor to what it offers in the purely human and social field.

Many a rough shock at first does the educated European receive! I remember well what I felt when my leisurely patronizing tone—that peculiar class-conscious tone of Englishmen abroad—was received on all sides by amused indulgence. I remember what I felt when I was first addressed as *a man* rather than as *a gentleman*. "This *man* wants so-and so"; "Here's a *man* saying so-and-so"; "Give the *man* back his seat, honey." By degrees however as I was buffeted into accepting my essential "status quo," just Anthropos Erectus among other anthropoids, I came to recognize what a great moral advance had been made in this particular. Reconciled to being a *man,* it was more difficult to slip naturally into the rôle of being a *guy.* "This guy wants his ticket"; "Here's a guy kicking about his seat." But even this has almost come now to seem no real derogation from primitive human courtesy.

It is not only women in America who benefit by this large equality. Young people, over here, of both sexes are given an indulgence and a consideration which is an absolutely new thing upon the face of the earth. The children of Manhattan, for instance—who can forget the audacity with which they bathe in prohibited fountains and burn bonfires under the very noses of the police? Those street bonfires have always seemed to me a brave symbol of the achieved freedom of youth in this country. How the little imps dance round them! And, to my mind at least, this fire-dance of the New York children is sufficient evidence that an atmosphere exists here less disciplined by the bureaucratic "verbotens" of organized paternalism, whether imperial, or Fascist, or communist, than anywhere else in the world.

One other commentary I would like to make on these solid advantages. Is the amazing power of public opinion over here to be included among these superiorities? This public opinion in America is, it seems to me, a psychic phenomenon which cuts both ways. Led by the press, and reflected in the press, it does *sometimes* put an end to abominable evils, but more often—one has to admit it— it sets itself to hunt down and destroy that free expression of individual genius upon which the life of our race depends.

On the other hand, over against this, it must be allowed that endless "queer ones," up and down this chaotic country, can live and die in their own extraordinary by-paths and back-waters, unnoticed, unspecified, uncatalogued; persons who, on the other side, would be smoothed out and pruned and trimmed and polished by the pressure of some little group or coterie or class. The feelings of such eccentrics in America must I suppose be more flagrantly outraged, their loneliness must be more acute, than would be the case abroad; but if they do manage to put forth their blossoms, like seedling peachtrees in Middle Western dooryards, they display a strange and spontaneous quality, the beauty of original sensitiveness thrown into sharp relief against the primordial waste of the landscape.

No doubt one of the great misunderstandings about Americans is due to the "protective coloring" with which people who do not fit into the standardized verdicts of their community evade the detection of their peculiarities. In England—with the weight of his class behind him—a man can be as eccentric as he pleases. It is indeed his joy and delight to assert his idiosyncrasies. English individuality therefore protrudes itself and fortifies itself where American individuality hides itself; but you have only to scratch one of these citizens and you'll find a prickly philosopher.

But, as I have suggested, over and above these obvious benefits to humanity of the American Scene there hover a thousand nuances of delicate intimation, which in my own opinion are of far rarer, far finer significance. But one has to wander like an old-fashioned "bagman," up and down all manner of out-of-the-way quarters of this country, playing the Quaker and waiting patiently upon the Spirit, to catch these more subtle flavors of the confused hurly-burly.

How, for instance, can the ways of such a continent be as inimical as these critics hint to the nobler motions of the soul when a man can wake up as I have done on many a Sunday morning in the most flagrant of all American cities, New York itself, and listen to the silence in the cool-blowing summer air, while the wind rustles the ailantus leaves at the window, lifting them up and letting them fall like undulating sea-weed in a vast green rock-pool? Sunday mornings in America are indeed halcyon seas of luxurious quiescence to anyone wakeful enough to be conscious of their peace. There is no deeper calm to be found in the depths of the ocean, in the heart of the desert. It is a psychic calm, produced by the relaxation of the quivering nerves of the most electric of all peoples. Such nerves when they do relax, relax to a level of abysmal somnolence unparalleled elsewhere, and out of these "fields of sleep" if the cool wind still blows what friendly sounds reach the ear! The echoing hoofs of the milkmen's horses, the siren-calls from the river, bringing rope smells and tar smells and the splash of waves at port-holes and the glittering, rocking sun-path to the horizon's rim, the twitter of sparrows, the murmur of pigeons—all these sounds as they come to us here, no less than anywhere else on the earth's surface, have the friendliness of those faint race-memories that Wordsworth loved to note as they came and went.

But it is the silence itself on these Sunday mornings rather than any sound, rather even than the mass bell from St. Joseph's or the bell-buoy in the river, that seems to be the sleep of the great, taut, tense city, relaxed at last, taking her fill of "deep and liquid rest, forgetful of all ill." That wave-washed mountain of delicate towers, what may be its multitudinous, its Atlantean dream? Millions of sleepers, in apartment houses, in tenement houses, in old doomed Dutch houses, under the spans of iron bridges, under the pillars of iron rails, lie horizontal and unconscious now, indrawn into the great cosmic diastole. Over it all the slippery sea-gulls sway and slide and are suspended. Over it all the white clouds journey, intent on voyages unknown to thought; over it all shiver those invisible air-waves that rise and fall forever through space, linking life to the secret causes of life.

I repeat once more—the essential spirit of America, its real contribution to civilization, is a psychic quality intimately associated with the geography of the continent, and far more involved with mystic nuances of feeling than with the making of Arrow Collars, Chevrolets, caskets, ploughshares, chewing-gum, Eastman Kodaks, dynamite and steel-rails.

Factories enough, industries enough, the traveler sees, from the old Dutch villages of New York State, through the small towns lost in the rich dark loam-lands of the Middle West, to the inhuman fastnesses of the Rocky Mountains; but these Mills of Progress no more really dominate human character in these places—its drifting resilience, its humorous patience—than they dominate the cosmogonic landscape which engulfs them.

For between this landscape and this character there has grown up a psychic reciprocity older than any science. What those old Indians breathed in from the earth-spirits of this land—an evasive sensitiveness in womankind, a rooted withdrawnness in mankind—can still supply its fluidity and its reserve to the modern mind that waits upon its spirit.

Americans themselves, isolated in particular portions of their native land, are ready enough to defend their predilection for New England, or the Far West, or the Old South; but what a wanderer like myself cannot help noticing is that the quality I speak of can be found in a measure everywhere you go, found in the most diverse places, be they prairie or desert, be they pastoral uplands or the littered debris of city environs.

The thing I am thinking of, with its blending of human and natural elements is what Walt Whitman had in mind when he used the term "calamus-root" to express the spirit of his democracy of the wild, of his camaraderie of the waste.

I have caught this "genius loci" of America, so furtive, so shy, many times off-guard and exposed. I have caught it in the upper reaches of the Hudson, when islands of green reeds and greener willows, backwaters of blue coolness and bluer irises, have broken through the mists of dawn.

I have caught it with a pang of capricious nostalgia, even in New York itself, when the name "Marion, Ohio," upon a crane-shovel has brought in a flash to my mind that Arcadian perspective of names, Bellefontaine, Greencastle, Terre Haute, leading out of the metallic labyrinth of Manhattan, like the milestones of a highroad, into solitudes of frame-houses, picket-fences, cows, chickens and red barns of the Middle West!

I have caught it above the muddy banks of the Mississippi where the city of St. Louis plants itself with four-square solidity, the richly gathered masses of the separate buildings rolling up, mounting up together ledge upon ledge, tier upon tier, as if enclosed, like the cities of old, by walls and ramparts—now seen all confusedly and vaguely imminent, through its own atmosphere of heavy smoke, penetrating all its interstices, the dusky pall of its identity!

I have always felt that there was something "rich and strange" and dimly formidable about St. Louis; and so apparently did the crowds at Le Bourget! Has not this city turned out to be the palpable fulfilment of that weird prophecy of Leonardo, quoted by Paul Valéry? "The great bird will take its first flight on the back of its great swan, filling the universe with stupor" and bringing "gloria eterna al nido dove nacque"—"eternal glory to the nest where it was born"!

What aplomb, full of old long sun-baked siestas of forgotten Congo dreaming, do those St. Louis negroes show, sprawling on creaking balconies, hunched up on rusty fire-escapes—great savage athletic bodies in flimsy modern clothes but with bare black feet, and women whose immense ebony faces seem to expand into the inhuman contours of idols between their jangling gilded ear-rings!

That wide steep declivity of slippery cobblestones descending to the water's edge—cobblestones not green with weeds or brown with mud, but of a forlorn phantasmal grey worthy of the very wharf of Lethe!

And those vast outlandish river-boats, whose winter quiescence has all the indescribable melancholy that belongs to old deserted wood-work, rain-soaked and sunbleached—the timber-life fled out of it and a sinister wraith-life entered into it instead!

All these things have something about them that passes from Nature to Humanity; and back again from Humanity to Nature.

I recollect finding myself once in Fargo, North Dakota, at a time when the great plains would naturally have been constricted under frozen snow. In place of this, long before her time, a strange uprising of the Spring Goddess had occurred. The atmosphere was full of a power that was like the presence of invisible flowing sap. The languid noon-winds seemed to carry on their breasts clouds of such impregnated balminess that one felt as though there were green shoots up there in the air.

I recollect skipping several paces down one of those long "dirt" roads in sheer childish happiness. Nor was this feeling lessened when, in the very lumber-yard of the freight-station I came upon the stone image of some early Viking settler, mildly receptive to that relaxing warmth, and close to this monument an old Dakotan who, himself like some decrepit Eric the Red, uttered the words: "I feels growth abroad, mister!"

Easy enough is it to pour forth pseudo-cultured abuse upon the thousands of prairie-lost "Main Streets" between Kansas City and Omaha. For civilization to "burn with a hard gem-like flame" it must undoubtedly have its roots in the deep past and its wavering decisions at some vital "parting of the ways"; but there are other moods, other conscious moments, other visions of the world which have also their human value. Life goes on, whether a man associates or does not associate his ploughing and sowing, his business and barter, his loves and his frustrations, with the Greeks and the Romans, with the theology of the *middle ages,* with the philosophy of the Renaissance! Grant that the intellectual continuity of the ages *is* broken, there is a primitive poetry of life, simple and natural, like the life of the aboriginals themselves, where the smoke rises from unlettered hearths and the corn is cooked and eaten on platters virginal of all esthetics. Men's thoughts can sink into themselves with a more earthy taciturnity, women's feelings can gather an am-

pler largeness, a freer grandeur, where they are not teased
and fretted by the insidious pressure of these layers upon
layers, strata upon strata, of old sophistries.

And in this life of bed-rock simplicity one psychic
quality profoundly essential to all great vision is not lacking, and that is a limitless *intellectual humility*. I have
always regarded "humility" as the most creative inheritance of spiritual Christian culture; and when I think of
the banked-up conceit of intelligent Europeans, so opaque
to the free flow of new ideas, I cannot help recognizing
that in the possession of this quality alone Americans release a hope of immense moment, not only for their own
future but for that of other races as well.

When I have sometimes wandered at night-fall past
the huge brazen boots and brazen trousers, past that tragically woeful countenance, of the Barnard statue of Lincoln in Cincinnati, I have known well enough that I was
face to face with a spiritual emanation from all these
dusty highways and "board-walk" hamlets such as was a
sufficient answer to the sophisticated accusations of the
old world. But not an obvious answer! An answer rather,
dependent upon what one has observed, round the Franklin stove in many a remote Arkansas hostelry, in many a
way-side Missouri station. Something coming and going
on these sad prairie-winds, something advancing and re-
treating with these drenching rains and burning suns, a
breath, a rumor, a movement in the air, a stir in the grass,
a whisper over the wooded fences, a wild-goose cry above
the tethered buggies in the meager squares, indicates to
one old-world mind at least that the human spirit can find
grist for its mill in a land where "Ben Hur" represents
romance and the Bible represents philosophy!

And the value of what might be called the American
"quota" to the psychic ascent of the human race springs

from the present situation. For here are all those "me-chanical improvements" with regard to the effect of which on human character sages are so suspicious. But here between these vast horizons and these staggering inventions the denizens of these multitudinous little country towns continue to live out their lives in almost Biblical simplicity. In such places there are no class divisions, no sophisticated vices. A spontaneous humanism such as would have delighted the soul of Rousseau himself answers to the clearness and freshness of the free-blowing airs. Hard-worked men and women seem to have energy enough left for an active friendliness such as makes the ingrown suspiciousness of old-world countrysides seem mean and bitter. It must be of this sort of primordial simplicity combined with hygienic science that Americans think, when in Berlin or Paris or Rome they cry aloud for their "home-town."

But if they are women perhaps they have an even more definite homesickness. For the feminine influence in American culture is quite a new thing in the world, so it seems to me, and a thing of extraordinary interest. The truth is that the *timbre* of masculine activities in this vast country is still attuned to the pioneer note; so that through all their politics and business and camaraderie there is that rough, untidy, adventurous casualness which men naturally assume when left to themselves.

And, except among professional students, the tougher "he-men" as they call them—the word itself is suggestive of what I am describing—are content to leave culture pretty much in the hands of their "women-folks." The result of this seems to be that all over this country the feminine attitude to life has invaded fiction and poetry and the decorative arts to an extent unparalleled in human history. And this feminine attitude is far less cramped and cynical and flippant than the attitude of a great deal of European literature. Not that it is in the least sentimental or banal. The poetry of Edna St. Vincent Millay, of Elinor Wylie, of Lola Ridge, holds its own with the best on the other side; while the fiction of Elizabeth Madox Roberts, Martha Ostenso, Zona Gale, Ellen Glasgow, drives straight deep honest furrows through the heart of many a mysterious field of human feeling quite remote from the experiences of the old world.

The casualness, the litter, the toughness, the pioneer chaoticism of the "he-man's" America finds its esthetic expression in Theodore Dreiser's work. But there is also a new group of "super-sophisticates," mostly young men, poets and critics, like E. E. Cummings and Edmund Wilson, who seem to combine the psychic imagination of this vast fluctuating crowd of women with a sharp witty rigorous attempt to turn into a kind of mocking beauty those aspects of modern American life such as radio, jazz, prize-fighting, aëroplanes, circuses, futurist patterns of steel and iron, streams of consciousness, "claviluxes" of color, which poise themselves like a phantasmagoric mist of acrobatic shapes, on a high stretched tight-rope, raised aloft above both masculine activity and feminine emotion.

This silly parrot-cry about Americans' love of money ought to be answered; and the way I shall answer it will seem to many Europeans a monstrous paradox in the face of the aggressive possessiveness and the resonant social "climbing" of the very rich and the *nouveaux riches* in this country. But it must be remembered that the vast majority of Americans are neither very rich nor *nouveaux riches;* any more than they are class-conscious "proletarians." They are that completely new thing in the history of our race, which one can only simply call American and leave it at that. Struggle for money they certainly do—

day in day out—but it is not, as it is with us Europeans,
for the sake of the palpable benefits that money brings
that they make it so fast and furiously. We Europeans
treasure it because it brings social prestige, attractive possessions, and above all leisure. But the American pursues
money for the sake of one of the craziest, vaguest, fan-
tasticalest *ideas* that has ever entered a rational brain.
He pursues it for the sake of what might be called
"power-in-the-abstract," an idealistic, subjective, cerebral
thing; a dream in fact without substance, without habi-
tation, an "airy nothing," a floating will-o-the-wisp!

This is why Americans who are making money leave
their landscape, their houses, their streets, their gardens,
their very automobiles, so littered, untidy and ramshackle.
They are pursuing something that is a fantastic ideal.
And how is this ideal of the average small-town citizen
to be metaphysically defined? I suspect that if we really
could get to the essence of it, this tedious European tag
about the Almighty Dollar would be proved the fallacy
it is.

Well! Is not this "power-in-the-abstract" something
parallel to the quests for intellectual truth, for esthetic
beauty, for sensual pleasure as we know them in the old
world? Average Americans are as completely devoid of
any epicurean "art of life" as were the monks of the
Thebaid! They have no taste for these things, no interest
in them. Gourmands, virtuosos in meat and drink, hardly
exist in America. Still less are Americans misers. What
money represents to them is something thinner than a
ghost, less ponderable than a cloud. It is not even power
in the European sense of that word that they are after
—not power, that is to say, over people, over things, over
the destinies of nations. It is, as it were, the Platonic idea
of power—*power for its own sake,* or if you will, the

diffused potentiality of power; the sense of being in a position to experience all human experiences; to give every form of privilege, every form of knowledge, every form of adventure, what they would call the "once over." It is in pursuit of this intangible Quest that, like so many standardized Don Quixotes they "post over land and sea," travelling—often with their whole families— not only from Salisbury Cathedral to the Parthenon, but from Mobile to Omaha and from Omaha to Detroit; while, for all their fantastic ideal of being *au courant* with every level of human *savoir-faire* from Dan to Beersheba, they leave their littered country and return to their littered country with no more palpable possession "added unto them" than as if some airy mirage, some Fata Morgana, had been luring them on.

For, deep down, out of sight of the vision of any European critic, there emerges from the subconsciousness of millions of quiet Americans a strange and mystic restlessness. There is quizzical humor about this restlessness. It is not discontented or morbid. But it is at the extreme opposite pole from anything materialistic or self-satisfied. It is a sort of psychic answer to some drifting whisper from the cosmos itself—flowing in from the unknown— prophesying incredible happenings. It is an abandonment, at once proud and humble, to some occult pressure in the air whirling up from the immense untamed landscape like a spiritual typhoon, a pillar of smoke by day and of fire by night, tornadoing forward in vast windy spirals towards the Uncreated.

What these European critics fail to discern are not only the Lares and Penates of cities as different from one another as New Orleans, Indianapolis, and San Francisco, giving each of them its own secret "genius," but the projected auras of the mass of isolated villages stretching from coast to coast. In these frost-bitten, sun-baked out-posts of Progress, there exist, between the "false-fronts" of the ramshackle "stores" and the boarded "sidewalks," quaint indurated characters whose crusty humors, un-revealed to a Sinclair Lewis, would still delight the soul of a Laurence Sterne or a Charles Lamb. The visitor from England or France, who knows such people at home, naturally sees nothing of them in hotels and Pullman-cars, and he returns to write his indictment of America from his impression of a handful of big buildings that could be hidden in one little fold of the Rocky Mountains or lost behind sand-hills in the smallest of Arizona ranches!

But the supreme mistake made by the European psy-chologist in summing up the American character is the mistake of assuming that the superficial braggadocio of this polyglot people is anything but skin-deep. In one gen-eration from his incoming a strange new reserve estab-lishes itself in the nature of an immigrant; a reserve that underlies all his *brio* and all his effusive slang. This is the primitive reserve of America. This is the mood of the high cheek-bones and caustic lips of the old aboriginals. And it is a reserve that is totally concealed from the "re-served" Englishman and the ironic Frenchman—con-cealed by the engaging candor and oratorical pedantry of the men who hide it! Sometimes I dream that it is a reserve concealed even from its own possessors. But, such as it is, it shares its secret with the astounding natural features of the land that evokes it. If American *culture* has a vaporous fluidity which it derives from its emancipated womanhood, American *character* has a rooted withdrawn-ness which it derives from its over-worked manhood.

Whatever may be felt about a civilization that combines such elements, the present writer cannot conceal his premonition that, in Walt Whitman's quaint and characteristic jargon, "divine things well-enveloped" are likely to be its issue.

SPEECH, COMMON AND PREFERRED *

Word-Manufacture in the United States

By Thomas L. Masson

It is undeniable that as our environment and our material equipment change, with the material progress of the world, we must create unceasingly new terms with which to express ourselves. Unabridged dictionaries, which formerly plumed themselves upon their importance in carrying about 100,000 words, now grow apologetic with only 450,000. Any scientific jargon, such as psychoanalysis, electricity, or biology, which cannot boast of its thousands of words, is a mere straggler behind the great army.

In the opening words of his essay "On Expression," John Galsworthy, who in 1924 was president of the English Association, remarks, "The soul of good expression is an unexpectedness, which, still, keeps to the mark of meaning, and does not betray truth." This power comes only through constant practice, constant study of the meaning of words, constant tracing of individual words back to their sources.

We are all the victims of vicious and unwholesome conditions which make it unfair to hold up a single individual as a bad example. These conditions are the outgrowth of expansion in printing, hurry, economic pressure, and the confusion in thought that comes from the enor-

* Reprinted from *The Century Magazine* by permission of the author and of the editors.

mous increase in words. Even as I write I am aware of
as much guilt as any one. But it will be a great step on
the road to recovery when teacher and pupil alike admit
their common fault, and work together for the right word,
for simpler and more accurate terms.

As far as the profession of writing is concerned, it requires a strong character to keep rehearsing one's words
all the time, and to do this while one is selling one's
wares at the highest rate. The English writers undoubtedly do this better than we do, because of their traditions,
grounded in the classics, and because their audience is
more homogeneous. As a typical instance of our own
shortcoming, I know a young American who attempted
years ago to make a living by writing. He had a fairly
good common-school education, and wrote with much
care. He failed, and his failure made him even more careful. He still failed, until one day his wife said to him,
"Why not write as you talk?"

Now it chanced that in his daily life he was what is
termed in the American language a regular guy. He mingled with all sorts and conditions of people, particularly
with sporting characters. And so, without more ado, he
sat down and wrote a story in the lingo that he knew.
He wrote what he heard, recreating it for his purpose by
a spontaneous talent which, up to that time, had been
dormant. His story was immediately successful. This
young man—now advancing to middle age—makes a
very large income, and if any philologist, burning with
word-zeal, should go to him and ask him to learn his
mother-tongue in its purity, he might blush with shame,
but fearing the loss of his bread and butter, he would continue to "carry on" in his own manner.

If now we contrast this American writer with, say,
Mr. Galsworthy, we shall see at once that Galsworthy

does not hesitate to write as he listens. Take any of his novels, and he reproduces the slang, the characteristic utterances of his period, just as all great novelists have done. But side by side with this, he is constantly rehearsing his words. He grooms his technic as if it were a thoroughbred. He is *en famille* with other writers.

On this side of the water, we have, quite naturally, writers who are equally painstaking. We have them, although some of our best writers, I am afraid, do not study their vocabularies. We can trace this defect—and it is a national defect—back to the public and private schools and universities. There is no method of teaching English practised in America at present—judging from results—that is worth a whoop. Is the English system any better? It would seem so.

No one is more keenly aware of this defect than are many of our own leading educators. Of course words must be classified, grammar must be taught, and certain principles established. If our leading educators have leaned too far in the direction of formalism and have been hoist with their own petard, it would be wrong to criticize them too severely, for almost invariably it happens that they know their failings better than we know them and are secretly trying to correct them while keeping up a brave front before the world.

For years the best among our educators have undoubtedly been trying to extricate our system of teaching English from the deadening influence of over-refinement, from the fatal tendency to stifle the minds of pupils with a mass of useless definitions, just as our lawmakers stifle us with an ever increasing number of laws; the passion for system grows by what it feeds on.

Our decadent tendency to run out into definitions is universal and deep-seated. We see it in science, in theology, in philosophy. It takes a man of very strong character to become a grammarian and not lose his soul. The reason lies in the fact that we never can fasten on any word a lasting identity.

When we try to group all our words into eight parts of speech, we have started on the road to Babel. The old grammars declared that a noun was the name of a person, place, or thing. That was correct for a person or a place, but when it came to things, the grammarian had to explain that a thing might be an abstract idea, such as love, or duty—something you could not see. Then again, the nouns had a habit of slipping away from their scholastic moorings and becoming almost anything else. The grammarians then thought that by giving a new name to the relationship of any two or three words they could develop in the young a renewed interest in language. Fancy that for intelligence! Putting salt on the tails of young eagles is child's play compared with it. Human beings in their search for expression are hideously reckless and wholly irresponsible. They will grab up any word or set of words to convey their meaning, with complete disregard for grammatical forms. A writer who has what we may term the feel of life and experience in writing does only what all human beings do, except that he does it better because he practises more.

A single example will be enough to show my meaning. In a screen version of Miss Edna Ferber's story, "Classified," the hero, a "mongrel" car-driver, admonishes the heroine, a flapper with a soul, to "cut out the eye-chatter." Here is a compound word coined to make a certain character alive. In this instance, both "eye" and "chatter" are nouns, and combined by Miss Ferber, they thus appear to be united into a common noun. Yet is this so? Don't they merely do their bit by helping to describe the kind of a girl she is, and therefore take on the quality of an adjective? It is interesting, by the way, to note that the word chatter is mentioned only once in the Bible; Isaiah 38 : 14 : "Like a crane or a swallow, so did I chatter." And Miss Ferber was writing only as Homer wrote, when he called Apollo the far-darter, Zeus the cloud-gatherer, Hera the ox-eyed queen, or ushered in the fair-tressed Demeter.

So it is with all words. At any instant they may change their form. An adjective may become a noun; a noun may become an adjective. At one time we were accustomed to react. Now everybody experiences a reaction. At one time region was an honest noun. Now we have regional advertising. A word is like a human being. It is likely at any moment to be anything that its sponsor wants it to be. A film is a noun. To film is not a noun. This tendency, in some cases very proper and highly useful, and in others deplorable, has undoubtedly been encouraged by those hidden magicians, the makers of newspaper head-lines. In a head-line, which is limited to a definite space, there may not be room for John Smith to commit suicide; but he may suicide. I suppose that the head-line "Lauds Wilson" appears a thousand times in this country the morning after any anniversary of the birth of Woodrow Wilson. A prohibitionist becomes a dry, and a real-estate man a realtor.

In this same story of Miss Ferber's, the mother, who is made to reveal an innate domesticity, is much distressed because her pretty daughter insists on referring to their home as "a joint." In desperation, the mother finally exclaims, "I won't have you call this dump a joint."

The word dump in American life is highly significant. Who was the wise man who defined patriotism as territorial prejudice? Here, in dump, we have that contempt for environment which comes from changing material conditions. It is the outward and visible word-sign of an inward spiritual restlessness. The plain people, who scorn expletives, constantly drag up words out of their inner consciousness which reveal their spiritual limitations. Any man you meet in the crowd, if he has occasion to address you, will call you "brother." In apparent contrast to this, but really due to the same cause, we have Pullman car porters meeting and formally protesting against being called "George," this common name offending their dignity. Nothing in the life of young people can take the place of a cultured home. Is it not plain that when Miss Ferber's characters are made to use the words dump and joint as applied to their lodging-place, they are unconsciously expressing their own lack? And is it not plain that if we are to purify our language we must purify our life?

Before a specific remedy can be suggested, however, for the undoubted slovenliness which marks so much of our writing and for the faulty teaching in our public schools, some brief reference should be made to what has already been done to correct our faults. Without doubt, three of the most useful and practical philologists in this country are H. L. Mencken, editor and critic at large, George Philip Krapp, author of "The English Language in America," and Frank H. Vizetelly, managing editor of "The New Standard Dictionary." Mr. Mencken first published his own book, "The American Language," in 1918. It was followed by two editions, each with notable revisions, the third issued in one volume. The merit of this work it would be difficult to exaggerate. It seems to me unfortunate that Mr. Mencken's reputation as an iconoclast should so overcast our sense of his value as a practical philologist. In ability and penetration his book exceeds anything else we have except Professor Krapp's more recent volumes. Both books should be in the hands of every American who wishes to understand the difficulties of the problem. Professor Vizetelly's works on "Errors in English," "Idioms and Idiomatic Phrases," and "Essentials of English Speech and Literature" are more broadly popular than the others, but all are useful desk companions, and, to any one interested in getting on intimate terms with living words, fascinating reading.

A more recent attempt to arouse the great public to our language and speech is contained in a volume of "Academy Papers." These papers are a reprint of lectures delivered before the American Academy of Arts and Letters by some of its literary members, including Paul Elmer More, William Milligan Sloane, William Crary Brownell, Brander Matthews, Paul Shorey, and Henry van Dyke. It shows quite clearly the futility of the super-cultured when it attempts to define that which is as broad as life and not to be confined within the narrow limits of the thing we have come to call "highbrow."

As the right of free speech is guaranteed by the Constitution, is it not clear that the professional critic, no matter how much culture he may have absorbed, cannot by comment or edict stop people from using the words they want to use? What is pure English or pure American anyway, if it is not what we make of it of our own free will, and this based on our purity of thought? And who is to determine this but ourselves? Not long ago I was asked to read and criticize a story by one of our most successful writers of fiction. In the space of about ten magazine pages this man had one of his characters "gesture" no less than five times. I pointed out to him that the word gesture was what my old school-teacher used to call a crutch word. It revealed the pathetic fact that the writer had not first created in his mind a living character, but only a Robot, manufactured from the assembled parts of a vocabulary which had become vulgarized. Most writers have their own familiar words, and it is not a curse on them if they have; but no really wise writer who hopes to grow will use expressions borrowed from others. I suppose that ten or twelve years ago one story in every four or five had a young gentleman in it who "flicked the ash from his cigarette." Now, thanks to the woman who is addicted to smoking, we have an even more frequent variant, a female character who flicks the ash from her cigarette.

As for favorite words, Mr. Mencken himself delights in "peasantry" as applied to the American moron, and as a relief falls back on "yokel." I think it was H. G. Wells who first originated the inverted verb as a beginning word to a sentence, which was followed in the motion-pictures by such an avalanche of came-the-dawns.

A number of British correspondents have amused themselves by making lists of favorite words of prominent authors. Wordsworth's favorite was solitary. Gibbon had a fondness for elegant, salutary, artful; and Mr. Chesterton is accused of important and uproarious. Dean Inge of St. Paul's not so long ago referred to this generation as spoon-fed, and this word is now creeping into use as a medium for ironical observation. Some years ago an American writer picked up meticulous, and thereafter it became the fashion. Since then scarcely a week has gone by in which this word has not been used by some one of us. As Sir Henry Hadow has pointed out, the expression "meticulous accuracy" is used as if the adjective had something to do with exact measuring, whereas it is in this respect meaningless. It comes from a Latin word meaning timorous or timid. Similarly our fiction-writers have for long delighted in intrigue, their characters becoming intrigued so persistently as to make us feel like throwing the book into the first filling-station we come to.

Mr. Adolph Ochs, owner of the "New York Times," in a speech before the teachers of journalism and the Association of American Schools and Departments of Journalism, said:

"Although we are very much interested in schools of journalism, we do not yet believe that the young men who come out of these schools are quite fit to come into our office and tell us how to run it. We like to know, however, that when they do come, they bring with them the ability to write good English."

That is true, yet on the same morning this speech was delivered, in a single editorial in the "New York Times," occurs irked (the Democrats in Congress are feeling irked), "let it be said," "showed a welcome access," "along the lines," "the strategic time," "it may be noted," and other literary "tags."

The word outstanding is now a great favorite. Mr. Edwin Markham refers to "one of the outstanding books of the season."

In defense of clichés, it is only fair to quote from Havelock Ellis in "The Dance of Life." After defining them, "We mean thereby the use of old stereotyped phrases—Goethe called them 'stamped' or *gestempelt*—to save the trouble of making a new living phrase to suit our meaning," he goes on:

"Yet the warning against *clichés* is vain. The good writer, by the very fact that he is alive and craves speech that is vivid, as *clichés* never are, instinctively avoids their excessive use, while the nervous and bad writer, in his tremulous anxiety to avoid these tabooed *clichés*, falls into the most deplorable habits, like the late Mr. Robert Ross, who at one time was so anxious to avoid *clichés* that he acquired the habit of using them in an inverted form and wrote a prose that made one feel like walking on sharp flints. . . . As a matter of fact it is impossible to avoid the use of *clichés* and counters in speech, and if it were possible the results would be in the highest degree tedious and painful."

I differ. The evidence is against Havelock Ellis. One may read any of the great English writers, Donne, Newman, Macaulay, Balfour, and while there is much that is dreary, their sentences do not show the hasty construction from which clichés are born.

This recalls the unfortunate case of Quiller-Couch, so often referred to by the purists, who wrote a book "On the Art of Writing" in which one chapter entitled "On Jargon" was—to the delight of his critics—itself full of jargon. It was in this chapter that he used the phrase "in our midst," which Charles A. Dana, the learned editor of the old "New York Sun," held up to such bitter scorn years ago. And to cap the climax, as Quiller-Couch might have put it, he concludes his "Jargon" with this telling phrase: "For the style is the man, and where a man's treasure is there is his heart, and his brain, and his writing, *will be also.*" The italics are mine.

If we cannot depend on the philologist, the grammarian, the schoolman, or the professional highbrow to solve for us the problem of purer speech, what are we to do?

Mr. Bernard Shaw has said that if there were no churches a right religion would spring up spontaneously from the combined needs of mankind. Similarly, if grammar were abolished, I am inclined to think we should be in better case. We should then begin to study our basic words on their own account; we should treat them with the respect due to their ancient lineage.

Indeed the improvements we hope for in our spoken and written word will not come from venerable and exclusive gentlemen in frock-coats who gather in select companies and discourse on diction, but they will come from two sources: from the main body of the people on the one hand, and from the small body of creative writers on the other hand.

How little do we understand that the universal tendency to imitate is what determines so largely the fashions of this world, not only in actions but in our thoughts! Sarah Bernhardt wore elbow-gloves to conceal her skinny arms, and elbow-gloves became the style. During the war the soft hat came in and the silk hat went out; then the word high-hatted was used to show the contempt that some people express for their fellows. The soft hat was further influenced by the motion-picture actor, W. S. Hart, whose hat was straight-brimmed, so that straight brims became not *the* style, but style as far as Mr. Hart was able to influence his period. The Prince of Wales wears his hat on the side of his head and is imitated by an army of young men. His bowler, circling the globe, leaves its progeny behind. Mr. George Harvey, years ago, wore the first tortoise-shell spectacles, and in a few years tortoise-shell Americans became an object of derision for Punch, the whole process resulting in a Harold Lloyd. Thus, as we say, it is to laugh! A generation ago Charles Dana Gibson created the Gibson girl, and every American female, no matter how lowly, tried to look like one. And now is it too much to say that every American girl who womanizes (why not *womanize?*) an office and delights us with her "colorful" (another fashionable word) personality, tries her "darnedest" to look a composite picture of Mae Murray, Gloria Swanson, Norma Talmadge, and Pola Negri, with, say, a dash of the Gishes.

It is a mistake, therefore, to assume that words spring full-blown from the soil; that is to say, from the mass of people. We shall find on examination that even one dialect itself is not a faithful copy of the speech of the people, but has been created by the mind of the writer, allowing of course for an original substance. Thus, when I asked Mr. Ring Lardner what his technic is, he replied that he listened. But scrutiny of the work of this remarkable writer will show that it rises far above the common speech, in the same way that Aristophanes and Shakespere created, from the body of material before them, the new forms, and gave them permanence as forms of true art. Professor Krapp shows that, although James Russell Lowell made seven rules for compounding Yankee dialect, in actual practice he did not keep to them, and Professor Krapp makes an analysis of Lowell's poem "The Courtin' " for this purpose. He adds:

"Further analysis of Lowell's dialect writing and of those of others who have written in New England dialect will confirm this conclusion. . . . In this poem, for example, the New England feeling is given more by rustic simplicity of the content of the poem than by the language of it, and the same observation could be made of a surprisingly large part of American dialect literature. Lowell's dialect in a story of the California gold fields would pass as Western dialect, and would seem not widely out of place on a cotton plantation in the South."

What happens is quite clear. A man who has the necessary gift for writing seizes on the raw material of life as he comes into contact with it, and out of this raw material fashions his production, makes it his own. His success may stimulate a host of writers to go and do likewise, and thus a new school, or cult, is started. The history of American dialect, and in particular of American slang, illustrates this literary principle. George Ade began with a small group of newspaper cronies who amused themselves by talking the slang of the Chicago newspaper offices and of the Middle West. But the genius of Ade made him recreate this raw material for his own use, and in doing this he took one of the oldest forms known, the fable. Wherever this sort of thing has been done by creative minds, they have always drawn from the common life about them; thus Lowell in his "Biglow Papers," Artemus Ward, James Whitcomb Riley, Charles Egbert Craddock, Peter Dunne, Ring Lardner, Sam Hellman, Wallace Irwin, and others. Where a writer or an artist chafes at the restraints imposed on him, and attempts to go outside of this ordinary life, and make exotic standards of his own, he fails in direct ratio to the attention he attracts within a limited circle. Miss Gertrude Stein has excited the high praise of a few admirers, notably Sherwood Anderson, by the eccentric form of her work, in much the same way that the cubists and futurists among artists and the imagists among poets have won praise.

Yet while these attempts are all extremely interesting and in many cases undoubtedly reveal a distinct advance in the development of true art, I can but feel that in the main our development must come from the common materials of life. Here are the opening paragraphs of Miss Stein's essay on England, which I presume is intended to be a revaluation of the genius of that much abused country:

ENGLAND

LEAVE OFF MORE TIME THAN THE HOPE WHICH ASSURES THE RENT OF A CUSTOM, THE SWEETNESS IS NOT THERE IT IS THE REASON LEFT AND THE MONKEYS ARE NOT MERRY. IF YOU DO HAVE EYES BLUE AND THE HAIR THE COLOR THEN IT EASY TO SEE THE HANDS.

ALL ALONG AND THE DAY, THE PRIZE IS NOT DRIVEN
AND THE SELECTING OF ALL THE COAL IS THAT

.   .   .   .

SO THE CLOTH IS ALRIGHT AND THE CARPET IS ENG-
LISH, PINK AND MOON, THAT SWEET SUGAR IS BROWN

Of this writing Mr. Sherwood Anderson remarks:
"For me the work of Gertrude Stein consists in a re-
building, an entire new recasting of life, in the city of
words. Here is one artist who has been able to accept
ridicule."

It would be a great error of literary judgment to belittle the value of Miss Stein and others of that limited
circle who, deliberately avoiding the main channels of a
vulgar popularity, go their own way and strike out beyond
the lines of formal and traditional endeavor. Their material failures are unimportant compared with the impulse
and courage which impel them to make their lonely trails.
At the same time, the biggest people have always used the
nearest and most commonplace material at hand. The rules
for writing laid down by Aristotle have scarcely been
bettered in all the years since he wrote.

The peculiar genius of the American people in the
"manufacture" of words is the result of pioneer conditions which they had to overcome; this made them in-
ventive and independent and—if we must say so—often
crude and over-vulgar. Thus we have to-day innumerable
phrases and terms which can but jar upon an ear cultivated even to a moderate degree. We are willing to make
things snappy, but not too snappy. We are willing to call
our sons and daughters by their right names, but not to
call them "brother" and "sister" and "Junior" and by
the more generic neologism of "kiddies." We have no
particular objection to "cafeteria" (from the Spanish

word for coffee-shop), but we object violently to "gro-
ceteria" and "drugateria," and even more to "pantorium,"
which, in the vernacular of the day, is ostensibly a parking
place for pants. We object to "low down," to "getting
one's goat," and—to move up a step into the language of
the more ambitious moron—to "citizenize" and to "fu-
neralize."

And yet these vulgarisms and many more which I refrain from inflicting on my tolerant readers are merely
fringes on a very extraordinary national gift which the
London "Spectator" refers to thus: "There is not, we
suppose, a thinking man who speaks English who has not
at some time felt his knowledge of the world and human
nature increased as well as his sense of the ridiculous
aroused and excited, by an 'Americanism.' "

This is, however, a rather striking exception to the
English run of criticism of our Americanisms. Dr. Robert Bridges, poet laureate, in referring to their comfort-
ing conviction that the English people are the "inheritors
of what may claim to be the finest living literature in the
world," goes on to speak of the menace which confronts
"our countrymen scattered abroad" and then refers to the
fact that this "menace" is "most evident in the United
States."

Messrs. H. G. Fowler and F. G. Fowler, authors of
"The King's English," and that more recent and more
delightfully stimulating work, "Modern English Usage,"
also warn their readers against Americanisms and take
Kipling to task for indulging in them. Apropos of this,
is it not true that Walter Pater refused to read Kipling
in order that he might not be corrupted?

To those who have been kind enough to read what I
have written, it is now, I hope, plain that the difficulty in
keeping the American language and speech pure does not

lie with the mass of people but with the small body of educated men and women who preside over our doubtful destiny: first, the experts, who are trying to reduce human nature to a system of grammatical imbecilities; and, second, the group of creative writers at the top of the heap, who do not care how slovenly they write so long as they are well paid. Much also might be said about the lamentable decline in the spoken word, a decline which dramatists attribute to the effect of the motion-pictures.

Among educated people in general, it must also be clear that, as valuable and necessary as the groundwork of philologists is, our progress will always be measured very largely by the increased attention given to the study of words by men and women who are actually creating our literature. And this applies to every one among our journalists and authors. When we see the men in charge of our public schools, who are so keen to make the language better, only getting into a deeper tangle of definitions the more they try to extricate themselves, and when we see our schools of journalism and the newspaper staffs of our leading papers ignoring constantly the ordinary rules of correct writing, we may well pause to ask ourselves whether our democracy, having been on trial so long, ought not to be sentenced to a term in "solitary."

It is our fatal fascination for adjectives and adverbs that undoes us. Our commercialized instincts constantly tempt us into superlatives, by reason of competition and high living. We think in terms of jazz. The Twenty-third Psalm is perhaps the most beautiful example of pure English in all the language:

"The Lord is my shepherd: I shall not want.

"He maketh me to lie down in green pastures: he leadeth me beside the still waters.

"He restoreth my soul."

In the twenty-nine words quoted, the two most prominent adjectives, "green" and "still," merely increase the
intensity of the nouns they accompany. I spare the reader
any attempt to show what a modern newspaper man would
do with these opening sentences.

In its surface aspects, the decadence in our language
is due to our extraordinary and hitherto unexampled
transportation facilities for words. Big words that sym-
bolized big simple ideas have been split up into masses
of small words, which are thought to be refinements and
thus to extend the human consciousness. The reverse is
true. Complexity of ideas is not extension but limitation.
The old scribes were bound by the necessities of their
work to make a severe choice of words, because the labor
involved was great. Now we have such a bewildering mass
of words to choose from, and so many writers have acquired such extraordinary skill in "bunching"·them, that
we have become the victims of a degenerate form of competition. The "super-salesman" is not confined to the
counting-house. He "cerebrates"—as they say—in the
author's den.

As far as the study of language is concerned, we may
easily abandon almost all of the intricate and misleading
grammatical definitions and classifications invented by the
grammarians and rhetoricians, and simply remember that
in a general way all words are either nouns or verbs; that
is to say, they symbolize things or ideas that are real or
permanent, or else they symbolize the action, the movement, or the development of those things and ideas. The
excessive use of adjectives and adverbs is always a sign
of weakness, indicating poverty of thought. Much more
than this, it reveals a lack of faith. The material splen-
dors and verbal superlatives of a godless people always
end in their being mental and spiritual paupers.

I have watched the process of degeneration in the vocabularies of our leading writers now for the past ten years, and have found that the grammarian who makes his pedantic protest against it has about as much chance as an Indian guide who tries to cross Niagara in a canvas canoe.

The cure? Dear friends, it lies with all of us.

THE DECLINE OF CONVERSATION *

By Albert J. Nock

THE more one thinks of it, the more one finds in Goethe's remark that the test of civilization is conversation. The common method of rating the civilization of peoples by what they have got and what they have done is really a poor one; for some peoples who have got much and done a great deal strike one at once as less civilized than others who have got little and done little. Prussia, for example, was relatively a poor State a century ago, while fifteen years ago it was rich and active; yet one would hardly say that the later Prussia was as civilized a country as the Prussia of Frederick's time. Somewhat the same might be said of Tudor England and modern England. The civilization of a country consists in the quality of life that is lived there, and this quality shows plainest in the things that people choose to talk about when they talk together, and in the way they choose to talk about them.

It can be taken for granted, I suppose, that a man has certain fundamental instincts which must find some kind of collective expression in the society in which he lives. The first and fundamental one is the instinct of expansion, the instinct for continuous improvement in material well-being and economic security. Then there is the instinct of intellect and knowledge, the instinct of religion and morals, of beauty and poetry, of social life and man-

* Reprinted by permission of the author and of Harper & Brothers, New York City.

ners. Man has always been more or less consciously working towards a state of society which should give collective
expression to these instincts. If society does not give expression to them, he is dissatisfied and finds life irksome,
because every unused or unanswered instinct becomes a
source of uneasiness and keeps on nagging and festering
within him until he does something about it. Moreover,
human society, to be permanently satisfactory, must not
only express all these instincts, but must express them all
in due balance, proportion, and harmony. If too much
stress be laid on anyone, the harmony is interrupted, uneasiness and dissatisfaction arise and, if the interruption
persists, disintegration sets in. The fall of nations, the
decay and disappearance of whole civilizations, can be
finally interpreted in terms of the satisfaction of these
instincts. Looking at the life of existing nations, one can
put one's finger on those instincts which are being collectively overdone at the expense of the others. In one
nation the instinct of expansion and the instinct of intellect and knowledge are relatively overdeveloped; in another, the instinct of beauty; in another, the instinct of
manners; and so on. The term *symphonic,* which is so
often sentimentally applied to the ideal life of society, is
really descriptive; for the tendency of mankind from the
beginning has been towards a functional blending and
harmony among these instincts, precisely like that among
the choirs of an orchestra. It would seem, then, that the
quality of life in any society means the degree of development attained by this tendency. The more of these instincts that are satisfied, and the more delicate the harmony of their interplay, the higher and richer is the quality of life in that society; and it is the lower and poorer
according as it satisfies fewer of these instincts and permits disharmony in their interplay.

American life has long been fair game for the observer. Journalistic enterprise now beats up the quarry for the foreigner and brings it in range for him from the moment the ship docks, or even before; and of late the native critic has been lending a brisk hand at the sport. So much, in fact, has been written about the way we live, how we occupy ourselves, how we fill up our leisure, the things we do and leave undone, the things we are likely to do and likely to leave undone, that I for one would never ask for another word on such matters from anybody. As a good American, I try to keep up with what is written about us, but it has become rather a dull business and I probably miss some of it now and then, so I cannot say that no observer has ever made a serious study of our conversation. In all I have read, however, very little has been made of the significance of the things we choose to talk about and our ways of talking about them. Yet I am sure that Goethe's method would give a better measure of our civilization than any other, and that it would pay any observer to look into it. For my own part, ever since I stumbled on Goethe's observation—now more than twenty years ago—I have followed that method in many lands. I have studied conversation more closely than any other social phenomenon, picking up from it all the impressions and inferences I could, and I have always found that I got as good results as did those whose critical apparatus was more elaborate. At least, when I read what these critics say about such peoples as I know, especially my own, they seem to tell me little with which I was not already acquainted.

II

Speaking as Bishop Pontoppidan did about the owls in Iceland, the most significant thing that I have noticed

about conversation in America is that there is so little
of it, and as time goes on there seems less and less of it in
my hearing. I miss even so much of the free play of
ideas as I used to encounter years ago. It would seem that
my countrymen no longer have the ideas and imagination
they formerly had, or that they care less for them, or
that for some reason they are diffident about them and
do not like to bring them out. At all events, the exercise
of ideas and imagination has become unfashionable.
When I first remarked this phenomenon I thought it
might be an illusion of advancing age, since I have come
to years when the past takes on an unnaturally attractive
color. But as time went on the fact became unmistakable
and I began to take notice accordingly.

As I did so a long-buried anecdote floated to the top of
my mind and has remained there ever since. I am reminded of it daily. Years ago Brand Whitlock told me
the story of an acquaintance of his—something in the
retail clothing way—junior partner in a firm whose name
I no longer remember, so for convenience we will make
acknowledgments to Mr. Montague Glass and call it
Maisener and Finkman. Mr. Finkman turned up at the
store one Monday morning, full of delight at the wonderful time he had had at his partner's house the evening
before—excellent company, interesting conversation, a
supreme occasion in every respect. After dinner, he said
—and such a dinner!—"we go in the parlor and all the
evening until midnight we sit and talk it business."

Day after day strengthens the compulsion to accept Mr.
Finkman as a type. This might be thought a delicate matter to press, but after all, Mr. Finkman is no creation of
one's fancy, but on the contrary he is a solid and respectable reality, a social phenomenon of the first importance,
and he accordingly deserves attention both by the positive

side of his preferences and addictions and by the negative side of his distastes. I am farthest in the world from believing that anything should be "done about" Mr. Finkman, or that he should be studied with an ulterior view either to his disparagement or his uplift. I am unequivocally for his right to an unlimited exercise of his likes and dislikes, and his right to get as many people to share them as he can. All I suggest is that the influence of his tastes and distastes upon American civilization should be understood. The moment one looks at the chart of this civilization one sees the line set by Mr. Finkman, and this line is so distinct that one cannot but take it as one's principal lead. If one wishes to get a measure of American civilization, one not only must sooner or later take the measure of Mr. Finkman's predilections, but will save time and trouble by taking it at the outset.

As evidence of the reach of Mr. Finkman's influence on the positive side, I notice that those of my American acquaintance whose interests are not purely commercial show it as much as others. Musicians, writers, painters, and the like seem to be at their best and to enjoy themselves most when they "talk it business." In bringing up the other instincts into balance with the instinct of expansion, such persons as these have an advantage, and one would expect to see that advantage reflected in their conversation much more clearly and steadily than it is. Where two or three of them were gathered together, one would look for a considerable play of ideas and imagination, and one would think that the instinct of expansion— since one perforce must give so much attention to it at other times—might gladly be let off on furlough. But I observe that this is seldom the case. For the most part, like Mr. Finkman, these people begin to be surest of themselves, most at ease and interested, at the moment when the instinct of expansion takes charge of conversation and gives it a directly practical turn.

One wonders why this should be so. Why should Mr. Finkman himself, after six days' steady service of the instinct of expansion, be at his best and happiest when he yet "talks it business" on the seventh? It is because he has managed to drive the whole current of his being through the relatively narrow channel set by the instinct of expansion. When he "talks it business," therefore, he gets the exhilarating sense of drive and speed. A mill-stream might thus think itself of more consequence than a river; probably the Iser feels more importance and exhilaration in its narrow leaping course than the Mississippi in filling all the streams of its delta. By this excessive simplification of existence Mr. Finkman has established the American formula of success. He makes money, but money is his incidental reward; his real reward is in the continuous exhilaration that he gets out of the processes of making it. My friends whose interests are not exclusively commercial feel the authority of the formula and share in the reward of its obedience. My friend A, for example, writes a good novel. His instincts of intellect, beauty, morals, religion, and manners, let us say, all have a hand in it and are satisfied. He makes enough out of it to pay him for writing it, and so his instinct of expansion is satisfied. But he is satisfied, not exhilarated. When on the other hand, his publisher sells a hundred thousand copies of another novel, he is at once in the American formula of success. The novel may not have much exercised his sense of intellect, beauty, morals, religion, and manners—it may be, in other words, an indifferent novel—but he is nevertheless quite in Mr. Finkman's formula of success and he is correspondingly exhilarated. He has crowded the whole stream of his being into the channel cut by the instinct of expansion, and his sensations correspond to his achievement.

Thus by his positive action in establishing the American formula of success, Mr. Finkman has cut what the Scots call a "monstrous cantle" out of conversation. Conversation depends upon a copiousness of general ideas and an imagination able to marshal them. When one "talks it business," one's ideas may be powerful, but they are special; one's imagination may be vigorous, but its range is small. Hence proceeds the habit of particularizing—usually, too, by way of finding the main conversational staple in personalities. This habit carries over, naturally, into whatever excursions Mr. Finkman's mind is occasionally led to make outside the domain of the instinct of expansion; for his disuse of imagination and general ideas outside this sphere disinclines him to them and makes him unhandy with them. Thus it is that conversation in America, beside its extreme attenuation, presents another phenomenon. On its more serious side it is made up almost entirely of particularization and, on its lighter side, of personalities.

These characteristics mark the conversation of children and, therefore, may be held to indicate an extremely immature civilization. The other day a jovial acquaintance who goes out to dinner a good deal told me a story that brings out this point. It seems he had just been hearing bitter complaints from a seasoned hostess who for years has fed various assorted contingents of New York's society at her board. She said that conversation at her dinner-table had about reached the disappearing-point. She had as much trouble about getting her guests into conversation as one has with youngsters at a children's party, and all the conversation she could prod out of them nowadays, aside from personalities, came out in the monotonous minute-gun style of particular declaration and perfunctory assent.

"She's right about that," my friend went on. "Here's a *précis* of the kind of thing I hear evening after evening. We go in to dinner talking personalities, no matter what subject is up. The theater—we talk about the leading lady's gowns and mannerisms, and her little ways with her first husband. Books—we hash over all the author's rotten press-agentry from the make of his pajamas to the way he does his hair. Music—we tell one another what a dear love of a conductor Kaskowhisky is and how superior in all respect to von Bugghaus, whose back isn't half as limber. Damned quacks actually you know, both of them. Good Lord, man, can you wonder that this country killed Mahler and put Karl Muck in jail?

"Well, we sit down at the table. Personalities taper off with the end of the soup. Silence. Then some puffy old bullfrog of a banker retrieves his nose out of his soup cup, stiffens up, coughs behind his napkin, and looks up and down the line. 'Isn't it remarkable how responsibility brings out a man's resources of greatness? Now who would have thought two years ago that Calvin Coolidge would ever develop into a great leader of men?'

"*Guests, in unison, acciaccato*—'Uh-huh.'

"Next course. Personalities pick up a little and presently taper off again. Somebody else stiffens up and pulls himself together. 'Isn't it splendid to see the great example that America is setting in the right use of wealth? Just think, for instance, of all the good that Mr. Rockefeller has done with his money.'

"*Guests, fastoso*—'Uh-huh.' "

My lively friend may have exaggerated a little—I hope so—but his report is worth an observer's careful notice for purposes of comparison with what one hears oneself.

His next remark is worth attention as bringing out still another specific characteristic of immaturity.

"But what goes against my grain," he continued, "is that if you pick up some of this infernal guff and try to pull it away from the particular and personal, and to make real conversation of it, they sit on you as if you were an enemy of society. Start the banker on a discussion of the *idea* of leadership—what it means, what the qualifications for leadership are, and how far any President can go to fill the bill—how far any of them has ever gone to fill it —and all he'll do is to grunt and say, 'I guess you must be some sort of a Red, ain't you?' A bit of repartee like that gets him a curtain call from the rest every time. It's a fine imaginative lot that I train with, believe me! I have sat at dinner-tables in Europe with every shade of opinion, I should say, and in one way or another they all came out. That's what the dinner was got up for. How can you have any conversation if all you are expected to do is to agree?"

III

It is a mark of maturity to differentiate easily and naturally between personal or social opposition and intellectual opposition. Everyone has noticed how readily children transfer their dislike of an opinion to the person who holds it, and how quick they are to take umbrage at a person who speaks in an unfamiliar mode or even with an unfamiliar accent. When the infant-minded Pantagruel met with the Limosin who spoke to him in a Latinized macaronic jargon, he listened a while and then said, "What devilish language is this?—by the Lord, I think thou art some kind of heretic." Mr. Finkman's excessive simplification of life has made anything like the free play of ideas utterly incomprehensible to him. He never deals with ideas except such limited and practical ones as may help get him something, and he cannot imagine anyone ever choosing, even on occasion, to do differently. When he "talks it business," the value of ideas, ideals, opinions, sentiments is purely quantitative; putting any other value on them is a waste of time. Under all circumstances, then, he tends to assume that other people measure the value of their ideas and opinions as he does his, and that they employ them accordingly; and hence, like my friend's banker, when someone tries to lead up into a general intellectual sparring for mere points, he thinks he is a dangerous fellow with an ax to grind.

This puts the greatest imaginable restraint upon conversation, a restraint which betrays itself to the eye of the observer in some rather odd and remarkable ways. I have been much interested, for example, to see that the conversion of conversation into mere declaratory particularization has lately been taken up in a commercial way. One reads advertisements of enterprising people who engage to make you shine in conversation. They propose to do this by loading you up with a prodigious number of facts of all kinds, which you can fire at will from the machine-gun of your memory. On this theory of conversation, a statistician with Macaulay's memory is the ideal practitioner of social amenities; and so indeed, with Mr. Finkman's sensibilities in view, he would be.

Another odd manifestation of this restraint is the almost violent eagerness with which we turn to substitutes for conversation in our social activities. Mr. Finkleman must not be left alone in the dark with his apprehensions a moment longer than necessary. After such a dinner as my debonair friend described it is at once necessary to "do something"—the theater, opera, cabaret, dancing, motoring, or what not—and to keep on doing something as long as the evening lasts. It is astonishing to see the amount of energy devoted to keeping out of conversation; "doing something" has come to be a term of special application. Almost every informal invitation reads, "to dinner, and then we'll do something." It is even more astonishing to see that this fashion is followed by persons whose intelligence and taste are sufficient, one would think, to put them above it. Quite often one finds oneself going through this routine with persons quite capable of conversation, who would really rather converse, but who go through it apparently because it is the thing to go through. When this happens, one marvels at the reach and the authority of Mr. Finkman's predilections—yet there they are.

My friend was right in saying that conversation is managed differently in Europe. I was reminded of this not long ago, when the German airship made its great flight to this country. Everyone remembers the vast amount of public interest in this event, and how the pilot of the airship, Doctor Eckener, was fêted and fussed over from one end of the country to the other. Three or four days after the landing, a friend of mine, a German banker, asked me to luncheon at his house. There were four of us: Doctor Eckener, his assistant, our host, and myself. We talked for something over two hours, largely about music, a good deal about the geography and history of the region around Friedrichshafen, and for half an hour, perhaps, about European public affairs. From first to last not one word was said about the flight of the airship or about the business of aviation or about the banking business. The conversation was wholly objective and impersonal; each one spoke his mind, and none of us felt any pressure towards agreement. I remember that I myself put out some pretty heretical opinions about the structure of music-drama. No one agreed with me, but no one dreamed of transferring to myself the brunt of his objections to my opinion.

This kind of thing gives the impression of maturity and, as far as my experience goes, it is as common in Europe as it is uncommon here. There has been much comment lately upon the attraction that Europe exerts upon certain American types. I am led to wonder if it be not perchance the attraction of maturity. Children may be delightful, may be interesting, may be ever so full of promise, and one may be as fond of them as possible— and yet when one has them for warp and filling, one must get a bit bored with them now and then, in spite of oneself. I have had little to do with children, so I speak under correction; but I should imagine that one would become bored with their intense simplification of life, their tendency to drive the whole current of life noisily through one channel, their vehement reduction of all values to that of quantity, their inability to take any but a personal view of anything. But just these are the qualities of American civilization as indicated by the test of conversation. They inhere in Mr. Finkman and are disseminated by his influence to the practical exclusion of any other. I can imagine, then, that one might in time come to be tired of them and to wish oneself in surroundings where man is accepted as a creature of "a large discourse, looking before and after," where life is admittedly more complex and its current disturbed in more channels—in other words, where maturity prevails.

One is impressed, I think, by the way this difference is repeatedly brought out in ordinary conversation in Europe and America—in the choice of things to talk about and in the way people talk about them. I am impressed by it even in conversation with children, though as I said, due allowance ought to be made for the fact that my experience with children is not large. Yet even so, I do not think it is special or exceptional. I have a friend, for instance, whom I go to see whenever I am in Brussels, and it is the joy of my life to play at sweethearts with his three daughters who range from seven to sixteen. My favorite is the middle one, a weedy and nonchalant charmer of twelve. She does not impress me as greatly gifted; I know several American girls who seem naturally abler. But in conversation with her I detect a power of disinterested reflection, an active sense of beauty and an active sense of manners, beyond any that I ever detected in American children; and these contribute to a total effect of maturity that is agreeable and striking.

IV

An observer passing through America with his mind deliberately closed to any impressions except those he received from conversation could make as interesting a conjectural reconstruction of our civilization as the palæontologists with an armful of bones make of a dinosaur. He would postulate a civilization which expresses the instinct of expansion to a degree far beyond anything ever seen in the world; but which does not express the instinct of intellect and knowledge, except as regards instrumental knowledge, and is characterized by an extremely defective sense of beauty, a defective sense of religion and morals, a defective sense of social life and manners. Its institutions reflect faithfully this condition of excess and defect. A very brief conversation with Mr. Finkman would enable one to predicate almost precisely what kind of schooling he considered an adequate preparation for life, what kind of literature he thought good enough for one to read, plays for one to see, architecture to surround oneself with, music to listen to, paintings and sculpture to contemplate. It would be plain that Mr.

Finkman had succeeded in living an exhilarating life from day to day without the aid of any power but concentration —without reflection, without ideas, without ideals, and without any but the most special emotions—that he thought extremely well of himself for his success, and was disposed to be jealous of the peculiar type of institutional life which had enabled it or conduced to it. The observer, therefore, would postulate a civilization marked by an extraordinary and inquisitional intolerance of the individual and a corresponding insistence upon conformity to pattern. For in general, it is reflection, ideas, ideals, and emotions that set off the individual, and with these Mr. Finkman has had nothing to do; he has got on without them to what he considers success, and hence he sees no need of them, distrusts them, and thinks there must be a screw loose with the individual who shows signs of them.

There is a pretty general consensus among observers that this picture corresponds in most respects with the actual civilization of the United States, and many of them deplore the correspondence. I do not deplore it. It seems to me important that Mr. Finkman should have room according to his strength, that he should be unchecked and unhampered in directing the development of American civilization to suit himself. I believe it will be a most salutary experiment for the richest and most powerful nation in the world to give a long, fair, resolute try-out to the policy of living by the instinct of expansion alone. If the United States cannot make a success of it, no nation ever can, and none, probably, will ever attempt it again. So when critics denounce our civilizations as barbarous, I reply that, if so, a few generations of barbarism are a cheap price for the result. Besides, Mr. Finkman may prove himself right; he may prove that man can live a full and satisfying inner life without intellect, without beauty, without religion and morals, and with but the most rudimentary social life and manners, provided only he has unlimited exercise of the instinct of expansion, and can drive ahead in the expression of it with the whole force of his being. If Mr. Finkman proves this, he will have the laugh on many like myself who at present have the whole course of human history behind our belief that no such thing can be done. But this is a small matter. The important thing is that we should then have a new world peopled by a new order of beings not at all like ourselves, but by no means devoid of interest on that account. So, whether the result be in success or in failure, the great American experiment—for just this *is* the great American experiment—seems to me wholly worth while.

GAIETY FOR THE SOLEMN *

By Irwin Edman

ONE of the pet illusions of the reformer and the intellectual is that it is impossible to be serious without being solemn. Those deeply concerned with alleviating the human lot or understanding the human scene have always been shy of laughter. The significant questions of human destiny are not to be approached with a smile. God, misery, and salvation are no joke.

The distrust of the light heart in contemporary thinking has been disastrous. The literature of social reform, of philosophy and religion—as well as the fiction influenced by them—has become increasingly melancholy and forbidding. The literature of the whimsical and gay has moved increasingly, sometimes to the verge of pain, in the direction of nonsense. On the one hand are the earnest seekers after truth or salvation whose solemnity frightens away or puts to sleep those who might otherwise have been saved. On the other hand are the frivolists who, having in their early youth decided that existence was in essence ridiculous, refuse to take any of its accidents *au grand sérieux*. Cherishing like a traditional clown their private sense of tragedy, they prefer to skim over the more amiable surface of things with an epigram or a joke. Thus a credo which, preached with a little winsome-

* Reprinted from *The Bookman* by permission of the author and of the editors.

ness and laughter, might have converted thousands is intoned to a sombre and impotent few. Comedy that might have been used, as Meredith insisted at its best it is used, as the polished tool of social betterment, becomes a nonsense void of all use and relative to no mortal concerns. The devil gets all the good jokes as well as all the good tunes. The philosopher, the theologian, the political prophet, are immured by a wall of impenetrable dulness from effecting the fortunes or clarifying the insights of mankind.

It is not hard to see why, for those plumbing the painful recesses of action or attempting fundamentally to alter its conditions, humor is at a discount and the humorist is regarded with suspicion. One may not always be disturbingly aware of what Unamuno, the Spanish philosopher, conceives to be the characteristic human agony, "the tragic sense of life." But once the hopeful elasticity of life is over, perhaps the most perduring of all feelings about life is that it is a serious, if not a tragic, matter. A little observation will steady the most elfin of mortals; by forty almost everyone is sober. The social worker or reformer has no patience with the glib smartness of the gilded literati. He has seen too much of the rending misery which constitutes the lot of a heartbreaking proportion of his fellows. Novelists like Zona Gale and Willa Cather, Sherwood Anderson or D. H. Lawrence, are endeavoring to trace the passionate hidden currents that flow below the conventional quiet surface of a man's being, or the fine compulsive threads which bound his days and make his destiny. They cannot be expected to pause for grimaces or bon mots. The contemporary philosopher has not time to amuse or to be amused if he is to make any sensible progress in piecing together a new intellectual house of life for his fellow moderns out of the shreds of decaying religions or the rough stones of a growing science.

Men and women engaged in such enterprises know there is something fatal and disorganizing about laughter. It arises, they know, out of the perceptions of the loose ends and crazy juxtapositions of living. Its echoes of mockery, its chortles of delight, have convulsed many a serious venture in the interpretation or the betterment of life. The psychiatrists have made us familiar with those painful cases where melancholy has rendered a patient absolutely incapable of action. Terrible doubt, such as Tolstoy's, may drive a man to the pit of nihilism. Skepticism, if it is not in the hands of so healthy a soul as David Hume, may drive a man mad through the hideous fantoms of his own mind. Any alienist can tell you what comes of taking life too seriously. No one has yet done justice to the dangers of taking it too lightly. But the serious minded know why they are afraid of giving play to their perception of the absurd. They might eventually come to take all existence as a joke. And in that grand engulfing farce, what would their own so absorbing activities become if not simply minor causes for amusement?

Small wonder then that the farceur is not at a premium in a scientific laboratory. It was not in the ribaldry of a tavern that Spinoza learned to look at time under the perspective of eternity. That very concentration and intensity that goes with the enunciation of grand thoughts or the achievement of great work, is inimical to the mood of the picnic or the clown. Say what one will about the business of being too solemn, high thinking is not produced during fits of giggles, and a joke is more dangerously out of place at events far more promising than funerals.

It is easy to understand, on the other hand, why

"the merry and bright" among mankind have been inclined to fight shy of those who were trying to save or enlighten them. The leader of a moral improvement society is not notably good company on a lark, and the practising philosopher is not commonly regarded as the life of the party. The light hearted may indeed well argue that in a world where no rational ends are clearly discernible, the only ends worth pursuing are those which come with their own clear certificates of joy. No bleak enterprise toward future bliss can compare with their own frequent moments of uncaring mirth. What would a perfect world be save one that gave its denizens precisely such a sense of truant wellbeing as the gay and the casual have even now? There is a finality about a laugh or a chuckle that is not to be found in the systems of the wise. A philosopher has to argue his case; a joke or a whimsy, if it brings so much as a smile, does not have to prove that it is amusing. A favored image of Olympus is that of the gods rocking with laughter. The great primitive poets could imagine no more divine diversion.

The light hearted may also have observed that for all the solemnity of the sages, conditions on the planet have not been radically improved since the dawn of written wisdom, and if at all, not necessarily by or according to the wise. Apparently, the grave have not secured bliss for others; they have even lost it themselves. Wisdom seems too often to have darkened the spirits or soured the tempers of those not content to regard with joy the diverting and pointless spectacle of human folly. The plain man, as Plato long ago pointed out, has distrusted all grave philosophers. The poet has distrusted all practical plain men. It is neither among the practical nor among the profound that the race has sought the instances and metaphors of happiness. The locus of contentment has been found rather in the careless blue eyes of childhood, the rapture of the lark, the sounds of singing men or clinking glasses in a tavern, or in the bronze savage lolling on white sands by blue waters under a tropical sun.

The gay can reckon up their assets with a jovial mathematics of remembered goods. But they are usually too busy experiencing delight to fret over its arithmetic, too intent upon it to criticize—or note the criticisms of the grave. The latter have likewise been too busy to do more than scold the happy vagabonds. In their pauses from their own unhappy labors, they have taken the time to envy the gay. They have never understood them. And in failing to understand them, they have missed the comprehension of one of the dear ingredients of that happiness which they were, so busily arranging for the race.

There is a danger in our own day that the world of ideas is becoming a feud between the happy trifler and the melancholy sage. A new Puritanism has come upon us, the cold morality of a machine age. It is precisely from these austerities of standardized work and standardized play that many are fleeing now to nonsense and satirical laughter. It is beginning to seem the more amiable part of wisdom to snatch at such gaiety as can still be found in the pauses of days that have been subdued to machines. There are moral values in abandon for a generation whom machines and formulas have robbed of all resilience. The whistling loafer, the irresponsible wit, have a lesson to teach the grave deacons of contemporary thought.

The loafer and the wit are, in the first place, characterized by insouciance. They are the born enemies of all dogmatism, the amiable foes of all rigidity. They cannot be dragooned by money or creed or ambition into solemnity; they will not crowd their bubbling spirits into a musty system of thought. The timid majority, coerced by a job or by an idea into slavery, look on these freemen with a concentration which is three quarters envy. The current popularity of a tramp literature is testimony to the hunger there is among us for a life that escapes the regular, the respectable, the ordained.

But to be a vagabond or to go to the South Seas is not to escape the mold or the treadmill. The missionary carries his drab Protestantisms with him to the Orient; one may wander far with a stay-at-home heart. There is, however, a more facile and certain form of vagabondage. Arthur Machen in "The Secret Glory" describes a boy who managed to bear the brutality and convention of school life by cherishing in his mind a white "secret glory." There is a less unctuous way of escaping from surrender to dulness or brutality. The comic spirit will keep one alive to the absurdity of those solemn conditions and conventions by which one would otherwise be spiritually enslaved. Equipped with the anti-toxin of laughter, one can live even in a standardized society without being too impressed by its standards. Perhaps to maintain gaiety rather than, as Pater supposed, to maintain ecstasy, is success in life.

The wits and loafers have another claim to the attention of the sober. For theirs is a gusto and exuberance that the serious minded too often miss. Much contemporary writing and thinking gives the impression that it has been done by tired men. The author of many an essay toward the betterment of the world seems to have gritted his teeth and girded his loins before he began. One can see him forcing himself heavily to sketch a design for a perfect state in which one imagines he would be much too weary to live. Even when the profound are happy, they never permit evidence of that fact to gleam across their professional pages. To read some of the most important of contemporary writers, one would think they had never had a gay moment or that they could not tolerate such a heresy among others.

No wonder the instinct of the common man turns away from all such melancholy saviors. From Rabelais to Robert Benchley he sees among the harlequins and pierrots an abounding vitality he has seldom observed among their more responsible brothers. For however various the forms of happiness may be, they are kneaded out of the dough of ordinary human vitality. The surest evidence of vitality is in the play temper, the surest instances of it in the playtime of the race. Certainly what makes the word "play" so completely delightful in its associations is its suggestion of abundance, spontaneity and freedom. In a really ordered society, all activities would be like those at present found in games, in jokes, and in the play of wits. One is grateful to those who even in a disordered civilization can take experience lightly, gaily, and with ease. If nature were not careless and civilization were not brutal, all life would be a perpetual diversion. Work would then be that of the happy craftsmen and would hardly be distinguishable from play. Thought would be a singing of the mind. Havelock Ellis hit upon one of the most apt of all the metaphors for perfect living when he described it as having the rhythmic freedom of the dance. Gaiety is the outward evidence of an inner vitality and freedom. It is a tragic comment on civilization that peace and eagerness are to be found chiefly in the amiable outcasts of society, not among the respectable and admired; among the triflers rather than the profound.

There is a further sense in which the perception of gaiety might be a lesson to the moralists. It was Nietzsche who pleaded powerfully for a joyful wisdom, though he was not the first. Indeed wisdom that has no joy in it may look to its title. For the absence of the latter is a sign that the pretended insight flows from some spiritual failure or feebleness. One may seriously suspect the grave philosopher, and that for two reasons. He is much too serious, and takes his theories much too seriously. It is a fair enough reason why other people should not.

Possibly the most sensible words ever uttered about love and immortality are to be found in the lovely and immortal dialogues of Plato. But it will be recalled that Socrates's glamorous speech about love is delivered to a party of wits slightly befuddled by drink. His grand and convincing fable about immortality is delivered just before the hour of his own execution, even at which terrible moment he finds it proper and possible to jest with his admiring, slightly shocked disciples. It is his jesting that makes the moment turn from terror to beauty. Again in the "Laws" which Plato wrote in his saddening old age, there is much less austerity than in its more youthful predecessor, "The Republic." By the time he was old and disillusioned, Plato knew that there could be no perfect state but that the spirit of play might make it less imperfect.

When a philosopher reaches a certain point of wisdom, he knows how tiny his wisdom is. He realizes the quaintness of a mite of intelligence trying to crush the universe into a system invented by his little mind. It is impossible to perceive the ridiculous save where there is a sense of proportion; a sense of humor may not be the most trivial though it is the rarest tool among philosophers. Likewise when the humorist makes the cosmos his theme, his sense of the ridiculous is itself a profoundly philosophical commentary. It is impossible to take the universe too seriously when a satirist lays his finger upon it.

It requires both maturity and good fortune to approach the world habitually with gaiety and exuberance. It requires maturity, because where there is little experience and perspective, any event or any idea is likely to appear monstrously more significant than any event or idea can be in the vast and pointless context of things. The mature have the capacity to be mellow because no passion or illusion any longer forces them to be sharp. But it requires, further, good fortune to be habitually gay or witty. When one is pelted by the blows of necessity, one cannot honestly be debonair.

Yet the gift of gaiety may itself be the greatest good fortune and the most serious step toward maturity. Our point of view has been tainted by the hard tensions of the Protestant tradition. We have been afraid to be happy where happiness was possible, because laughter seemed to have in it the mockery of devils and gaiety the sinfulness of the damned. Our saviors and sages have been depressing; our wits and our warblers have been exiled as foolish and have made up their minds to be as foolish as they could. It is possible, however, to conceive of a wisdom tinctured with lightness and mercurial beauty. Professor Eddington's recent exposition of "The Domain of Physical Science" is a masterly example of how to be at once dancing and profound. There are writers, such as Barrie and Milne at their best, whose gaiety is simply the gentle voice of their sense of the infinite pathos of things. A world peopled by Pollyannas would be ghastly; one inhabited by the grave deacons and moralizing secular saints of the day would be even worse. There is a graceful middle way. One finds it in a few writers. They are those whose wisdom seems to be an intelligence turned glowing and joyful. They seem to have fought their way through (not to have evaded) all the jagged passes of the spirit, and reached a high golden eminence from which they could look down with a tingling serenity. The tingling is their humor; the serenity is their wisdom. They do not see less far, the W. H. Hudsons, the Havelock Ellises, the Shaws, for seeing with merriment or jubilation or wit. They are too serious to be crabbed or puckered or cross. They are the consonant spokesmen of nature. They suggest the primary article of wisdom: to be like nature, in the face of annual death and defeat, to be resurgent always with a gay vitality.

CHILDISH AMERICANS *

A Diagnosis of Our National Malady

By Joseph Collins, M.D.

Our chief deficiency as a people, our most conspicuous national shortcoming, is a condition of mal-development to which the name Adult-Infantilism is given. There is much to indicate that we are a nation of adult-infants, and not a little to prove it. Adult-infantilism is responsible for more social maladjustment, more family discord, and more intellectual vagrancy than any disease, derangement, or other disharmony of mind and body. And the number of people thus afflicted seems to be increasing. Why should this blight have come upon us and whence has it come? What is it and where is it leading us?

The gravamen of the charge is sustained by our individual and national conduct, by our literary and artistic life, by our prejudices and beliefs, our boastings and our satisfactions, our gregariousness and our restlessness.

Who has not heard the child say to his companion, "My house is bigger than yours"—"I can run faster than you can"—"My father can lick yours any day"—"My doll can talk and yours can't"?

Parents pretend to correct this boasting, but in reality it often amuses them. Carried into adult life, it is manifest when Mr. Jones adds a wing to his house after his

* Reprinted by permission of the author and of Harper & Brothers, New York City.

neighbor has added a side-porch to his own. It prompts such statements as "There is not a man in the world who can lick Tilden," and "Jack Dempsey is the greatest fighter the world has ever seen." It makes the visitor from Dallas or from Cleveland sneer at the Cathedral of Chartres because both steeples are not identical, compare the Corniche road unfavorably with Lakeside Drive, and it suggests to the New Yorker that the picturesqueness of San Gimignano's moldering towers is not a patch on that of lower New York.

It accounts for that self-satisfaction with which we hold aloof from the affairs of other nations, and for that self-esteem which leads us to believe in the superiority of our institutions and the righteousness of our conduct. It is the basis of our determination to regulate man's conduct by legislation—to say what he shall not teach and what he shall not drink. We have more colleges and universities than any other country of the world, and yet we are the worst educated, the least cultured. We have more churches, chapels, and civic-centers than any country of Europe, yet we are swayed by religious prejudice that transcends the understanding of Europeans. We have a climate that has no equal, yet we flee from it as though its atmosphere were mephitic. We have comforts that kings might consider luxuries, yet it is real punishment for us to stay at home; we have wealth and occupation, but little of that peace of mind surpassing wealth which the sage finds in meditation.

Why? Because so many of us are emotionally infantile.

II

What is meant by Adult-infantilism? The condition and conduct of an individual who, having reached maturity of physical development, remains infantile in his responses to the demands and obligations of life. One may be infantile on the physical, the intellectual, or on the affective side, but the term ordinarily is limited to lack of development in the field of the emotions. Bodily infantilism is usually so apparent that it does not need to be pointed out; dwarfs, pygmies, and midgets are its victims. Intellectual arrest of development is equally obvious, and a man whose mental faculties have not kept pace with his age is labeled "moron" without aid of physician or psychologist. But infantility seizes chiefly upon the man or woman whose emotional (affective) make-up lags behind his or her physical and intellectual development. It is all the more dangerous because it is not usually accompanied by any obvious manifestation and is not considered an infirmity. Indeed, such emotional backwardness is often accepted as engaging, attractive, amusing. The adult-infant is not aware of his handicap, and often goes through life ignorant of his part in the disaster and misfortunes he encounters or causes. He blames them on fate, on the malignity of others, on unfair treatment. His limitation prevents him from looking to himself for the cause, and he is likely to engender children whose burden will increase proportionately with their inability to cope with it.

We are adult infants, and we enjoy it. We do not experience pleasure or fulfillment in the thought that we are grown-up individuals prepared to meet struggle and hardship. We think that the longer we remain impervious to life's warning the luckier we are; that if life would only spare us its blows we should be happy.

Children do not like to carry a thing to its logical conclusion; they do not like to think connectedly or protractedly; they do not like to think at all. They like to have others do it for them. Grown-up Americans experience similar likes and dislikes. They leave it to their aldermen and legislators, their priests and their newspapers, to think for them.

Children are notoriously gregarious; they shun solitude. They wish to be in the limelight and to have the attention of others directed toward their activities. The good fellowship of which we boast, our "rotariness," as it were, our "clubiness," is carried over to our adult life from early associations, from barn-clubs, dancing-classes, smoking-behind-the-shed-clubs, school and college clubs.

When we play we bring into our games a dignity and soberness that children have when they play "father and mother," or we go to the other extreme and display a jovial exuberance and enthusiasm which is neither becoming nor really felt. These are typical childish traits. However, there is a process of adjustment or of unconscious rationalization that takes place in the mind of the "player" and influences his attitude, for it is no rare thing to see an American man who in his own country carries his office-mask of sobriety to the golf links become boisterous and garrulously gay when on the links at Cannes, Le Touquet, or Inverness.

Who has not seen at one of the big football games a dignified-looking, elderly gentleman throw off his coonskin coat, scale the ramparts, grasp a megaphone, and lead the cheering? His emotions will no longer tolerate repression. He is a boy again, and glad of it. And he is one of a great army of adults who regard such games seriously. We aver that football engenders courage, teaches fair treatment of opponents, develops backbone and will power, which is all buncombe. It does not do any of these things. Fewer heroes are recruited from football fields than from factories, and the man who displays signal courage or bravery when it is called for is

more likely to have spent his spare time in college reading Keats and Baudelaire than charging upon the gridiron and breaking opponents' ribs.

Foreign visitors to this country, especially those from
countries where reality has competed successfully with
romance, are amused at American men, gray at the temple and thin in the neck, who, when asking the where-
abouts of their wives, say, "Where are the girls?" and
amazed when they hear stately matrons refer to their hus-
bands as "the boys." The American is reluctant to ac-
knowledge that he has lost his hold on youth; he wants to
be playful, and his wife wants to be kittenish.

Our childishness is most conspicuous when we are
abroad; our wit banal, our conversation trivial, our conduct herdish, our thoughts superficial. Our aim is to be
seen, heard, and envied. Who has not seen Americans
in the smoking-room of ocean liners, in cafés of Ritz
hotels, in Maxim's, or at Monte Carlo, acting like schoolboys at their first party? How straight-laced an American
captain of industry can be at home, and how loose-laced
abroad! Hence, our reputation for naïveté and credulity.
Europeans tell us we are clever and resourceful, but they
tell one another behind our backs that we are childish.
Would anyone who has the intuition and discernment that
M. Caillaux is reputed to have, comport himself as he
did in Washington last October if he were not convinced
that we are babes?

We are as infantile regarding our laws as we are about
many other things. There is no better way to encourage
the average child to do something than to forbid him to
do it. Immediately he bends his energies and concentrates
his thoughts on accomplishing it. There is no surer way
to make us thirst for alcohol, which in reality most of
us do not need and few of us formerly craved, than to

tell us we can't buy, make, or drink it. We advocate speed laws for motor cars, and we break them when opportunity presents; but we are insistent that others should obey them, and we are secretly glad when we see a policeman handing a summons to a reckless motorist. If that is not a childish trait, then there are none.

There are few things more torturing to a child's pride and self-respect than to be different from other children, or to have to dress differently. Self-consciousness invades the soul of the child made to wear clothes not popular with other children. Originality and individuality are taboo among children—and they seem to be so with us. Let a woman carry a walking stick or a man wear spats anywhere save in a metropolis, and they will receive disapprobation as heartfelt as it is manifest. Note one of our conventions to which we bow the knee: straw hats shall not be worn after the fifteenth of September. Sometimes we have tropical weather then and later, but that does not matter, for if we wear a straw hat after that date boys will jeer and men will gibe. We are continually conforming to conventions that we may not suffer the opprobrium of being thought "unlike" others. And we carry this fear and compulsion to the higher concerns of life: we regard individuality of thought and sentiment in others as "queer" and not quite decent.

Our thought is standardized because we refuse to grow up and think for ourselves; we are unable to purge ourselves of the fear of ridicule. This is particularly true of our literature. One can hardly picture James Joyce, Dorothy Richardson, T. S. Eliot, Marcel Proust, Tchekhov, Gogol, developing in this country. When one of their type originates here we treat him as a pariah; we call him bad names, we impugn his personal morality, and we warn the public to shun him.

Emotions are budding in the child; their blossoms are ready to be gemmed as soon as he reaches the age of discretion; they need only attention and guidance so that a stately tree hung with copious fruit may result. But in the same manner as they are budding in the child, they are repressed in adults. We are a nation of emotionally repressed people, and nowhere do we display Adult-infantilism so conspicuously as in the direction and management of our fundamental urges, our primitive instincts. The American man is reputed to be the best provider and the poorest lover in the world; the American woman the best looking and the least temperamental. Neither perhaps merits the reputation. But we treat the genesic instinct like a stepchild; we feed it, but the food is of the plainest—no spicing and little care given to the serving of it. Love is something to be proud of when firmly bitted, securely curbed, and thoroughly groomed. Uncurried and unbridled, it is sure to run away with its mount. It has to be "trained." We pretend it is indecent to train it; immoral to guide it when it is being put through its preliminary paces; immodest to discuss it. We are loath to display the manifestations of love, and we throw a cloak of secrecy over the one passion of man which connects him directly with God. This has always been a puzzle to those who have not studied New England's origins, while those who have see little hope of breaking down these inveterate prejudices by other than extreme measures. If our thoughts were no more occupied with sex and its natural entailments than our conversation is, there would be nothing to fear. It would make for an emotionally insensitive nation, for whom the most marvelous and ennobling of natural functions— and one which is nearest to the supernatural—would have no more meaning than the necessity of ordering food so that we may eat. But such is not the case; we regard love as one of the most beautiful of emotions until we come in contact with it, and then shame, reluctance, modesty, puritanism, or whatever one wishes to call it, enters into play and makes us attempt to revert instantly to the time when we believed in Prince Charming and were contented with the stork myth. It may be the fault of our education—it is more probably the fault of our ancestry—but there prevails in America a feeling that love, emotional response to beauty of any sort, is something we should not discuss or display except within rigidly conventional limits. We ignore or make light of life's greatest responsibilities—and that is a childish trait.

III

Our personal achievements and accomplishments evoke a similarly childish, emotional response. We pride ourselves grossly and turbulently on what we have done; we experience a glow of satisfaction when we have succeeded in defeating an adversary; and we are loud in our self-praise and laudation. So are children. "I got the best mark and I am the cleverest of all," is the note that echoes through our masterful lives. Our impulsiveness, our generosity, our lavishness, our egregious hospitality, are all hang-overs from childhood. They are laudable impulses, praiseworthy possessions, priceless gifts, but they should be *transformed,* not merely transferred from childhood.

"Be sure to come and see me when you come to New York" we say to a man who, ten minutes before, was a stranger; and when he comes we dine him, cocktail him, and parade him till he is cast down in his digestion and puffed up in his pride. A pianist or a prize fighter, a politician or a priest, a royal wife-hunter or a republican

wife-beater, a Coué or a clown are received and fêted
by us royally. When we are in their countries we are
sometimes chagrined that our hospitality is not recip-
rocated, our exuberance not retaliated.

It is asserted that American people will succumb to
anything, reasonable or otherwise, if it is sufficiently advertised; they will overstep any limit, too, if the bait is
fashionable or popular. We have had more "crazes" and
"fads" in our country in the past fifty years than any
other country can boast of in twice that time.

Forty years ago the "whole world," save all paralyzed
and epileptic, was on roller-skates. Once this fair country
was dotted with "rinks"; now there remains but one in
Philadelphia to recall this skating urge of our parents.
A little later we nearly forgot how to walk in our enthusiasm for "wheels." It was no uncommon sight in
New York of a Sunday morning to see thousands riding
up and down Broadway and Riverside Drive. Bicycles
have given way to the craze for motor cars; it is a poor
man indeed who cannot take his family out on week-end
motor trips. Mah-Jong swept the country two years ago,
and its popularity might have endured longer had not
"cross-word puzzles" dethroned it. And now we are so
absorbed in "listening in" to cheap music and cheaper wit
that we have no time to loaf and invite our souls.

And we do not confine ourselves to passing enthusiasms
over pastimes and sports, which threaten the harmony of
our spiritual life. In no other country can doctrines of
supernaturalism develop in such brief time and thrive
to such wondrous extent. Waves of mysticism have passed
over us and turned our beliefs and our hopes in directions that had not been foreseen by the established Church.
Last winter New Thought was the great topic of conversation; this had been somewhat prepared for by the

Coué craze, which made parrots out of human beings. But these were as naught compared with the excitement caused by the vulgarization of Freud's theories, over which the country is still exercised.

We are constantly shifting our viewpoints, because we have little focusing power. A passing idea attracts our attention, but we cannot concentrate on it—we are too afraid meanwhile that another idea may go by unnoticed.

Children never remain long at one thing; they tire of it as soon as it has yielded its first glamour of novelty, and their attention and interest are directed toward the next thing until that, too, loses its savor. We are as bad as children in this respect. We cannot withstand leisure, nor can we find within ourselves or within our books, in people or in environment, appeasement and satisfaction. We charge the atmosphere with making us restless, but we are restless because of our distractibility, our continual seeking for new sensations, anticipating that the morrow should bring something that to-day has not brought. Satiety comes in the wake of prosperity: we build palatial homes in the city and country which affront the eyes of the foreigner; but we tire of them if our days are prolonged and our children sell them as soon as we pass on. In most parts of this country it is rare to find a house in which a family has lived during three generations, and the New Yorker who lives in the house in which he was born hardly exists.

This lack of stability from one generation to the other is one of the gravest phenomena of Adult-infantilism. We are justified in laying this charge to our parents; they are responsible for our infirmity. Had they treated us wisely, or even fairly, we should be able to follow in the footsteps of their forebears and grow up into men and women of balance, of maturity, of poise.

The men who wrought to transform us from a group
of colonies to a nation were the forebears of those who
in the nineteenth century wrote their names indelibly
upon the annals of time. Why does our mental equipment and emotional endowment compare unfavorably with
that of our parents and grandparents? There is scarcely
a man in this country, with one notable exception, who
is carrying on as his distinguished father or grandfather
did in lighting the world, in building its railroads, in
diversifying its commerce, in transforming our resources
into capital. There is a reason for this. Parents in their
love and in their imbecility have thought that it made
for the welfare of their sons and daughters to spare them
the trials and hardships that they themselves endured.
Many of these parents have lived to see their sons refused entrance by universities. Many others have been
obliged to devote their time and money to persuading
the modern Delilah to spare their sons' hair.

What an interesting chapter the rise and fall of any
one of our "first families" would make! I recently visited
a tomb which in its grandeur compares with that of the
great Florentine pawnbrokers in the Church of San
Lorenzo and with the Panteon de los Reyes in the Es-
corial. It contains the remains of one who three generations ago laid the foundation of a fabulous fortune by
transporting us, our goods, and our produce. Time has
shown that he had vision, imagination, courage, decision,
and determination—and many descendants. Have any of
them displayed a tithe of the qualities of their great fore-
bear? Their names are frequently in the "society" columns of newspapers, but the "news" connected with their
names is often not to their credit.

I am not contending that genius is or is not hereditary.
I am stating that good blood ought not to peter out in

one or two generations, and that it does not in any country save our own. There is something, apparently, in this land of the free that is capable of destroying the fine fiber of personality, of disintegrating the higher moral faculties, if allowed to envelope the growing child. For lack of a more specific name it may be called parental over-solicitousness.

It is the way the past generation has brought up its children spiritually and materially, and the way the present generation is bringing up its own that is responsible for our personal and national infantilism. The care that wealthy parents expend upon their children is love's labor lost. Parents and teachers pay as little attention to their children's emotional development as they do to their vocalization or their carriage—that is, none at all. Then they are astonished that their children do not realize that "beauty is truth, truth beauty," and that they do not speak melodiously or walk gracefully.

There is only one way to facilitate emotional maturity: provide the adolescent with cares and responsibilities. On the other hand, there are many ways to facilitate emotional immaturity, and the most effective is to wrap the budding emotional soul in the cotton-wool of paternal oversolicitude.

One of the reasons this country had a Washington and a Lee, a Franklin and a Lincoln, an Emerson and a Thoreau, a Poe and a Whitman, a Vanderbilt and a Vail is that they were not brought up in hothouses; they were not swaddled in silks and furs. Their colds did not cause parent-panics, and their bilious attacks were not beyond the reach of sulphur and molasses. They were not rushed to the mountains or the sea when the sun grew hot, or to Florida when the days grew cold. They were allowed to meet the hazards of life, and made to rely in a measure on their own invention to surmount them. They had to face the problems which God or man, fate or accident set them. But to-day we solve them for our children, and then we wonder or weep when our children cannot solve those problems which present themselves after they have flown from the nest, or are making ready to fly.

While we witness the abolition of social distinctions the world over, and vaunt our democratic disregard of birth and privilege, we say to our son or daughter, "Don't play with so and so, dear, he is not 'nice.' " Or we say to each other, "You know, Julia and Charles can't live in Sandown; their children have no one to associate with. Their neighbors are all Poles and chauffeurs."

We display an anxiety about the physical welfare of our children which would be justified were they made of sugar, salt, or tobacco. We shelter them until their twelfth year from all outside influences that we can thwart, and even then we strive to keep their contact with the world very limited. During this plastic age, they are studiously kept from contacts, environment, and experience that would stimulate their emotional growth and invigorate it. Then we are astonished that many of them are punies, parasites, perverts. If parents lack vision and perspective, how can we expect children to possess qualities that must be bred into them unconsciously with the first smile and the first frown?

IV

There is an appalling side of matrimony which is disturbing the minds of many people: the increasing frequency of divorce in this country. More divorces spring from Adult-infantilism than from adultery. When a man realizes that his wife is a doll, with the reactions of a child in the body of a woman, he quickly curls himself up into a cocoon or he seeks the companionship of someone who will give him emotional stimulation or appeasement. It is the same with a woman who has had it brought home to her that her husband is a "stuffed shirt," who whistles tunelessly while shaving, blows soap-bubbles while bathing, becomes panicky when his temperature rises above one hundred and two, and won't play unless he can be the leader. Jealousy, cruelty, alcoholism are as naught compared with Adult-infantilism as a wrecker of marriage.

In young women Adult-infantilism takes on an attractive aspect and appeals to man's sense of protection. The girl whose lisp is "too cute for words," who plays at being a child when she is old enough to have one of her own, who looks appealingly to men for assistance and comfort is the one from whom men should fly as they would from the plague. But they don't. The woman-infant attracts them. They rail and theorize against the girl who is not afraid to look after herself, who has neither leisure nor inclination to camouflage her personality that it may please the other sex, and who scorns artifices of conduct as much as she loathes affectation.

"My daughter, you know, is such a child," is the customary admonition of the mother to her new son-in-law, or it was until yesterday, and that's the pity of it! The speech I heard oftenest from women during my professional life was, "You see, I knew very little about life, its entailments and responsibilities, when I married. My mother did not tell me anything."

The adult-infant woman who marries may experience when her first child is born a far greater thrill than she had when she received her first doll, but apparently she soon finds the responsibility too great, the care too confining, the energy required to bring him up more than she can supply; and the child is given over to nurses. It is be-

yond belief how little parents see of their children these
days. Of course I mean parents that are well-to-do.
Parents who think they can buy character for their children from nurses and teachers harbor a delusion from
which flows the unpardonable sin: bringing children into
the world and then neglecting to orient them on the road-
way of life.

It is obvious that the life of a nation is dependent exclusively on the lives of the individuals who compose it, so
the handicaps of the latter are directly resultant from those
of the former. An individual carries his infirmities and
qualities into his public life—and the public life of some
hundred and fifteen million people compose these United
States as a nation. Therefore, it is not astonishing that the
man who suffers pain because his house is not so large as
his neighbor's should belong to a nation which becomes
much wrought up when it discovers that it cannot have
the largest airship in the world, or which prides itself on
having the biggest city, the tallest buildings, the longest
bridges, and the fastest automobiles in the world. Dimen-
sion, size, weight, and speed are the slogans of our country, and they compensate for ideals, for art, for true greatness.

We display, to the average European, an ignorance or
an apathy toward foreign affairs which is astounding.
Magazines or books that attempt to cope with this apathy
are regarded as "highbrow," and receive neither support
nor encouragement. Stray facts regarding foreign policies,
like facts about foreign customs, are gathered from newspapers and from persons who are not qualified either by
experience or knowledge to speak informatively.

One reads, in the newspapers, at intervals, that a man
whose name is prominent in business circles has just returned from a trip to Europe. He is eagerly questioned by

reporters as to "conditions abroad," and there usually follows, on the part of the traveler, a long, detailed, forceful, and sometimes plausible argument which tends to explain not only facts regarding other countries, but their hidden and mysterious psychologies. Not a voice is raised in protest as to the wrongness of such argument; the public either shrugs its shoulders, thinking, "What do I care? These foreigners should take care of their own affairs, just as we, good Americans, take care of ours," or else accepts it all blindly.

It is only occasionally that politics have any meaning save "to keep the newspapers busy" and "to provide jobs for a lot of men who could not otherwise make a living." The fact that politicians are running our nation and that upon them falls the responsibility of shaping its destiny, makes little or no impression. To follow the trend and achievements of the country requires maturity of mind which involves emotional maturity. That is what we have not got; the happy-go-lucky attitude is so much easier. We would rather play golf or go to a football game than vote; and we cannot take the time from radios and movies to inquire into the merit of constitutional amendments. It is always time enough to rise up in self-defense when our statesmen strike at our most cherished possession. We, moral men and true, find it much easier flagrantly to break the law prohibiting the manufacture and sale of alcohol than we do to co-operate in getting it changed or modified so that we, moral men and true, can face ourselves as such in the mirror.

Youth is dogmatic and tenacious of its opinions. It takes years of experience, of hard knocks and sound thinking to reach the conclusion that there is some good in all evil and some evil in every good. To children things, ideas, and persons are all of one piece: good or bad. Tolerance is a virtue to which they have no access, and their opinions have the rigidity and stubbornness of the inexperienced. It is only in later years that resiliency of mind and indulgence of heart modify the sternness of our youthful judgments. Can we say that we have reached maturity when we reflect upon our attitude toward Negroes, Jews, and Irish Catholics? What is the explanation of our hatred of them? It does not exist among other peoples. In what country of the world could the Ku Klux Klan thrive and operate as it does in the United States? Can anyone imagine such excitement and participation in fundamentalism in France or in England as we have displayed during the past year? We have two political parties: the members of one oppose the other, but neither can tell wherein they differ. A Republican is a man who believes in a protective tariff, but when the Democrats are in power the protective tariff still prevails. Our political views, as well as our religious beliefs, are for the most part emotional attitudes. Judgment does not enter into their conclusions, it leaves the road free to prejudice and to what we call tradition— that is, to our father's ideas and beliefs.

What does a child do when he has nothing to do or nothing to play with? If he is very young, he cries to attract attention or to manifest his boredom. If he is older, he clamors for help; if he is too old to do either, he sits in an armchair and broods, his feet dangling over one of the arms, or he seeks solace in drink or drugs. When questioned, he says, "I have nothing to do, no one to play with, I am tired of my old toys and books; I have nowhere to go." What do we grown-ups do when we have amassed a competence, are bored with the newspapers, and cannot find any new movies? We go to Europe by the tens of thousands, we rush *en masse* to join touring parties, we are forever carrying our sterile minds and tired bodies to other lands. We exclaim "How lovely!" as our gondolas glide through the Grand Canal; "how queer!" when we look at the habitués of the Café de la Rotonde, "how terrible!" when we listen to the guide's toneless explanations of the Tower of London, and we hope it won't be long before we are back in Claridge's, in Montmartre, or at the Lido.

One of the most conspicuous traits common to all the examples chosen in order to illustrate the extent to which we are adult-infants is that there is everywhere a lack of moderation, of measure. We take things in their extreme, we push a situation to the point where it can no longer hold but has to give way under the pressure we inflict upon it. We drink to excess, or we are total abstainers; we talk continuously, or we are mute; we are ardent churchgoers, or we maintain that religion has lost contact with the living reality from which it derives validity and truth. We play too hard, and we work too hard; we condemn others, or we praise them beyond their merit. We contend that the countries of Europe should pay us what they owe us in full, or that we should wipe the debts completely off the slate. People are "hateful" or "wonderful," and things are "terrible" or "marvellous." There is no middle-ground where good and evil mingle and blend, and make for thought and perspective. We are a nation of people whose emotional qualities are not measured against corresponding intellectual possessions and we display the former to the detriment of the latter. It was not always so; it is a comparatively recent development. It is a corroding result of our colossal and too easily won prosperity. What if we should have to distribute our money that we may rid ourselves of this recently acquired infirmity?

The die is cast, but we need not despair. Recognition and detection of the causes of a malady are half the cure. Materially, we have made great strides in the past hundred years; we have reached a position in the financial world of which we may be proud. But we may have more legitimate cause for pride when other nations no longer regard us as a conglomeration of business wizards, unbeatable polo-players, peerless cup-defenders, whose days are given over to making money and whose nights are devoted to listening to the American eagle shriek our praises.

SHORT SKIRTS *

By Hugh A. Studdert Kennedy

ONE lovely afternoon in June, some twelve years ago, I was passing under the Admiralty Arch in London, out of the bustle and roar of Charing Cross, into the comparative quiet of the Mall and St. James Park. It was a warm day, very warm for London, and the sunlight seemed to dance on the leaves of the plane trees, and catch up a soft mist from the earth. I was walking along and enjoying it all with that quiet satisfaction a Londoner feels when his London is running true to form, when, suddenly, looking up I saw a woman turning out of one of the little side roads leading to Birdcage Walk, and coming towards me. The moment I saw her I almost stopped where I stood. She was obviously a woman of grace and refinement, beautifully gowned in the mode of the day, save for the outrageous fact,—for so it seemed to me,— that the sleeves of her dress were completely transparent from the wrists to the shoulders.

Well, it was a shock, but I pulled myself together, and was walking on without, I hope, any undue exhibition of emotion when I noticed to my regret that several of the passers-by were not acting with a like restraint. First one here and one there, quite frankly stopped to look after her. Then they began to follow her. Then the small crowd, with its inevitable snowball tendencies, began to draw a

* Reprinted from *The Forum* by permission of the author and of the editors.

large crowd, and before she had gone fifty yards some
fifty people must have been following her. I shall never
forget the look of bewildered terror which came over the
girl's face when she realized that she was the centre and
cause of it all. She quickened her pace, but so did the
crowd; then some small boys began to jeer, some youths
began to jostle her, and it was easy to see what would
happen. Before I knew what I was doing I had pushed my
way through the crowd, enlisted the services of the inevitable policeman stationed at the corner of Spring Gardens,
and between us we got the half fainting girl into a taxi.
The rôle of knight errant was new to me, but I carried it
through with an efficiency which surprised myself, and by
the time I had deposited her at Queen Anne's Mansions,
where she was staying with her father and mother, she
had tearfully explained to me that they had just arrived
from New York, that every woman in New York was
wearing that kind of dress, that she never could have
dreamed that such a thing would happen, and that she
would never get over it.

I could not help recalling this incident very forcibly,
last year, when on a very similar summer day in June, I
found myself once again passing under Admiralty Arch
out of the whirl of the motor busses into the blessed green-
ery of St. James Park. Everywhere one looked, dotted
about the lawns, under the shade trees, walking along the
Mall, leaning over the bridges across the Long Water, and
feeding the ducks, were girls, not in gowns with transparent sleeves, but in gowns with no sleeves at all; in
gowns that did not come an inch below the knee; in gowns
devoid of necks and only very transparently supplied with
backs.

Well, I remember, I hired a chair from an ancient but
watchful attendant at the price of twopence, and, taking

it under a tree, sat down and watched it all. Ten years before, one lone girl clad after a fashion which at that moment would have been regarded as almost Quakerish in its modesty, had created something bordering on a panic in this very place; women had openly dubbed her a hussy; men and boys excited by the brazenness of her costume had openly followed her, with intentions which were not honorable, and more undemonstrative passers-by had wondered what the world was coming to.

And this was what the world was coming to,—bare arms, bare knees, bare necks, and, yes, bare backs too. What *was* it coming to? And yet, as I looked out from my Olympian seat under the tree, I could not help but note how unconcerned everybody seemed about it. It may have been fancy, but it seemed to me that the air was purer and cleaner than it had been ten years before, as if an unholy pressure had been relieved, and impudent hocus-pocus shorn of its imaginary power. Legs were everywhere, arms were everywhere, necks and backs by the round dozen and score were everywhere, and yet the men and boys passing back and forth were going about their daily walk and conversation just as if nothing were happening, just as if the world around them was not coming to anything out of the ordinary, after all.

And so, as I sat under my tree I thought of many things, and I remember recalling how, several years ago, a great artist told me an interesting story. We were talking about this very matter of women's dress, and how entirely it was a question of the point of view. He remembered, he said, one day when he was a young art student that a curious thing happened at the life class he was in the habit of attending. The model was a young girl of singular refinement and beauty of form, and the class was drawing her undraped figure. She was a good model, and had been sitting motionless for half an hour or so, when, suddenly glancing upwards, she saw the face of a man peering at her through the skylight. She had been posing for half an hour before a class of fifty men, yet when she saw this face at the skylight, with an outraged cry, she threw a wrapper around her shoulders, jumped from the platform, and withdrew in tears to her dressing-room.

Now the artist has always been regarded as necessarily a man of looser morals than the man who follows some other calling. It is an absurd assumption, of course, but it arises from the fact that the average human being, dragooned into a show of "respect" for the "mysteries" of women's dress, cannot conceive of anyone who does not give the rap of a button for it as anything but immoral. The fact is, of course, that artists are not less moral than other men, but have, on the contrary, gained a certain measure of freedom from that incubus of mystery which makes for, as it is intended to make for, the excitation of desire. The human mind resents the acquisition of this freedom. Whatever this so-called life force is, which, as Bernard Shaw says somewhere, takes us by the scruff of our necks and compels us to create after its kind, it will fight every step of the way against any movement tending to shake off the shackles of mere animalism, and make for a larger and higher interpretation of life.

A hundred years ago the "womanly woman" had perhaps reached her most "womanly" expression. The women of Jane Austen's day were almost completely preoccupied with questions of sex. They had it for their every thought. They sewed a little, cooked a little, read French a little, played the harpsichord a little, languished a great deal, had the vapors whenever necessary, and, as a last resort, went into a decline. But whether they sewed or played or had vapors, it was always with some very gallant gentleman or gentlemen in view. And as to the very gallant gentlemen, they were so gallant that a chance view of my lady's ankle was sufficient to put them into a cold sweat, while anything more was sufficient to persuade them that they had been transported out of the world of everyday life into the half-world of everyday life, which existed, a hundred years ago, just as it does to-day, and just as it had done since the beginning of time.

I remember as I sat on that twopenny chair under the shade trees in St. James Park asking myself if after all it was a degenerate age in which I was living. A boy and girl passed by, taking a short cut across the grass towards the water. He was a healthy looking youngster, with a sunburnt laughing face and curly hair, and she, free and lissome, kept pace with him. In dress she was everything she ought not to have been, according to the standards of a dozen years ago. According to the standards of Jane Austen she was nothing but a wanton. As I watched them, they suddenly went up in smoke, and in their places I saw my lady and her gallant gentleman of a hundred years ago. They seemed to have only one thing in common, one thing to talk about, one reason for existing. And he bowed over her little hand, and she blushed underneath her ringlets, and the great preoccupation of all the ages was enthroned with power. Next moment they had gone their way, and the boy and girl of this present hour of grace were back again. They had stopped in front of me, and he was kneeling on the ground and supporting her foot on his knee, tying her shoe string and they were both laughing. "Well," she said as she steadied herself with her racket, "it was a pretty even fight, but I won, fair and square, didn't I?"

It was a pretty even fight. The words came to me with a strange new revealing. I remembered too, some twelve years previous, in the days just before the war, I had sat with one of the leaders of woman's suffrage, and debated with her the whole question of the "liberation movement," as we called it then. They were burning churches throughout the country, in those days, blowing up bridges and doing all manner of things they ought not to do, and the cry of sex warfare was to be heard on all sides. Yet this mild-voiced, mild-mannered woman insisted to me that the one aim and purpose of it all, however little men and women seemed to be conscious of it, was equality and coöperation. "We must have equality and we must have coöperation, because only thus can we obtain completeness, and that is after all what we are all seeking, and must one day attain."

And so, as I sat there under my tree, and the sun began to sink down behind Constitution Hill, and the ancient but watchful attendant began to pile up his vacated chairs, I seemed to get a new light. In spite of the fulminations of so much constituted authority, I began to see this younger generation as "some holy thing." It is a conviction that has grown in strength ever since. Every woman is a potential man, and every man is a potential woman. The woman of to-day may not have envisaged this as something to be demonstrated; she is, nevertheless, setting about its demonstration. With unerring, if unconscious wisdom, she is doing the first things first, she is getting rid of the mystery of the flesh. It may appear to her very often as an exaggerated form of sex indulgence. The arbiters of fashion may think that like a homeopathic dose every attenuation adds to its potency, yet the man who twenty years ago was fired by the suggestion and mystery of the clothed form finds himself unmoved in the presence of so much nakedness, because it is unashamed.

The point is a fundamental one. Last summer I was in Paris. I had not been there since the war, but in the days before the war I had known Paris well. From a little front room in the Rue Descartes, in the Quartier Latin, I had seen the world go by, and fared forth at all times of the day and night to mingle with it. Every phase of Paris life fascinated me, and so, when I came back to it, last summer, I sought to mingle with it again. Change of course had been everywhere, but that is away from the point; what is to the point is just one experience,—a visit I paid one hot August evening to the Casino de Paris. The great theatre was filled to overflowing—with Americans. Fathers and mothers from,—to judge from the conversation around me,—every State in the Union were there with their families; college students, boys and girls, schoolmarms and maiden aunts, a very respectable and utterly wholesome crowd. They were out in search of adventure; they thrilled with the thought of being real devilish. Often had they heard and read of the terrible things that were to be seen at such shows and here they were actually going to see them. Some of them looked as if they wished they had never come. "Momma" was obviously disturbed; "Poppa" obviously determined to see the thing through; "Son" tingling with wild expectation; "Daughter" triumphant. Directly behind me was a family party from Vermont, and I shall never forget the despairing gasp which came from the mother of the party and a maiden aunt when the curtain rose on the first scene. It was a masterpiece of color and light, but as each successive girl mounted the dais, and, throwing aside a gorgeous wrapper, posed unclothed from the waist up, these two sterling women could see nothing in it but an outrage on decency.

Now, I am not concerned to defend such shows,—I

really dislike them, not because of the shows themselves, but because of the audience,—but I am concerned with their effect upon the audience. The first hour at the Casino de Paris was atrocious. The audience was an indecent audience; but gradually a change was noticeable. The horrified gasps, the semi-hysterical giggling, the "Land's sakes!" the "Good nights!" died away. The mother from Vermont became silent, and I had almost forgotten about her when the curtain went up on a scene which was supposed to be the climax. It represented the interior of a Roman bath. Whatever may be thought of such exhibitions, there can be no doubt that it was a perfect picture, a Leighton, a Collier, or an Alma Tadema. The lighting, the setting, the faithfulness to detail, the draped or half draped figures of the women, their pose and movement were all characterized by a very excellent restraint. Suddenly, at the top of the marble steps leading down to the bath a young girl appeared; she paused for a moment, and then, throwing aside her wrapper, descended the steps, unclothed, to the water's edge.

And then I became conscious that Momma was speaking.

"My, isn't she just beautiful," she said happily.

"She sure is," was Poppa's reply.

I looked round at Daughter; she was looking straight in front of her, and for some unaccountable reason, her eyes were filled with tears. Then I glanced at Son; he was holding sister's hand. I could not help asking myself then as I have often asked myself since,—had these people risen or fallen in the scale of morality since they entered the theatre? They had surely risen. They had gone to look for darkness with a candle, and behold there was no darkness.

The incident to me is typical of this day and age. The

lack of morality is not in the nakedness but in the shame, and the shame grows less day by day. The question of sex is really occupying thought far less to-day than at any time in history. Where a hundred years ago a woman had but one preoccupation, to-day she has a hundred. And so when a Prince of the Church declares, as he did recently, that he is shocked at "the unparalleled depravity of woman's dress," and declares that he is "at a loss to explain the universal decadence which has swept over the world," the woman of to-day is apt to answer him shortly enough. Some time ago, I was in a street car, in a far western city. Two young girls came in, and took a seat diagonally across from me. They were evidently returning from some afternoon concert, and were animatedly discussing the program. Almost opposite them sat what can only be described as a simpering youth. As one of the girls crossed her legs, and displayed a pair of sturdy bare knees, the youth simpered still more. He tried to attract her attention, and finally did, but the next moment, collapsed. The expression of contempt on the girl's face was most successful and the most potent I have ever seen.

That expression of contempt is on the face of woman, to-day, whenever she is faced with the prurience of man, and man is rising to the demand that woman is making upon him. The struggle is ever towards completeness. For the most part, it is a blind struggle, the instinct of the leaf that turns towards the light, but just in proportion as it becomes more conscious, does its success become more rapid. For untold centuries, men and women have been seeking this completeness materially, but the more surely do they through such means scale the heights, the more certainly are they hurled from them into the depths. "Who told thee that thou wast naked?" is still the demand of

Reality from those who, through the ecstasy of the senses, have sought to achieve the heaven of completeness.

No transitional period is desirable for its own sake, and as far as the relation of the sexes is concerned, we are passing through a period of transition, a period in which license is, more often than not, mistaken for liberty, and old-time "faiths" vanish in a peal of laughter. And the laughter is the most wholesome thing about it. The surest way for the world to rid itself of the hocus-pocus of sex is to laugh at it.

> *A lady with a lamp shall stand*
> *In the great history of the land.*

Well, the lady has come, and she is standing. And her skirts are short, and her arms are bare. As to her back, I cannot see it, for her face is towards me; but on her face, upturned to the light of her lamp, is shining the glory of a new era.

THE DOGMA OF "BUSINESS FIRST" *

By Stuart Chase

ONE hundred and twenty-six years ago my great-great-grandfather was living in a farmhouse with a pitch to its back roof and a great fireplace, ovened and wainscotted, in the town of Newburyport, Massachusetts. He lived in a community that raised the bulk of its own food, built its own houses out of local materials, and spun and wove most of its own clothing. Withal, it was good food, durable and comely clothing, and housing of a unique and lasting beauty. On High Street were the square white houses of the shipbuilders, and out along the country roads were the farmhouses with their well-sweeps and their dipping eaves. And lovely as were the houses of the shipbuilders, lovelier still were ships (soon it was to be clipper ships) which they built. In fact, upon an astonishing amount of the materials which passed through the hands of the men and women of Newburyport, and the other New England towns—upon iron work, pewter, glass, woodwork, textiles, masonry—was stamped an authentic and enduring beauty which all the banalities of the traffic in antiques cannot efface. Reasonably well fed, snugly housed, and with articles to his hand for daily use which now are jealously guarded in museums, my great-great-grandfather lived his life. Anon he hitched up and went over the hills to the town meeting. The steam engine was yet to come, the first textile mill was yet to

* Reprinted by permission of the author and of Harper & Brothers, New York City.

be built in New England, the industrial revolution was waiting to be born.

A century and a quarter later, after the most stupendous increase in the technical arts which the world has ever seen or is ever likely to see, I look about the place where I live in New York City, and out of the window of that place where the sun never rests, and wonder what, in terms of the life more abundant, the industrial revolution has done for me. How much more rewarding, not only in respect to beauty and the things of the spirit, but in absolute material comfort, is my existence than that of my great-great-grandfather? My housing is drearier and more inconvenient, my food is softer and less succulent, my clothing is uglier and infinitely less durable; the day-by-day pressure of the sights and shadows and odors about me is depressing, and cumulative in its depression.

In the matter of income, my great-great-grandfather was not above the average of his community; quite possibly, as a farmer, he was below it. The joint income of my wife and myself is probably three times the average of the community in which we live. Compare the average householder in New York to-day with the average citizen in Newburyport in 1800, and where does the advantage, in terms of the good life, lie? Look abroad out of these sullen canyons to other cities—Chicago, Pittsburgh, Cleveland, St. Louis, San Francisco, New Orleans—to the suburban cubicles which girdle modern cities, to Main Street, to the farms of the cotton belt and of the tobacco belt, aye, to Newburyport and its outlying farms as they are to-day. What tangible improvements in well-being, beauty, and happiness has a century of unprecedented invention brought to the inhabitants of these places? I ask the question. I know that it has brought some well-being, perhaps a great deal to some people. But, looking into dead walls from my apartment window, I wonder again what are the gifts which Arkwright and Stevenson and Watt have placed in my hands. The amazing thing is that I should wonder at all. There is a machine now which can make plows thirty-two times faster than the black-smith of Newburyport could ever fashion them, a machine which can make cotton sheeting one hundred and three times faster than my great-great-grandmother could ever spin and weave it, and we have in the energy released by the engines and turbines of America, the labor of three billions of slaves, or nearly thirty servants for every man, woman, and child in the country. Engineers have assured us that technical knowledge is now available, which—if it could be put to work—would banish poverty, double or treble the standard of living, turn ugly cities into noble cities, and by means of giant power and decentraliza-tion bring the culture of the town to the countryside.

Why has this not been done? Why do I look out at my blank wall, why are millions infinitely worse housed in slums, why does the tobacco grower of Kentucky abandon the losing struggle against the marching weeds? This is a question not lightly to be answered, a complex and baffling question. But my guess is this. It has not been done because an economy like that of Newburyport, for all its lack of engines, was well within the range of hu-man capacity to administer, being in fact the immemorial economy of self-sustaining groups the world round; but the economy of the machine with its immense distances of transport and its great clots of workers who make no food, and of food growers who make nothing else, has proved to date, except in time of war, to be beyond human administrative capacity. Or better, under the prevailing system of business enterprise, it is held that the machine needs no master with an eye single to the

welfare of the group; and whatever potential administrative capacity there may be accordingly never gets a
chance to function. The prime charge upon every politician
is the welfare of business in terms of monetary profit;
only in passing and incidentally may he regard the welfare
of the whole community. For it is held as axiomatic that
what is good for business is good for everybody; what
hurts business, hurts everybody. When Adam Smith spoke
of the "invisible hand" which directed this consummation, he little realized that he was founding what has
come to be almost a new religion.

> Thus God and Nature formed the general frame
> And bade self-love and social be the same.

The learned Smith and the business men and the politicians may of course be right. Perhaps by scrupulously
safe-guarding self-interest and anarchy in business we do
secure more in net welfare than we should by any other
method. All other methods are, to date, largely a matter
of theory because, since the coming of the machine, business anarchy is the only method which has been tried.
The Russian experiment is too young to give any sound
evidence on either side. But what we may conclude without fear of contradiction is that if business anarchy is the
best way to regulate the machine, while it may keep a
few more of us alive per acre of crop land, most of us
have not gained anything compared with Newburyport,
if, indeed, we have not lost. If this is indeed the best
way, it is painful to contemplate the results of any other
way. Where would a hundred years of co-operation or
state socialism or some combination of these two with
laissez-faire have landed us? With two-thirds of the
families of America now beneath the line of the United
States Department of Labor's budget of health and de-

cency, presumably most of us would have long since starved to death had the three billions of power slaves been in any other hands than those of business. Not many of us die of starvation and perhaps, Mr. Coolidge, that is proof enough that yours is the wisest way.

Whatever its ultimate wisdom, anarchy is by definition and by practice wasteful. Nor should business anarchy reflect any exception to this rule. It may not prove unprofitable to take inventory of certain major leakages and losses which are implicit in the going economic structure. Down what blind alleys has technical knowledge gone; what dams have choked and diverted the free flow of invention and discovery; what are the three billions of slaves concerned with that they have not time to destroy these slums, uproot these weeds, build me a decent house in a noble city?

II

The factor which is primarily responsible for the dispersion of energy is, I suppose, the lack of community and regional planning. That the rush of the pioneers to conquer a continent must inevitably be planless is as manifest as is the fact that absence of plan makes for an incredible volume of waste. Cities sprang up on the wrong sites, crops were grown on the wrong soil, factories were built in the wrong places, railways paralleled and choked waterways, forests were butchered to the glory of fire and flood, long hauls displaced short hauls, gas wells blew their billions of cubic feet into the air, pools of unemployed workers began to form, while the machine diluted its output with a tremendous tonnage of ugly, flimsy, shoddy, jerry-built, and generally adulterated products. "Everything turned to profit. The towns had their profitable dirt, their profitable smoke, their profitable slums, their profitable disorder, their profitable ignorance, their profitable despair. The curse of Midas was on this society: on its corporate life, on its common mind, on the decisive and impatient step it had taken from the peasant to the industrial age. For the new town was not a home where man could find beauty, happiness, leisure, learning, religion, the influences that civilize outlook and habit, but a bare and desolate place, without color, air, or laughter, where man, woman, and child worked, ate, and slept. This was to be the lot of the mass of mankind; this the sullen rhythm of their lives. The new factories and the new furnaces were like the Pyramids, telling of man's enslavement rather than of his power, casting their long shadows over the society that took such pride in them." Thus the Hammonds conclude their exhaustive study of the coming of the industrial revolution to England. It was not greatly different in New England or generally in urban America.

Of all the great American cities, only Washington was planned for comfortable living rather than for selling real estate by the front foot. No local region has ever been planned at all and, save for a brief interval during the World War, no budget of national requirements has ever been cast, or the productive capacity to meet these requirements assessed. It is only the sheer fecundity of the machine which has permitted such a sprawling, haphazard growth. If every engine stripped its gears tomorrow, in a few days most of us, in our present geographical location, should begin to starve. In a month we should be dead. Without steam and electricity Newburyport could take no such chances in hurling its people to the economic peripheries, could afford no man power wasted on the shoddy and the jerry-built, could tolerate no excess industrial structure—twice the fields or twice the blacksmith shops or twice the shipways which normal demand called for—nor maintain the luxury of a reserve squadron of unemployed workers. Its economy forced a moderately accurate adaption of production to requirements, and the dependability of the plan is evidenced in the time which still remained, after stark necessities were met, to elaborate and beautify, and stamp upon the output the seal of craftsmanship.

To plan for a continent is a harder task than to plan for a town. During the pioneering decades it was folly to ask for any plan at all. But as the Pacific was reached, some rough appraisal, some conscious attempts at coordination were certainly not beyond human capacity. Regions have been planned from Mesopotamia down. More American cities might have followed Washington— and Paris. Waterways might have been aided instead of strangled. The people through their Government might have controlled the exploitation of natural resources. As invention and the technical arts expanded, the coordination of national economic life might have become the more competent and accurate. Dreams, yes. But only so was it possible to outdistance Newburyport, only so could the fecundity of the machine create an accelerating reserve of welfare for the whole community. But the religion of private enterprise said no.

Take New York City for example. The congestion of its streets puts a premium on death and injury, and adds enormously in transportation cost to every article the city dweller buys, and to every structure built. I know a building where four hundred bricklayers stand in rows, trowel in hand. Yet so great is the pressure of traffic below them, that never more than a single hour's supply of bricks can be stored in advance—which means a constant stream of trucks delivering hand to mouth. And when the trucks are halted in a traffic jam—as they often are—the masons stand idle. But that idle time goes into the cost of the building. As land values shift, it has become a recognized practice in New York to look on construction as a short-term investment. Thus, instead of lasting its hundred years or so, buildings erected twenty, even ten years ago—perfectly sound buildings many of them—are being torn down and scrapped. New buildings spring up, only to be scrapped, undepreciated, in their turn. Consider the colossal cost, the gigantic waste of such a program. Consider the cost of digging a subway, which, when it is finished, far from relieving congestion, has only accelerated it. Consider the cost of furnishing water, gas, sewage, electricity, telephone service, foodstuffs to a city so badly planned; think of the unbelievable number of bottlenecks through which all these services must pass. Think of the plumbing which has to be renewed on the average every eight years, at a labor cost twice that of the original installation. Yet the technical arts can tell us how to install plumbing which will last a generation. Consider the absurd terminal facilities, the half-loaded milk wagons, the hauls and the cross-hauls, the additional cleaning due to the lack of smoke prevention. Above all, consider the enormous parasitic population of New York: the middlemen, the speculators, the ticket scalpers, the prostitutes, the bootleggers, the dope peddlers, the flunkies, door openers, wash-room dusters; the purveyors of the ultra, the modish, and the snobbish.

In Newburyport there were no parasites, there were no problems of congestion, of subway building, of cross-hauling, of short-term housing investments, of idle bricklayers standing four hundred in a line. There were no seasons of unemployment when half the clothing workers walked the streets. There were no business cycles. There was no importing of bulk foodstuffs over half the world. There were no spirited campaigns, supported by expert psychologists, for the smashing of sales resistance. There was no installment buying. These merry things cost unbelievable sums of money—and what is more to the point than money, they cost *man power*. What the machine, what the industrial revolution have done in effect is to permit New York City to support a large population of idle, an enormous population of working parasites, and a colossal extra force of useful workers kept busy by the congestion and planlessness of the urban area. No little of the energy of the three billion slaves goes down this trapdoor. The technical knowledge is available to plan cities, to plan regions. Mr. J. Russell Smith alone, one suspects, could tell us how to double living standards. But there is no private profit to be made from such plans. They are proscribed.

III

I am convinced that it is the lack of regional planning which constitutes the main reasons for my failure to gain on my great-great-grandfather in anything like the ratio that productivity per capita gains. Most of the productivity goes into bridging the fissures in the underlying chaos. But this is a large, general and, no doubt, an arguable indictment. It is possible to outline certain other leakages of knowledge more specifically.

Consider for instance the concern of the science of physics, chemistry, and biology with modern warfare. As everybody knows and as corporation income tax returns make quantitatively evident, war is good for business. War has always driven some men mad, but never, until modern science took charge, has there been such

a malady as "shell shock." Science as applied to warfare
is well on its way to shrivel up the nervous systems of
those it does not kill. Gone in battle are the virtues of
strength, determination, skill at arms—aye, of courage.
A little man with a leaky heart valve pushes a button
somewhere miles away, and the strength and skill and
courage go hundreds of feet into the air together with
fragments of arms and legs and viscera. Of the ten million killed and the twenty million wounded in the late
crusade for democracy, how many received their hurt in
hand-to-hand struggle such as the Romans knew? Probably not one per cent. The ninety and nine were stricken by
the engines of science.

Furthermore, with the development of psychology, the
importance of civilian morale in war time is being given
its due weight—which means that applied science must
not only be directed to the destruction of armies and
navies, but to the destruction of the civilian morale that
supports them. Which means the wiping out of cities, the
utter terrorizing of general populations, behind the lines.
Competent technicians are at this moment giving their
undivided attention to the most efficient means of destroying London, Paris, and Berlin. Yet when it was recently
proposed in Washington that army engineers should design, and army privates should build a bridge across the
Potomac, thus salvaging a little of their technical education for the community, the construction industry rallied
to a man, and in convention assembled, resolved that the
project was an abomination; that construction undertaken for any other end than private profit threatened the
whole fabric of the republic. So the army engineers were
happily permitted to go back to their plans for blowing
the bottom out of the Suez Canal.

Consider next the extent to which the technical arts

have been overborne by quacks bent on the profitable exploitation of new knowledge. On the skirts of every advance in physics, chemistry, biology, and medicine hangs a well-organized group of astute men of business ready to capitalize with useless and often dangerous drugs and devices the wide publicity which the new discovery has received: vaccines, radiations, glands, salvarsans, vitamines, and even the electron. Let J. B. S. Haldane, the noted English biologist, state the case: "For every dollar which we can spend on research and publicity together, the food-faking firms have a thousand for advertising 'scientific' foods. . . . The faker is already on the market with radiations to cure rheumatism and make your hair grow. These are mostly harmless, but probably the sale of X-ray tubes which may cause cancer, will some day be as carefully regulated as that of strychnine. . . . There is no serious reason to believe that any of the rather expensive products of the sex glands now on the market, and often prescribed by doctors, are of any value except as faith cures."

Consider the mauling which science receives at the hands of the high priests of the Nordic saga. In primitive society men who rose to the chieftainship of the tribe looked suspiciously at aspirants from the ranks. So they frequently invited in the royal medicine men to help them hold their power. To-day men of property, of so-called Anglo-Saxon stock, and thus possessing prestige and power, find their possession threatened by radical labor movements, by an incoming horde of shrewd foreigners. They appeal, as always, to the medicine men. But a little difficulty presents itself. The emergence of science has relegated to a twilight zone the gods and myths invoked by the old-time medicine men. Science is on the throne. Softly; what does the commonalty know about science?

Only enough not to blow out the gas, and to read scientific supplements in the Sunday newspapers. Good. Science, for the mass of men, is only a new mysticism; a shift from elves in glades to elves in molecules and air waves and germ plasms. And with a zeal which would have distinguished them in the days of the Aztecs, the modern medicine men proceed to "prove by the aid of science" that the Nordics are the anointed race, that present class distinctions are eternal and unchangeable by virtue of the chemistry of the germ plasm, that heredity is everything and environment nothing. In brief, they summon science to support each and every prejudice of the American man of property. Meanwhile, on some of their pronouncements science has come to no conclusion at all, while on the balance the drift of impartial evidence points to diametrically opposite conclusions. More and more, for instance, particularly since the behaviorists began laboratory experiments on new-born babies, it appears that environment as reflected in acquired habits, is the shaping influence on character. But gullible millions swill down this witchcraft, and thus is the new knowledge traduced again.

Consider the predicament in which applied psychology has landed. Psychology is not yet a full-fledged science, but it has made important and far-reaching advances in the past few years. The behaviorists, the psychoanalysts, and the industrial psychologists are laying the basis for profound changes in the technic of group control. Where is this new knowledge being principally utilized at the present time? In the offices of advertising agencies. Today as never before the man with something to sell knows how to turn into cash three fundamental aspects of human nature: the desire to attract the opposite sex, the desire to exert power over one's neighbors, the desire to get safely and honorably to heaven. In brief, the higher salesmanship has captured applied psychology, horse, foot, and guns. And the very knowledge which might render us significant help is turned against us to create new wants, new desires, new forms of waste. (Some psychologist should write, as he starves, a monograph entitled: How To Build up Sales Resistance. No one will read it now, but in a hundred years he will have a statue in the market-place.)

The consumer at large has to-day no standard of reference by which he can determine quality of goods. Only through the painful and wasteful method of trial and error can he hope to separate the shoddy from the sound. The shoddy makers can say as impressive things about their product as the conscientious manufacturer. A certain roofing concern fabricated a great stock in anticipation of Government orders during the war. The stock, after careful test, was rejected as inferior. Nothing daunted, the company, by means of a high-pressure sales campaign, disposed of the whole order to the general public. Yet here and there in well-equipped laboratories an enormous volume of data as to consumer products and their relative values for specific uses is being accumulated. The Bureau of Standards at Washington has been making such tests for years. As a result, the federal government saves a hundred million dollars annually by purchasing materials, not on the stimulation of high-pressure salesmanship, but according to specifications laid down by the Bureau. For building materials, textiles, clothing, soaps, cleansing fluids, lubricants, motors, paper stock, ink, stationery, hardware, leather goods—for nearly every kind of thing which the common citizen uses—the government pays a lower price for a more durable product

—a price *below* the usual discount for quantity orders because of the standards and specifications determined by the Bureau.

To date, unfortunately, it has not been the policy of the government to release this knowledge to the country at large. Imagine the tearing of beards in the business world if it should. The Bureau of Standards in its laboratories has found out which makes of textiles stand up and which go to pieces, which paints and varnishes are good and which are bad, which inks keep their color and which do not, what types of filling station pumps invariably give short weight; but so hallowed is the conception of private business that this knowledge has remained locked in government files, serving only government purposes.

"Sure," said an ex-Ford employee, "if I went on tightening up nut number 999 any longer, I'd have become nut number 999 myself." Industrial standardization is one of the mightiest achievements of the new technology, but it is a two-edged sword. Applied with due regard for the human equation, it promises the elimination of untold duplication, confusion, and waste, and a tremendous gain in the general standard of living. Applied only from the point of view of the maximum profit in dollars, it can readily become an unmitigated curse. True to the formula of business *über alles,* it is the latter course which industry has pursued to date. Thirty years ago when Frederick W. Taylor was laying down the principles of Scientific Management, motion study was frankly an experiment. It promised well from the standpoint of increasing output, and nobody knew what it would do to the employee. To-day we do know. Not completely and finally, but psychologists in industry have already developed the general laws governing the effects of rhythm, sound, vision, fatigue. They have estimated that of the million man-years lost annually in America by industrial accidents, a full half of them is preventable. We have a body of knowledge sufficient to fix the limits of factory standardization. Is it applied? It is not. With very little exception it is unutilized, wasted knowledge.

Nor is the standardization of the goods which the factory worker makes in much better state. Obviously, the great values here are maximum standardization in all intermediate processes: standard gauges, measurements, tools, supplies—combined with minimum standardization in those end products where variety adds to the spice of life. As Cornelia Stratton Parker puts it, "I see no reason why the æsthetic spirit of the nation would be degraded if we all used 21-inch sewer pipes instead of some 22-inch, but I don't want to see all women wearing the same hats." These values find little place in the going business structure. There is an appalling lack of standardization in intermediate processes and in end products, like sewer pipes, where standards have only virtue —a lack fostered by trade secrecy and the desire to secure competitive advantages. The United States Chamber of Commerce so far forgets itself as to assess this waste at one-quarter of all industrial effort in America. Meanwhile there is over-standardization in many end products where variety is essential. Standardization is a magnificent technic when rightly used, but in the hands of the business motive it has so far succeeded only in running amuck.

One more item, and our inventory of the perversions of knowledge, while by no means complete, must end. Under the acquisitive organization of industry, society shares in new engineering devices, but only to a degree, and only after a period of maximum obstruction. Chief

Clerk Woolard of the United States Patent Office states the case, "There are countless numbers of patents which, if in operation, would much cheapen the articles they could produce, but they are intentionally shelved to prevent competition. Concerns operating under old inventions for which they have expended great sums to erect plants, buy up these new and cheaper methods to prevent competitors from getting hold of them. They then tuck them away in their safes, never to be used."

New inventions may not only be suppressed; they may be presuppressed. A concern may get patents on a whole series of processes in order to tie up the field for the next generation or more. The weighing scale industry is said to have secured advanced patents (by taking them out on some foolish toy) sufficient to close the door to anyone else for twenty years. The ultimate social loss of this one case alone has been estimated at a hundred million dollars.

IV

A member of the United States Tariff Commission in a recent book has put the challenge squarely up to us: "The business world knows no waste unless the saving can be accomplished at a profit. What cannot be salvaged at a profit is not waste in the economic sense. As well talk of the waste of atmospheric nitrogen." And there we are. To release the data of the Bureau of Standards would be alarmingly unprofitable for many corporations. To restrict patent monopolies would stagger the balance sheets of many more. To put the army to building bridges congeals the vitals of the private contractor; to liquidate the blah of advertising would shrink untold dividend checks; to make durable goods would lessen turnover.

For every obstruction, every hindrance to the free flow
of knowledge has been, so far as may be, capitalized at
substantially what the traffic will bear. It earns a profit
and is not waste in the business sense. To break its grip
and bring technology to the direct relief of the community
is treason to business principles and, therefore, un-
thinkable.

But as the inventory of planlessness and thwarted
knowledge unrolls before us it almost moves us to the
brink of treason. Why should we bow meekly before a
dogma which, measured by its concrete results, has netted
us so little in a century and a quarter? Why should we
accept as an act of faith the somewhat preposterous
theory that a few hundred thousand business men, each
working within the high walls of his own back yard
with never a look at the world outside, can provide the
community at large with more and better food, shelter,
and clothing than anyone else ever could?

Why dogma at all? Why does it have to be pure individualism versus pure collectivism, or pure coöperation?
Why all the blood and tears over the "thin entering
wedge?" Governor Smith of New York wants the state
to develop the waterpower of the St. Lawrence, which
the state owns. Owns, mind you. He is willing to let the
distribution of that power remain in the hands of private
business. Technically the combination is admirable. The
dams and the turbines can be built and operated more
economically by the state than by any private company,
while distribution can quite possibly be handled more economically by those already skilled in the technic. Yet for
this proposal, Governor Smith is held little better than a
Bolshevik. Mr. Charles Evans Hughes on behalf of the
Petroleum Institute has just petitioned the Government
to let oil production go on committing harikari—at the

rate of three needlessly wasted barrels for every one reclaimed—because private enterprise must not be interfered with.

On all long-term projects dealing with the exploitation of natural resources, private business simply cannot afford to wait to exploit them systematically and with a minimum of waste. Forests have got to come down, oil fields gush, the cream to be skimmed from coal and minerals, instanter! The principles of profit demand it. Yet whenever and wherever it is proposed that the community handle such exploitation because only the community has the resources and the credit to develop the project according to technically sound principles, the thin opening wedge is brandished, and a thousand editors sniff treason. And so with any fundamental proposal for community planning.

There are doubtless many things that private business can do better and less wastefully than anyone else can do them. There are other things which the community through its government can do best. And still other things which coöperative groups within the community can excel in. It does not stand to reason that there is any one divine way of economic behavior for one hundred and sixteen millions of people over three thousand miles of continent. The assumption of high sanctuary by the theory of business anarchy is undoubtedly as much stuff and nonsense as one hundred per cent state socialism.

It must be more than a little of a bore to be a business man dedicated to a lifetime of unrelenting greed. No wonder he and his fellows go into conference, or play golf on the slightest excuse, or take specials to Florida, or wear paper hats, or grow maudlin about Service. There they stand, each in his own trough, a herd across whose backs no statecraft can hurdle. Good, decent citizens mostly, but their dogmas are costing us all that the machine and the industrial arts and the billions of power slaves might have done for us.

And I guess—it may be a wild guess—that until we smash those dogmas Newburyport will continue to hold its own.

A STRANGE NEW ENGLAND *

By Dane Yorke

"THE wares," once ran a motto on the front page of the
Boston *Post,* "are not improved by their seller's shouting." So New England believed in a day not long gone
by, and persistently set her face in stern pride against
anything that savored of self-exploitation or of an appeal
to the outside world for favor or regard. This trait was
particularly noticeable in New England's attitude toward
the charms of her own countryside. "These Yankees,"
lamented one observer, "have never had the advertising
habit; they never participated in a real-estate boom; they
have believed that New England is better than any other
country and that everybody else would just naturally
recognize so plain a fact." New England, in short, was
the despair of the booster and rather gloried in the fact.
Said Robert Frost in his poem, "New Hampshire":

> I met a Californian who would
> Talk California—a state so blessed
> He said, in climate none had ever died there
> A natural death . . .

New England's scorn of such self-advertising enthusiasms
spoke in Mr. Frost's ironic comment: "That's what comes
of being in the market with a climate."

* Reprinted from *The Independent* by permission of the author and
of the editors.

While his refrain, "It never could have happened in New Hampshire," was almost a platitude. Nothing seemed more of a certainty than that the advertising boom-and-boost spirit of California and Florida, "never could have happened" either in New Hampshire or elsewhere in steady-eyed, quiet-mannered, proudly individualistic North-of-Boston. But note well that I use the past tense. It was in 1923 that Mr. Frost published "New Hampshire" and during all of 1926 that State—and all of New England—were very busily confounding the prophets.

The debacle, if such we may call it, was officially ushered in on May 28, 1926, when a Maine newspaper, under the headline, "New Hampshire Citizens Making Desperate Struggle to Offset 'Come to Maine' Movement," recorded the fact that $50,000 was being raised by public subscription to add to a special publicity fund of $25,000 already granted by the New Hampshire Legislature. The Maine paper further commented:

This summer the other New England States are looking to Maine for the inspiration of Coral Gables. Maine is the first New England State to definitely launch a Business Boom program. The others are wistfully watching our progress and are hastening to take steps to offset our publicity broadcasting.

By June that "hastening" had resulted in the amazing spectacle of Maine, New Hampshire, and Vermont flaunting themselves on the pages of the great newspapers of the country in advertisements—sponsored not by individuals, but by State publicity committees—that shouted their respective recreational charms like competing sideshow barkers. In July, New Hampshire, stealing a march upon the others, gathered a party of 130 newspaper men and women, "representing every State in the Union except four"—one wonders if those four omitted were sister New England States!—and proudly conducted them throughout her domain in a tour of self-exploitation of which the staidly conservative Boston *Transcript* remarked, with approval, "New Hampshire's advertising stunt may well attract the attention of the country wherever big things are being done to attract prosperity. It is unique in every sense." Almost a direct answer to that Boston *Post* motto earlier quoted was the publication that same month by the Maine State Department of Agriculture of a list of farms for sale—many of them of the "abandoned" type—under the remarkable caption: "Gold Mines of the East!"

It is unnecessary to particularize further. The fanfare dazed even the boosters. As one of them remarked, almost incredulously, in a statement published in September, "Who would have thought five years—or even two years —ago that $300,000 provided by State, municipal, and private subscriptions would have been spent in 1926 to advertise New England's advantages and attractions!" Who would have, indeed? Or that Massachusetts this year would vote to fall in with North-of-Boston in "a program of State-wide advertising in 1927!"

But strange as is the mere fact of that advertising, there have been other New England manifestations even more odd. To recur again to that passage from Robert Frost's "New Hampshire," New England has had climate but she never "sold" it—except, perhaps, in the form of ice to India! Truthfully speaking, New England has had an abundance of climate. Mark Twain spoke feelingly of its infinite and unpredictable variety; General Grant half jested of its "nine months winter and three months cold weather"; even Henry Adams dwelt upon its harsh contrasts as cultural disadvantages, while historians have repeatedly described the Pilgrim settlers—and, by implication, their descendants—as having had to face the rigors

of "an inhospitable climate and sterile, rock-bound soil."
New England never resented, particularly, she never
glossed nor minimized such things. But she does today.
A former mayor of Boston has been urging, with wide
editorial approval, a "strong" program of communal advertising stressing the advantages—and only the advantages—of that same climate. Under the headline, "Maine's
Newest Booster Movement," the daily press recently noted
the request of the Maine Public Health Association that
the National Weather Bureau at Washington include "in
its weather reports a comparative showing of the actinic
ray content of the sun's rays in various parts of the
country. If this is done, Maine may be expected to compare most favorably in a comparison of this health-giving
quality of its sunshine." And the suggestion then followed, that to compete with Florida's "Land of Sunshine"
slogan, Maine call herself "The State of *Purest* Sunshine!" More striking still, a well-known New England
newspaper, in a "Brag and Boost Your State" editorial,
proclaimed New England's climate as "Best on earth
for seven months of the year and *yet more lovely* the
other five months *for those who like* the colder winters."
(The italics are mine.) I happen to be one of "those who
like" the New England winter; even so, the naïve euphe-
mism of that phrasing calls irresistibly for emphasis. But
then, listen to New Hampshire—Robert Frost's New
Hampshire—crying in a State advertisement:

What a place to live! To bring up the children, to retain
health and win happiness in the sunshine of the great outdoors!
To raise your own food and gather it fresh from tree and vine;
to learn to know the flowers and the birds! . . . Come! . . .
Revel in the wonderful air and scenery of the "Land of Scenic
Splendor!"

If New England were in the market with soil and climate only! But she hawks other wares as well. The Yankee has been persistently called cold. In my own experience the criticism is based on misunderstanding; the New Englander is not demonstrative or effusive, but he does have a quiet friendliness, almost shy in quality, that is genuine and most likable. New England has been aware of her reputation for frigidity and for years has gone on her way, unnoticing. But today, a hotel advertisement before me says anxiously, "There is nothing cold or stiff about the atmosphere of this hotel—the management *insists* on a *policy* of warm-hearted cordiality." "Our community," contends a chamber of commerce booklet, "is an ideal New England village with modern homes, with democratic and progressive citizens who always give strangers a most cordial reception."

Perhaps it may be thought these are simply isolated instances. Here is the depiction of an entire State. The quotation is from the Boston *Transcript's* account of the newspaper men's junket earlier mentioned. The date is July 17, near the end of the "stunt":

"Every person a booster for New Hampshire" has been the advertising slogan for many months, and there has been an amazing response in these past few days. Scores of towns and cities have vied with one another in placing before the visitors their respective scenic and community merits. . . . Men, women and children have cheered themselves hoarse in their demonstrations of cordiality. Everybody has been eager to see to it that the visitors have had the best possible impression of the people. To the warning, many times expressed from the platform by prominent members of the visiting party, "You are too conservative in New Hampshire," there has been the response of local speakers that the State is fast awakening to the value of advertising and the need of hearty co-operation.

What a picture! Proud New England apologetic; taciturn New England cheering itself hoarse in its efforts to please; stubborn New England abandoning its own inner light of free-necked individualism to listen meekly and sheepishly to the criticisms of outsiders because, forsooth, those same outsiders can give—publicity!

And what is the purpose of it all? A leading newspaper of Maine speaks frankly:

Why are the people of Maine interested in carrying on a campaign of publicity? It is to induce people of other States to come to Maine to spend some of their money. We are not trying to get vacationists and tourists to come here only because they have a good time and improve their health. It is their money the people of this State are trying to get.

True! Impelled by a severe industrial depression that has affected practically every level of her population, New England for the first time has seriously turned—for revenue—to "the tourist business." It is a radical change; the country whose prides have been her town meetings, her long rosters of eminent men and women, her great industries and her even more remarkable educational resources, whose glory has been the title "Mother of republics," that country is today trying to live up to the slogan, "The playground of the nation." What a rôle for Puritan blood!

Naturally, she seems strange. Back in 1683 old Cotton Mather was saying, "Shall I not endeavor to shine by good Example? Yea, and orally upon just Occasion, as well as practically always, bear a Testimony against the Levity of the Young Generation?" But in 1926 other leaders are shouting,—the quotation is actual,—"We must boost New England by advertising *or any other means* that will do the trick!" and some of the "other means" are as strange—in New England—as would have been the mast of the *Mayflower* serving as a Maypole in Morton's Merrymount. Perhaps that may seem hyperbole. But consider this: For years the proud and invariable totem of New Hampshire has been the stern-featured Old Man of the Mountain, the Great Stone Face. But last May the newspapers announced:

New Hampshire will be represented at the Philadelphia Sesquicentennial by a smartly attired model of a winter-sports girl, inviting people to the Granite State, the playground of the country.

The Great Stone Face supplanted by "Miss New Hampshire—with the latest kind of a shingle bob!"—the Maine official State folder saying coquettishly, "For *social* diversions come to Maine!"—Vermont insisting "Coolidge-Land *is* Vacation-Land," while her thoroughly representative son, Calvin Coolidge, is busy all summer long in learning how to fish in an Adirondack lake. Certainly, it all betokens a most strange New England!

FREE AUTO CAMP GROUND *

By Oscar Lewis

It is less than a block from the court house, an area of
wooded ground beside the river. Three years ago, when
the town council met and made the momentous decision,
it was a pasture. In the fall, children gathered blackberries
from the tangle of vines among the willows and about
the bases of the cottonwoods. The city of Manton leased
the property for five years, at an annual rental of $75,
and there were those who said the town fathers had made
a bad bargain. They were wrong; it was the sort of investment buyers of oil stock hope they are making when
they persuade the salesman to let them in on the "ground
floor." Any merchant will tell you that it was the best
thing the town ever did. Let us see why.

Manton has a population of less than fifteen hundred.
On a certain recent summer night, the free camp ground,
by actual count, provided accommodations for more than
two thousand tourists. Throughout the four summer
months of last year there were hardly a dozen nights when
the transient population camped along the riverbank did
not equal, or nearly equal, the number of permanent resi-
dents. Something had happened to the town which no
one, a decade ago, could have foreseen: it had gone into
the tourist business. Without unusual natural attractions,
without present or historical importance, without water-

* Reprinted from *The New Republic* by permission of the author
and of the editors.

falls, or caves, or mineral springs, it had become a tourist centre.

It became a tourist centre through the accident of location. Such things are far from unusual. In the old days, quiet towns on canal or river or overland stage line were jarred to renewed life by sudden increase in traffic, and everyone west of the Mississippi remembers what the coming of a railroad has meant to hundreds of struggling villages. It has been a common phase of America's growth, this spectacle of towns taking their sustenance and waxing fat from the arteries of trade. Manton and its free auto camp ground are part of a new chapter to an old story. The source of its prosperity is not canal or railroad or stage line. It is a state highway, a twenty-two foot ribbon of concrete, that winds with the sinuous grace of a serpent out of the low hills from the south, crosses the river bridge to the centre of town, turns to the right at the court house, and fades away, like the diminishing flight of an arrow, straight up the centre of the valley.

At the court house corner, the metal emblems of two transcontinental highways point the way for the moving lines of tourists. During the summer months one can stand at this corner and in an hour count the license plates of thirty states. But the mere fact of its presence on the heavily traveled state highway is not responsible for Manton's altered economic life; within fifty miles to the north and south the concrete bisects a dozen other towns and villages, and beyond the multiplication of refreshment stands and gasoline pumps, these have undergone no changes since America began driving past their doors. They are on the main line, to be sure, but it is their misfortune to be way stations, and it is division points only that the automobile tourists transform.

Manton, without attractions of its own, is a tourist centre because it is midway between two authentic tourist centres. A hundred and fifty miles to the north is a famous national park; almost the same distance to the south is one of the best advertised cities in the world. From May to November the license plates of America flicker past in unending double streams, one headed from the city to the park, the other, the park "done," straining ahead toward the city. In either case, the tourist is likely to have been seven hours on the road when he approaches Manton. He has not started until the sun was well up, and he has stopped for lunch on the way. It is past the middle of the afternoon when he sees the first of the signs the town fathers have installed along the highway for miles on both sides of Manton. *Municipal Free Auto Camp. Free Water. Free Lights.* As he continues, the signs grow more frequent, cunningly reveal attractions hitherto unmentioned. *Free Shower Baths. Social Hall.* The sun's approach to the horizon adds its persuasion; the tourist eases his foot from the accelerator as he drives into Manton. If the camp ground is not too awful; if it is not another barren field, swept by dust-clouds. . . .

A single glance at the tall cottonwoods, the green fences, convinces him. He holds out his hand to warn the car behind, swings off the concrete, down the incline, through the hospitable, wide-open gate. A quarter of an hour later the white smoke of another campfire is curling through the dusk toward the spreading branches of the cottonwoods. Thus informally, Manton becomes host for the night to a family from Pennsylvania, or Maine, or Georgia, or Kansas, or from nearby Oregon or Arizona.

Manton's attitude toward its guest is a curious one. Having gone to no little trouble and some expense to induce the automobile tourist to stop, the town leaves him strictly alone. Manton's welcome is official, a community greeting. It is seldom supplemented by individual friendliness, even by curiosity. Not one Manton citizen in ten visits this transient, gipsy community by the river from one season's end to the other. It is not that he resents the transformation of his town, the constant presence of strange faces in stores and on the streets, for he mentions these with pride. He takes a satisfaction, individual as well as civic, in the fact that, having gone into the tourist business, Manton has done so successfully, that the free camp ground and the number of its patrons do not suffer by comparison with any town within a hundred miles. Though they do not fraternize with the tourists, the townspeople neglect no opportunity to preserve their goodwill. Tourists by automobile are like tourists in general. The auto camper buys as he goes, and Manton merchants, the grocers and butchers and bakers, the restaurant keepers and dealers in automobile supplies, and to a lesser extent a half dozen others, depend on them for a constant and profitable market. Extra clerks are hired during the tourist season, stock moves from the shelves at an accelerated speed.

For six or seven months of the year Manton merchants supply the needs of the town and the surrounding country, the limited requirements of rural families who in general buy only what they cannot produce themselves. During the remaining months the stores are crowded with transients from the camp ground, who produce nothing and buy everything they need. The tonic effect of this trade penetrates into every part of the town's economic life. Each day the humming streams of traffic deposit a new market in the backwater of the auto camp, and directly or indirectly a large part of Manton sets to work supplying its needs. Farmers of the district find a dependable local market that did not exist a few years ago, and fruit and dairy products now are rarely shipped from Manton to city wholesalers. Like a thousand other towns from Maine to California, Manton by assuming the unfamiliar rôle of tourist centre has found its business life stimulated by new and vitalizing currents. It is still a bit confused by its new part, even on occasion a trifle resentful. But it has been learning its lines industriously, and there has been no talk of quitting. The salary is good and sure, and the show seems likely to have a long run.

What of the camp itself? To leave Manton's main street on a summer evening and pass through its gates is to pass—one must use the old phrase—from one world to another. One passes from the workaday world into the world of holiday, from the routine of the hotel serving room into the banquet hall itself.

The glow of many campfires lights the bases of the cottonwoods, and the air, the cool breath of the river in it, carries the scent of burning wood, of food crisping in the pans above the brick fireplaces. The darkness softens and subdues the scene and one passes down the long corridors beneath the trees with a sense of having left strict reality behind. But though the setting is a curiously fitting one for lightness and carefree good humor, one discovers that the holiday spirit is a restrained one. Through the streets of this city-for-a-night pass unhurried figures bound casually on definite errands of finding water hydrants, shower baths, the woodpile. One sees at once that these are not blundering, curious amateurs on a holiday; they are seasoned campers, accomplished and matter-of-fact, in fact, a little too finished in their routine.

The passage down one of the dim streets is like a journey between rows of closely built suburban cottages whose fronts have been removed, revealing the accelerated functioning of the domestic machinery as the dinner hour approaches. From the shadow, one may safely look on while a family, which an hour before was on the highway, finishes preparations for the evening meal. The rolls of baggage have been removed from running-board and rear luggage carrier and the equipment of a complete camp drawn magician-like from them. The khaki tent is stretched with creaseless tension on its umbrella pole, the thrown-back flap revealing blankets folded with precision on the camp cots. Blackened vessels simmer above the fire and the mellow aroma of coffee fills the air. A gray-haired woman, khaki-clad, presides casually over the scene. She leisurely sets the table, peers into one of the pots, stirs and tastes the contents of another, slices half a loaf of bread. One looks unsuccessfully for a holiday zest in her manner, for some evidence of her realization that she is not between the familiar walls of her kitchen. She is, perhaps, three thousand miles from home, in a town of which she had never heard, on the far rim of a continent she had never hoped to cross. One wishes she would not take the experience so calmly.

Her husband returns from the Manton stores, deposits paper bags and in the light of the gasoline lantern unfolds and studies a road map. Presently two sons appear with damp towels and dripping hair from the showers, and the steaming dishes are put on the table.

The husband speaks: "The book says the last thirty miles into Yosemite ain't paved."

"We'd better get an early start," answers his wife, decisively. "I don't want you driving after dark through them mountains."

The three males laugh at Ma's nervousness. The meal is finished; in a quarter of an hour the dishes are washed;

in another fifteen minutes this unit of the camp is in darkness. It will be astir at six, by seven-thirty the group will be on the road again, Pa at the wheel, reading mileage on roadsigns and calculating time, Ma regarding from the tonneau a snowy peak of the Sierras, wondering meantime about her chickens.

It would not be safe to call this group typical of Manton's overnight guests, for a nation has taken to the highways and every type swings down through the gates of the camp ground. Ma and Pa may have had as neighbors for the night on one side a Princeton professor and his bride, on the other a group of migratory laborers from the Arizona mines, headed north toward the Puget Sound lumbering towns. For in this former cow pasture by the river, Manton is playing host to America.

CHANGING FASHIONS IN HISTORY *

BY CLARENCE WALWORTH ALVORD

WAS it Napoleon or some wittier Frenchman who threw off the cryptic judgment: "What is history but a fiction agreed upon?" Whoever the author, his words contain a profound, though only partial, truth. The fiction exists not only in the traditional narrative of past events but also in the astigmatic vision of the historians themselves. The affliction is incurable, since it is innate in the relation existing between the students and their subject of study, the social torrent madly rushing they know not whence or whither. Creatures of their environment—children of the present, heirs of the past—they are tossed, like derelicts, hither and yon upon the stream of life. Their horizon is limited, and haphazard is their view of it. Surely Henry Adams was correct in declaring that social change appears unmoral, meaningless, and chaotic. So it must always appear unless historians can discover some high place upon which to raise themselves above the circumambient flux.

Real stability amidst the ever-changing has been desperately sought by brilliant scholars—but all in vain. Hence comes fiction. There has been developed a clever and apparently learned method of procedure by means of which historians succeed in deceiving themselves and in convincing others that their opinions concerning what

* Reprinted from *The American Mercury* by permission of the author and of the editors.

has happened and what is happening conform to reality, that objective truth has been at least approximately secured. The mental operation is complicated and can only be acquired by a long and painful novitiate, but possibly it can be sketched in simple terms.

The first process is to cut off in imagination the piece of human experience that is to form the subject of investigation. This stretch of the social current, after being isolated from previous and subsequent developments, is still further simplified, lest the brain be paralyzed by receiving at one time too many sensations. To this end the historian casts aside as useless for his purpose much of the life he finds, the literary and philosophical, sometimes the religious, phenomena, the sickness and health of the people, their methods of business, in fact every activity which may distract his attention from observing the more serious events which in his eyes are alone worthy to be laid on the altar of Clio.

His amputations are drastic, since his sole object is to explain how the conditions which he thinks he finds existing at the close of his chosen period came into being. Possibly the mental operation in its entirety may be best illustrated by a concrete example and a simile. Say the Revolutionary War is the phenomenon to be explained and the forces which created it are to be discovered in the colonial experiences. Our scholarly man imagines himself stationed on the mountain top of the Revolution, whence he looks over a scene where personal and mass motives and inhibitions, private and public desires and fears, accidents to individuals and crises in the British Empire are twisted and interwined like the flora of a tropical forest. The prospect appears disheartening. But wait: the historian produces his magical telescope; he places it to his eyes, which end depending upon his special interest. The transformation is miraculous. Only those phenomena that he finds of interest to himself are focussed in his tubular blinder.

But the process of self-deception is not yet completed. The events of the past are seen on parade, moving in succession before his eyes. They must be forced to assume the relation of cause and effect. The historian, not being able to accomplish this by any known method of logic, has recourse again to imagination, and ascribes to the forces which he thinks he understands a purposive power to will the ends he desires to explain. This process is called teleology, a word borrowed from that very scientific discipline, theology. In this manner a most satisfactory explanation is reached. The origin of the American Revolution is traced back to old England, whence were conveyed to Jamestown and Plymouth the disintegrating energies that in the course of their development were predestined to disrupt the Britsh Empire. The historian has accomplished his end. All the history of the American colonies from its origin to the point of observation is centered around one line of purposive force pushing society towards the War of Independence.

After our seeker of the truth has thus expounded to his own satisfaction and for the edification of the masses his thoughts on the metamorphosis of colonies into States and States into a nation, he runs down the course of the social stream in search of another period of belligerency, for in his mind wars assume an exaggerated importance and constitute the major part of history and transform all the rest. On the top of the Civil War he places himself and gazes intently through his magical glass at what he takes to be a valley of the less important features lying beneath him. Again the system of eliminating his nonessentials and of magnifying and combining his selected happenings is applied. To him all lines of development end in the War between the States. The germs of disruption are discovered in the Federal Constitution, the Southerners are distorted into conspirators against the Union, the Mexican War is their artful contrivance.

At the present moment in the stream of time students are making their observations from the crest of the World War, and some of them are beginning to interpret the events of the last few decades in terms of that great conflict. The Spanish-American War is raised to the dignity of the pivot upon which public opinion turned. All unconsciously, you and I and all of us were, for years, bearers of the malign forces of a world's cataclysm. It may be so.

II

The foregoing has been the process by which the traditional interpretation of American history has been laid down. The point of view expressed very exactly the opinion of thirty or more years ago, for in the eyes of older generations wars appeared like dams obstructing somewhat the current of the social stream and therefore offering to observers a convenient place for studying the flow of events. Could an historical interpretation be confined to the generation that gave it birth, its limitations could be disregarded. Unfortunately, the obscurantisms of the past are blinders on the souls of men of today, and retard the clarification of their vision.

Particularly is this the case in the field of history, where authority and prestige exercise an unwarranted influence. Historians take too eagerly an oath of allegiance to tradition and make only sporadic and half-hearted efforts to shake off the shackles laid on them by their forerunners. It is certainly strange that the twists and turns of exposition, the *crescendo* and *diminuendo* of narratives, written by the generation of Sparks and Bancroft guide historical thought even today; and as for Francis Parkman, whose pages drip red with gore, his books contain the law and the prophets for practically every professor of history in the country.

But historical astigmatism resulting from this bellicose view of the past is not the only distortion from which the accepted story of America's evolution suffers. The wars have been observed too exclusively from a narrow and limited geographical location. Birth and environment have been determining factors in selecting for the watch-tower the gilded dome of Massachusetts' capitol. Boston undoubtedly offers many advantages to the sight-seer, but one would not select it for a point of vantage from which to examine the antics of the madding crowd of Charleston, South Carolina, or even the ups and downs of the political gang in Chicago, Illinois. Yet this is what has happened in the writing of American history, because a disproportionate number of our foremost historians—Sparks, Bancroft, Parkman, Fiske and Channing, to mention only a few—were born in New England, or at least received their training at Harvard or some other parochial institution of the Northeast. Massachusetts has been by them written large over every page of our national history.

I am not disposed to offer at this time any criticism of the telescope method of our observers of social dynamics. Some *modus operandi* is evidently necessary. The element of relativity in so-called historical truth can never be eliminated, for the character of their phenomena and their sources of information compel historians to employ some means of eliminating what may appear to be irrelevant forces and events. For this purpose the teleological view, is natural, since it lies within the nature of the social flux. Yet it must not be overlooked that the perspective in which the historian sees the events and the meaning which he reads in them are dependent upon the location in the social flood whence he chooses to direct his observations. The myopia arising from a geographical monopoly is slowly being cured by the dispersion of interest in matters historic to all sections of the nation. New England, together with the Middle States, still exerts a predominating influence upon historical studies, and no doubt will continue to do so for generations, or at least so long as the graduate schools of the Northeast attract by their higher cultural standards and their greater facilities for research young men and women from all parts of the country. The rapid growth of the great State universities of the West, however, is bringing nearer the time when the long endured leadership will be questioned and finally contested with success.

Before the year 1914, upon which we shall hereafter base our historical calender, students of society were emancipating themselves from the war obsession, were broadening their outlook to embrace the whole gamut of social life, and were following the lead of the Germans in directing their research to explain civilization as a whole. A reaction against this diversion from the older school has already set in; and fife and drum, or rather bomb and gas, history is again in the ascendant. How long it will remain so, it is impossible to foretell.

But neither the evils inherent in a belligerent world view nor the blessings of its opposite, *Kultur-Geschichte,* constitute the subject of this essay. Our minds are occupied with the selection of the most available social mountain-top upon which to erect an imaginary observatory of American life. The problem of selection is made complex and intricate by the conflicting opinions entertained by various groups : economic determinists, political historians, sociologists, psychologists, modernists, and others representing every conceivable nuance of mental obliquity. Never again will historians find themselves so much in accord concerning the subject matter and the meaning of their science as were the students of fifty years ago. So mutually repellent are opinions today that one is inclined to seek refuge among the historical modernists whose sole interest in the past is its contribution to the present. They level their magical telescope, complacently, through their study windows and take note of only those forces that move directly towards their eyes, thus making a stringent application of the doctrine of relativity. They may be wise; but the result is necessarily limited to personal opinions on things in general, for no two scientists are in agreement concerning the constitution of the present; and as to a knowledge of the future so closely involved in its meaning, the advocates of this new departure in historical research, if I understand them, make no claim to the clairvoyance of an H. G. Wells. Pessimistic as I am about attaining to even approximate truth in history, I find it impossible to make myself over into a pragmatic historian, and so I must continue my search for a better spot on which to build my observatory than is offered by my desk and swivel chair.

III

It is quite evident that the aim of all researchers in dusty volumes and mouse-eaten manuscripts has been to discover the succession of events that have been apparently thrown off by the central current of American evolution.

The older historians thought they had hit upon this in the cataclysms of war; the economic historians are certain that the struggle for existence and well-being in a given geographical area will afford the stream of human activities for which we seek. Others make different proposals. There is one intriguing point of view that has become the credo of a very active, though young, school of historians, and it is my guess—I am a Massachusetts Yankee—that in time its opinion will prevail. Unless I am deceived, there will take place in the near future a revolutionary change in the history fashions of America. The greatest event that ever occurred in the New World, and indeed one of the most momentous in the history of humanity, was the settlement of the major part of the North American continent by people who spoke English. Some historians are declaring in categorical terms that in the peaceful conquest of the continent there can be found the true key to unlock the secret of our national growth and that, therefore, the story of our country should be woven around the westward movement. Instead of erecting an historical observatory amidst the destructive engines of war, they urge us to mount the high places of the continent, from where we may follow the progress of the constructive forces of planting and growing. We should concentrate our attention on men clearing the forests, locating towns and cities, and constructing means of transportation.

The history of the colonists has been too long obscured by the battles' smoke. A clearer understanding can be obtained from the top of the Appalachians. From here we may observe the activities of the human freight deposited upon the Atlantic shore by ships from the Old World. Hardly have new villages been built, when the first frontiersmen enter upon the long trail leading into the West.

Slowly at first and then with accelerated steps they make their way through the forest. For a short period they pause at the foot of the mountains; but their numbers increase, the spirit of competition arises, the desire for wealth drives them, and soon a few undertake the hazardous climb. The wide expanses of the Ohio Valley lie spread before their eyes. Thousands now follow, each buoyed up by the hope of discovering some fertile meadow wherein to raise his home.

As observers we must ourselves hasten across the great inland valley of the Mississippi and take a station on some snow-capped peak of the Rockies, whence we may watch the triumphant march of an army of pioneers mustered from all the nations of the world. Not yet is the valley conquered, when the loud shout of gold echoes from hill to hill. The march becomes a mad charge. Wildly, heedlessly, the multitudes hurl themselves at the mountains; they scramble through the dangerous defiles and spread themselves over the sunny lands of California.

In his first observation from the novel and Western lookout the historian is bewildered by the confusion of the once orderly landscape; mountains shrunk to hills, hills to plains, strange peaks appearing on the horizon; events familiar from the days of childhood have undergone curious transformations and are arranged in a new perspective. The world of his tradition is metamorphosed; all is topsy-turvy. Many well-trained historians can discover no path of truth leading through this uncharted wilderness, and so they continue to follow the well-worn road surveyed by the Fathers. Their guide-books are still appearing from the press, even while younger and more imaginative pioneers are boldly blazing the trail of a radical interpretation.

Let us follow the guide of the younger men amidst the scenes of the strange landscape. First, it will be noticed that Massachusetts and her Puritans cease to cast their shadow over all events of the past. Evidently we are not in a world of Yankee manufacture. The founding of Plymouth and Boston is no longer magnified by local chauvinism and antiquarian zeal. They were only early examples of similar communities established by the English-speaking people at every stage of their advance westward. Age and priority cannot secure for them an exaggerated emphasis, since, for an understanding of the history of the American people, they are from many aspects less illustrative than others, for instance, New York, Philadelphia, Detroit, Chicago, St. Louis, New Orleans, and San Francisco.

The soul of the true American is not to be discovered among the New England hills, for the Yankees, shut off in a corner, were contemplating the perfection of their own conscience, while the miraculous birth of a new people was taking place to the south of them. The valleys of Pennsylvania and Virginia rocked the cradle, and the river banks and prairies of the Ohio guarded the days of childhood. More clearly than did the ancient scholastics do we see the genesis of this new nation: in its soul is mingled the psychic life of all the folks of the world, memories of the British Isles and of lands of a more guttural speech and more æsthetic spirit; into its consciousness has been poured the thought of the highlands of Central Europe and of the lowlands to the east and south; into its brawn have entered the dusky races of Africa and Asia. All united have been the progenitors of this youthful people called American. Who can place on the scales the value of what any one of them has contributed?

IV

While gazing at the new picture of the past, we feel dropping from our eyes the scales of the institutional complex which half blinds the people and historians of all nations. Actual government is never identical with the communal graveyard wherein lie the stereotyped institutions. Most of the bonds cementing society are not to be found in the book of statutes; folk customs and habits are stronger than law. The soul of a people expresses itself outside of their constitution. One who has watched the pioneers staking out free land, making their own rules and regulations, creating a true democracy, shaking off the shackles imposed by the fathers, is in no danger of sharing the popular delusion that the American government, Athena-like, sprang full grown and unchangeable from the heads of certain Jovian wise men. Clearly the blessings and evils of America can be traced more justly to the Western frontier than to Philadelphia.

In their new perspective the wars, which have always been represented as high peaks, will be recognized with difficulty, for when placed in comparison with the conquest of a continent, they are reduced to truer proportions as mere incidents in a greater achievement—the building of a nation. The Revolution seems to rise hardly above the general level, being obscured by the transmuting energies molding contemporary society, the call of the prairies, the gestation of democracy, the transformation of customs and manners; all these would have acted just as powerfully, would have accomplished their end just as effectively, had the separation from the British Empire been postponed a few decades, or occurred without hate and bloodshed. The War of 1812 and that with Mexico were conceived in the West and were expressions of an imperialistic will. The Civil War was a struggle for supremacy between two economic sections: in its origin is apparent a weakness of democracy, which can find no cure for a national disease except by recourse to irrational emotions and the frenzy of popular madness, in this case with vast and incalculable damage to one of the contestants.

Certain aspects of our history sadly neglected by the earlier writers stand in the foreground like high hills, and over many of them hangs a haze, the breath of economic selfishness and dishonor. All the varied relations with the Indians, the fur-trade, the purchase of land, the consequent speculation, are striking features. To the historian with literary aspirations a description of the dreary national land policy will offer serious difficulties; but he will find his compensation in the romantic trek of the Mormons across the dry lands, in the picturesque rush for gold, and in accounts of the daring speculators in timber, cattle, mines, and railroads. The new subjects of interest are innumerable, and many of them are both intriguing and momentous.

Such is the appearance of the new fashion in history that will some day be found acceptable by the American people. In many places it is being already taught. Its point of view lies somewhere between that of the older school and that of the one advocated by the radical modernists. There is in it a genuine effort to maintain the judicial temper of the former, to interpret the past in its own terms; whereas there are concessions to the latter in the long view of evolution, in the recognition of continuity, in the just criticism of the oblique vision that is broken by arbitrary periods. The value of the new truth revealed by such a radical transformation of the national story must not be too greatly exaggerated. It may or may not approach close to reality. Who can say? There comes to my mind a pregnant sentence by Henry Adams in a reply to a would-be critic: "I have written too much history to have faith in it; and if anyone thinks I am wrong, I am inclined to agree with him." Without making the Western interpretation a matter of faith we can, I think, accept it, without mental stultification, as a novel guess in relativity, made by historians who have caught a different vision of the meaning of the past, as they drift, buffeted by shifting winds and tumultuous waves, towards an uncharted destiny.

COMEDY AND THE AMERICAN SPIRIT*

By Langdon Mitchell

It has been said that the only reason for man's taking a wife is that without one life is too untroubled. And so, perhaps, the only good reason for a playwright's taking to the lecture platform is that if he throws himself into that dreadful vortex, he will be asked troublesome questions, and regarded with contempt if he can't answer them.

Some years since, lecturing, for the first time, on the drama, to a class of university students, I made record, with no little interest, of the many questions asked me. The class was not small, many outsiders coming in for one reason or another, and accordingly, I rather flattered myself—that is, at the go-off—that I was doing very pretty work, reading "Hamlet" and Aristophanes in a semi-original translation, and commenting on both in my own vein. It is agreeable, and by no means difficult, to be pleased with oneself. There seemed no cloud on the horizon, no storm approaching. But one day (it was after the third lecture), a student of the university, a rosy young woman, came up, and used the fatal phrase: "I don't see why."

"I don't see why Hamlet made such a fuss about his mother's marrying his uncle? Why shouldn't she have?"

A fine-looking, athletic, tow-headed, young man, em-

* Reprinted from *The American Mercury* by permission of the author and of the editors.

boldened no doubt by the first questioner's presence, then approached me and said:

"I think Romeo and Juliet were a pair of dubs: Weren't they?"

These were the first large, heavy drops of the approaching storm, and presently it broke in a downpour, a hard hail of queries.

"What is Comedy? Why do you dislike the newer drama?"

"Well, see here, Professor, is High Comedy just a description of the goings on of rich people, and if so, why 'High'? What is Low Comedy, anyway?"

"Why do you say realism is dead and done with? We thought realism was the last, best thing."

"We wish you would explain, and *clearly,* why you think the American people do not like what you call 'pure' Comedy."

"People in real life don't talk poetry: so why the 'poetic' drama?"

"When a brick falls on a man's head and knocks him out, you say it isn't dramatic. I'd call it dramatic, believe me!"

If I had, now, to answer these questions, I should, I think, begin by saying: a play is a rational dream, dreamed waking and on purpose, for the pleasure of it. And, hoping to avoid the guilt of a formal definition, I should say, further, that just as Tragedy is something partial, something composed in a special mood, so, too, is Comedy. True, the writer of tragedies may introduce the comic element into his play, but he will see to it that these scenes shall not be alien to the mood he writes in, and the feelings he wishes to arouse. And the writer of comedies may, and often does verge upon the tragic; but, in a general way, he, too, will seek to be true to the comedic conception of life, and the tone which follows upon that conception; in short, he likes his dream to be not only rational, but also harmonious within itself.

Comedy, when the spirit of it is pure, is then, the product and fruit of a special mood; something partial and particular; a certain temper and way of thinking and feeling evoked in certain men at a certain time by the spectacle of life, or by as much of it as at that moment they choose to look upon. I suppose it may be best put in this way, that the comedic mind takes it that nothing is final, irretrievably wrong, hoplessly and helplessly bad. There is, it asserts, no despair, no death; or, if there is, it is a good despair, a friendly and desirable death. There is, in short, no possible posture of affairs but admits of a good outcome. And Comedy has no hesitation about the means we should employ in order to remedy a bad state of things, insure the good outcome, and let the curtain fall on it. A little virtue and common sense is the means, the cure-all. A slight degree of moderation, of prudence, a little ordinary and even cool kindness or goodwill; not to be a ramping egotist: not to be stone-blind to the fact that there are others in the world; this is all that is needed to make men happy.

II

Supposing, for the fun of it, that I am right in these not inconsiderable assertions, that is, that Comedy, when not adulterate; not, for example, timid, tasteless and middle-class in temper, or not of a duplex mood, weeping copiously for the worst of reasons; or not merely a rollicking horse-play; suppose, I say, that Essential Comedy is the voice and expression of something purely rational: and that her virtues, which she regards as moral hygiene for all the follies of life, are pagan virtues, as they clearly are—how, then, will the American regard this very rational Comedy? Will he be pleased with it? Will he take to it, as not so long ago he took to "The County Fair," or to that play which is so entertaining, the play, "Turn to the Right," of Mr. Winchell Smith?

Of course, when I ask will the American take to it, as he took to these things, I mean will he find his own ideals expressed in it, will it be to his taste? I am constrained to believe that it will *not* be to his taste, and that he will feel inclined to look askance at it, as at something alien to the spirit of his Americanism, and therefore antipathetic. He will do this in the face of Pure Comedy for the simple reason that its way of looking at life is rational and nothing else. Whatever solution it offers for the evils of our lot, is, therefore, a purely rational solution, and necessarily, the virtues it extols are purely pagan. He will feel and say to us, "If common sense and moderation are all that are needed, Christianity is impugned. There is another Way of Life: a better way. The rational way, the way of moderation. And, this won't do. It won't do, because it isn't the truth." If we go about to jeer and make light of this attitude of the American mind, we are in the infancy of culture. What we should rather do is to note the fact, and find out what bearing it has.

Looking at the thing in this way, it may be asked, where do we meet such Americans? Of course, nowhere, and yet everywhere. America is not merely a geographical boundary. America is a spirit; the spirit of a certain race and culture. I know how much in certain circles this idea is, at present, disrelished. The Egyptian and Syrian arrive here, and naturally it is their country. "What is this American stuff? Who are Americans, and why do they have a special spirit? America, they say, is an international union. As for Anglo-Saxons, Nordics—but why speak of them? They are going the way of the bison. The land will be ours, and is now."

Mr. Israel Zangwill, an author living in England, feels much in this same way. And why not, for he is one of that great race, the Jewish race, which now governs the world? He speaks, therefore, with a truly Roman assurance and solemnity to us about ourselves: much as a Roman consul might have spoken to the ancient, uncivilized, foolish and painted Britons.

Mr. Zangwill speaks, or writes thus to us Americans in No. 652 of the Haldemann-Julius Booklets. The thing within our borders which has irritated him to utterance is the Ku Klux Klan. It seems to him to be un-American. And as he is an internationalist living under the protection of the British flag, and has spent some months in this country, he feels that he knows what true Americanism is; or ought to be; knows the American spirit; and accordingly he instructs us, not without the Roman air of authority I have mentioned, to the effect that we should not think of America as a nation, but as a continent. And he indicates to us that we must dismiss from our minds the false and ridiculous notion that we are a race, a people, with our own culture, our own ideals; for, we are, evidently, nothing more than many races and peoples thrown together on one continent. And he concludes by fervently begging us to qualify our independent nationality, and altering the Constitution, to embrace internationalism. In doing which things, he tells us, we shall be true to the American spirit.

We who were born and bred here are a little disinclined to listen very long to these excellent internationalists, and their conception of what we ought to think, feel, be and do. We know pretty well who and what we are, and what we want. We know the American spirit. We know it, be-

cause we have breathed it in from the earliest years; and
sometimes even later in life, we feel called upon to criticize and oppose it in certain of its manifestations. But we
never doubt its existence. We know it is not international.
We know it is the spirit of a people : our own spirit.

III

Americanism is, then, a spirit, and, as we all are aware,
it is sometimes sentimental, cynical, and even other and
less tolerable things. But, for our present and limited purpose, it is preferable to take the American spirit in its
strength rather than in its weakness.

The ideals and habits of mind of our people, are, as I
have said, Christian; deeply and prevailingly so. And this
Christianity of theirs, is, of course, their strength. But,
it is not their only strength; for, in certain regions of
thought and activity they are not Christian, and yet are
constructive and powerful. In order to explain it, we
might, I suppose, say that, save the so-called Friends, the
Quakers, we are imperfectly christianized. Only compare
us with this pious people : for in them there seems to be
no remnant or crumb of the original barbarian left. But
with the rest of us, there remains a stark something of the
Viking, or Saxon sea-robber; something as little Christian as the Bill of Rights, or Thomas Jefferson.

And thus it comes about, that, touching certain political, or moral matters, we are rational, and nothing else.
In our feeling about these matters, we are cynical, pragmatic, indifferent to theory, and opposed to what we call
idealism, opposed to any Christian solution of the problems presented.

The young students whom I quoted spoke in this rational or common-sense vein and their questions were elemental, and went to the root. For they were speaking in

the fulness of their own American spirit. And never more so than when they said: "Why were Romeo and Juliet not a pair of dubs?"

Nothing could be more natural than for an American to think Romeo and Juliet a pair of dubs. Let us take it in this way: many of us have suffered the sad experience of co-education. Sad, for this herding together of the young bulls and the heifers is a great cooler-off. The edge of strangeness is dulled. The blue of the distance, it may be recalled, disappears when we approach the mountain. The mountain is then no more than a pile of rocks—and all mountains are alike.

Thus, when our young man is thrown into the closest non-connubial intercourse with a lot of young women, seeing them hourly, and often when he'd prefer not, and necessarily losing his male attribute of the pursuer, he presently finds himself indifferent. And after a year or so, his emotions becoming generalized, he becomes continently promiscuous: I speak of a spiritual promiscuity. Romance, naturally, there can be none, for there is no surprise, no novelty, no fear, but only a highly accurate, and close-at-hand, inch-by-inch perception that women are not deep or mysterious things, differing by an entire inner world from men, but just people, in a pool, or on a team, and often in the way.

It may be that Shakespeare, when he wrote "Romeo and Juliet," wished to justify co-education as a means of abolishing romance. For, clearly, "Romeo and Juliet" treats of the first love of those who have not been co-educated; of that sort of romantic first passion which is in itself an excess; and, as such, easily creates a catastrophe. For Romeo didn't *like* Juliet. He didn't know her well enough to like or dislike her. He adored her—nothing more intelligent. We Americans do not altogether believe in, or approve of, excessive and irrational adorations of anything; not even of young women. The cold rationality I referred to comes at once into play. But romantic passion is irrational or nothing. Well, the American regards the romance of it as silly; and the less said about the passion of it the better.

Thus co-education and our new and deliciously naked and photographed bi-sexual athleticism produce a Spartan state of affairs. The Spartans were no more romantic than they were honest. And so, the American spirit, possibly not without wisdom, regards that famous two as a pair of dubs. A Spartan would have regarded them in the same way.

Taking "Hamlet": There is no reason—no American reason—why the Queen should not marry her dead husband's brother the day after the funeral of her dead husband. She might defer the wedding out of a just regard to the opinion of mankind, but myriads of excellent and virtuous American widows defer nothing. From one bed they leap to the other. Americans being, as I say, in this matter rational have no horror of a second love following hot-foot on the first. It would be otherwise if we had a respect for passion. But we lack this, and define our feelings by the special name we give it. If passion squares with the law, it is all right. If not, it is immoral. In the first case it is love: in the second infatuation.

The consequences of this attitude are far-reaching and profound. The whole of our literature shows it. In view of that literature, and remembering what American ideals are, it appears to me indisputable that the American spirit, whether Christian and mystic, or purely common-sense and rational, is not easily congenial to the "Tragic" or "Comic" of Europeans. If our people were less sterile in creative art, we should perceive this more clearly; the

examples of our own American way of thinking and feeling would lie to hand. As in time, no doubt, will occur,
when we shall have created more freely in our own image.
All I wish to do, at this point, is to suggest, and try to
make it clear, that when the untutored American mind
comes upon the essentially tragic, or the essentially comic,
they are not altogether to its taste, and why this is so. But
any such generalization needs to be qualified.

The theater is a civic institution. And, in our larger
cities, where this form of entertainment flourishes, the
population being largely of foreign birth and breeding,
views life as foreigners do or may. Accordingly, the
plays of New York may at some future period attain popularity in that city, but fail of it in the country at large.
The comedies of Congreve were relished only in the London of his day.

IV

But how much more, and more winning and delicious,
there is in Comedy than what has been said, or even suggested. For, after all, Comedy, like life itself, is most
blessedly various. There is no reason why it should always be *pure* Comedy, severely rational, or severely anything. Some men like to mix the possible with the impossible, carefully disguising the latter, and then you have
Farce, than which few things are more entertaining.
Other men mingle the rational with the romantic, and
you have Poetic Comedy of a sort: "The Tempest" or
"As You Like It."

Even Molière, when in "Alceste," a comedy of the
purely rational kind, he failed to carry his audience with
him, harked back to a something broader, to a mood of
more geniality. But, in view of our somewhat commercial-

ized theater, it should not be forgotten that he was never untrue to himself: that is, he would not regain his popularity by a lie, by a stroke of sentimentality. On the other hand, if ever a dramatist took pains to entertain his audience, he was the man. And one of his means of entertainment was the creation of character, especially of such characters as are not so singular and eccentric that an auditor will say, "No doubt there are such birds, but I never have seen them."

Molière avoids these rare birds, these eccentrics, because they have so little bearing on life as we know it. The seeing of them on the stage entertains, but the entertainment is shallow: we soon forget what we saw, and refuse to see it twice. What gives us the most pleasure is to see a character, who, we can swear, is no infrequent occurrence. The truth is, the knowledge of character is so important in daily life that an audience, taking nothing else on the stage seriously, takes that so. For even illiterates know that the men and nations which understand character are successful. The lack of that native understanding runs through the whole of German literature; you may almost say that because of it the Germans lost the war. The English, inexpressive as they are, and stupid as we stupidly think them, know men, understand character. And, thus, we are led to perceive that it was not by chance that they produced Shakespeare.

So, for the dramatist, everything depends on the choice of his characters. On that, and on his natural, delicate, creative sensitiveness to the supreme need of not "forcing" these characters. A character, let us say, once chosen, is thereafter no puppet, to be moved hither and yon at the will of the master of the show. He is, rather, something which abounds so much in his own sense that his inventor or creator must be a quietist in regard to him:

must wait in silence, and listen till he speak or act, and then with exactness and humbly put it down. But the great comedian selects his characters well at the start. He does not inject into lovely comedy a villain of such violence or vulgarity that he will break the mood, and, in action, turn all to blood and tears.

Turning to Shakespeare for an example, I know of none better than that scene, the seventh of the second act of "As You Like It," where, a table being laid with eatables, in the forest, and the young and starving gentleman, Orlando, seeing it to be so, he enters with his drawn sword, resolved to eat, let the unknown host say what he may. The exiled Duke is, however, himself eating, or about to do so. Turning to the scene you will see that it hangs on the slippery edge of a duel, in which a death might easily come about. What keeps it from this violence, what keeps it Comedy, is simply the good sense, the humane moderation of feeling and self-control of the exiled Duke.

In the "Uncle Vanya" of Tchekhov, the same spirit is at work. The play is forever on the edge of a pathos which would carry us presently beyond even tears, into a world of cruel despair. But, exquisite artist as he was, the Russian dramatist keeps it comedy.

V

But there is in every play a something even profounder than the matter of the characters chosen: namely, the sort of man the creator of all these human shadows is, in himself. How does he regard the world of action and feeling, the world of men? How does Shakespeare regard love? Is it, as conceived by him, always a cause of ruin? Is it never what the Elizabethans called fancy, irrational, as wild as a weather-cock, but easily to be brought to a good issue?

Those exquisite, decorative, dove-colored and wide-winged little people of the night air, whom our children call "millers," since a bloom of the finest flour covers and beautifies them—this wild and wandering people, beholding with their innocent eyes a great and adorable sunrise in the midst of circumfluous shadow, flutter and fly toward it, and are presently, as we fear, singed to nothing in the heat of our kerosene lamp. Well, Shakespeare has, sometimes, the lamp lit, and the window of his play open to the human moths of his imagination; but, being really an American, and therefore born kindly, as well as before his time, he permits no tragic incineration. Rather, he seizes the lovers, so foolishly in love with love, and, as a man would a moth, he turns them loose on the freedom of the dark. The curtain then falls, and the audience goes home, reminded that pining away for love is no such great matter.

What do we gather from this? Clearly that Shakespeare was a poet, but not sentimental. We are supposed to know nothing of his character. But, in a play played, the author's character comes across to the audience as it were the blast of a trumpet. Wycherley, aside from his limpid prose, is a callous and cruel fellow. You feel it when you see his play. And Tchekhov—was there ever such an unstrained love of humanity, such a rational tenderness, such sweetness of nature? If I should say the Mohammedan Arab could not create in the spirit of Tchekhov, should I not thus make clear that the man's character was a product of Christianity?

High Comedy, which my students asked me about, is not with us a thing of class, since in our country classes are fluent. But, though static classes are absent, we have, none the less, the higher and the lower sorts of human beings. High Comedy is, then, plainly, a Comedy that deals with men who are superior to the rest of us. That is, it deals with relatively perfected creatures, with what used to be called their manners, the ways and customs of them. And Low Comedy treats those people whom we Americans do not dare to call low, but know they are. It might be called the Comedy of the unfinished man; or, if we must be scientific, the Comedy of the relatively less complex.

It was asked me why I disliked the new drama. By this I judged was meant the newer American plays, and the impressionistic drama of Europe. The answer to the question is a simple assertion in denial: I like the newer drama more than the drama of thirty or of twenty years back. It is freer, for one thing; more intellectual; a less restricted form; and, when it is expressionistic, or even merely fantastic, it has more depth and scope. It is, too, less debilitated by the sterilizing influence of French realism. It is more inclusive, and more poetic than our earlier drama.

"But no one talks poetry in real life," so why, I infer, should we write poetry into the mouths of the people in a play?

I suppose that the wild notion that the "poetic" is a matter of words comes from the baneful mouth and empty mind of some professor in a State college. I put him as low as I can. The "poetic" is like the comedic, or the tragic: it is a mood, but, as I have indicated, more inclusive than either. The man who has it not, in some form, is dead to the world he lives in. The nation which lacks it is sick, or miseducated—educated out of it, as we, with all our natural and inborn gift for poetry, have so patently been. It is true that Shakespeare wrote in blank

verse, and used much imagery. But the reason why
Shakespeare is a great dramatic poet is not here, or but
in part. Seeming to beg the question, he was a poet because he regarded life and the universe poetically; which
is, however, merely a short way of saying that the beauty
of it all gave him an infinite delight; thrilled, satisfied,
and filled him with enthusiasm. And that he regarded this
beauty as *significant*.

Beauty, defined by the definers in so many ways, whatever else it may be, is certainly either the presence of life,
in perfection; or it is the representation, the re-creation in
art, of such life. Death is ugly; so is carrion, and so is
a junk-heap. So are many criminals. Most stupid, and all
envious people are ugly; and, in the invisible moral world,
cheating at cards, or cruelty to a child, is, we all feel, an
ugly habit. The plain American thinks it so. He speaks
of cheating as a "dirty" action. He speaks of "foul" play,
and "fair" play. Beauty is, I repeat then, either the presence or the expression of life in perfection. Naturally the
arts busy themselves with it. And the drama without it is
something self-restricted, and infinitely less pleasurable.

Take it in the simplest way: Al Jolson in his black
make-up radiates good will and amiability, and is in
every motion one of the most graceful of human beings.
So here you have moral beauty, and physical grace. And
our citizens pay four dollars and forty cents to see it.

The dramatist who can combine beauty with action
will have the American audience at his feet. For that audience has now, since long, shown in every way it can
that what it most likes is the fullness of life in action:
and that way of looking at life, which we find in great
poetry. And, poets, apart from their images, their hende-
casyllables, or their free verse, are those men who are
natively in love with life. They praise life. That's what

they are for. It is their function. But the French realism
of which I spoke disrespectfully was not in love with
life. And, accordingly, it sterilized literature wherever its
influence prevailed.

Of all people, we needed it the least. For our literature
has, now for this thousand years and more, been fearless
in that truer and higher realism which consists in a
boundless delight in reality; in all realities. It has always
called a "spaed a spaed"; which, being interpreted, means
a bitch a bitch. From Beowulf, through Chaucer, Mar-
lowe, and the refined but heaven knows realistic Miss
Austen, to the last novel, or play, our literature has been,
and is, prevailingly, powerfully, fearlessly, and giftedly
realistic in this, the only possible sense: it rejoices in
reality.

Besides which, whatever good there may have been
for us in the French movement has long imparted its influence to our novels and plays. The younger Italians, the
younger men of Central Europe, have done with it ages
ago. If you as much as mention it, they put you down as a
noodle. They are living in, or at least they are preparing,
a new Period. Must we then still chew on this twice-
chewed cud? It reminds me—I speak like, as it were, a
political orator—it reminds me of a story:

When the Indians of the Red Bud Agency complained
to their agent that they were starving, this sarcastic fellow asked them why they didn't kill and eat a certain lean
and sickly dog which hung about the camp? The reply of
one Black Cloud, a dignified wit, was, that as to the dog
in question, he was, firstly, so lean that there was nothing on him to eat; and, secondly, they had already eaten
him. "And," continued Black Cloud, "among the Sioux
it is not the custom to eat the same dog twice!"

The American spirit is at times inconsistent, inchoate,

confused; no doubt, it has its worse side; its appalling sentimentality, and its insane frivolity; even its cruelty, as our humor sometimes indicates. We are a prosperous people; and prosperity, the being at a lusty and perpetual picnic, is a great trial to man or nation. We exhibit, therefore, the horrid faults I have put down. And another I have failed to put down. We are little contented. We hardly know how to live, to live well and in happiness. But our people have poetry in their very souls; the poetic attitude to life is the attitude they understand. Races do not change. And the past of our race shows where it is gifted: not in painting or sculpture, possibly not in philosophy, but plainly and assuredly in politics and poetry: in the poetic drama.

THE GREAT AMERICAN ART *

By Thomas Craven

Abroad it is called the cinema; in picturesque American it is the movie.

Go to London, Paris, Rome, Berlin, and Vienna, and you will find that these sensitive peoples of the Old World, the very ones who are supposed to love and foster the traditional arts, have succumbed to the movie, and not, let it be noted, to films of their own manufacture, but to the exclusively American product—to the acrobatics of Fairbanks, the amours of Valentino, and the unique waggery of Chaplin. The conquest of England has been swift and overwhelming: witness the triumphal entry of Tom Mix into the city of London, and the protestations of British producers. Even the valetudinarian Hardy has broken silence to deplore the American incursion; and from the Island of Free Trade come rumblings of a prohibitive tariff, or a Parliamentary act to restrain the exhibition of all pictures save those controlled by British capital.

At last America can boast of an original art, an art as indigenous as ice-water and the red Indian, an art without antecedents or refining tradition, a spectacular and extravagant affair measured, not as the other arts are measured in terms of intelligence and enlightening influence, but in miles and millions—and most important of all, an art consistent with the ideals and energies of the

* Reprinted from *The Dial* by permission of the author and of the editors.

nation from which it sprang, rising from ignominious poverty to win in a few years the patronage and exploitation of the elect. You will remember, perhaps, that the founder of the Astor fortunes, John Jacob himself, was a dealer in furs, and that out of hides came an aristocracy; similarly was Mr Adolph Zukor, the great movie magnate, a furrier, and to-day he stands out as the progenitor of a new and more powerful social order—an aristocracy of art.

It was in 1893 that Mr Edison devised a machine by means of which light was projected through a succession of photographic films upon a screen, thereby endowing the American people with a new medium of expression. Strange to say, the Americans did not adopt the medium with the alacrity which might have been expected. The kinetoscope was a clumsy instrument apparently of slight commercial value, and the initial development of its resources was slow and unpromising. In 1910 improvements both in the camera and the films assured the merchants of substantial returns, and production increased ominously; in 1913 the eccentric comedy and the western melodrama came into vogue, and the new industry became an important factor in our national culture. But as yet the moving picture had no pretensions to art—it was simply a novelty and an ingenious and profitable plaything. In 1915 Mr D. W. Griffith produced the first feature-film, The Birth of a Nation, and the movie passed into the realm of art. During the last decade the industry has multiplied to such bewildering proportions as to require a John Maynard Keynes to explain its financial magnitude. Fortunately it is primarily the art of the movie with which I am concerned, and when I say that the vested interests are estimated at more than one billion, five hundred million dollars—the fourth largest business in

America—that every week one hundred thirty million people pay six hundred million dollars to enjoy this new art, and that ninety per cent of the films shown abroad are American, I shall have said enough.

The simplest concept of art is the theory expounded by Tolstoy, according to whom art is a means for communicating certain states of the soul, but mind you, elementary states—the homiletic infection of parables, the sentimentality of Dickens, the pathos of lowly illustration, and the touching piety of folk-songs. Tolstoy believed that most of the alleged great art of the world is nothing more than organized artifice, and that its appeal to the senses is based on pernicious hypnotism, or the power to evoke the sensual instincts. To him art was a moral agent, and he refused to countenance anything beyond the comprehension of peasants. One would think, inasmuch as the movies are largely conceived and performed by peasants, or their American equivalents, that the new art of pictures would fit into Tolstoy's scheme, but such is not the case. I find no evidence in the films that any one has ever seen, felt, or experienced anything worth communicating.

From a less primitive point of view, art should contain a measure of intelligence and should demand of its audience a certain amount of understanding and cultivation; through the honest conviction which brings it into life, it should be a protest against cheapness and vulgarity; it should, by reason of its beautiful forms, rouse in man the spirit of emulation, make him intolerant of baseness and shams, and sharpen his susceptibilities—in short, it should act as a civilizing influence. The movie does none of these things. It is the only art in history which exacts nothing from the beholder, and renders impossible the participation of the higher faculties.

There is yet another form of art, a sham art wherein

accepted decency and conventional morality are employed as motifs for scurrility and wantonness. Under the mantle of righteousness, and with the sanction of its official censors, the movie engages as "a sense of duty" to expose evil and the dark alluring ways of sin, pursuing its course to the very limit of barbaric extravagance. Artificiality lies at the root of all its productions, and nothing real or convincing ever comes out of its gilded studios. Partly through the nature of the medium and partly through the stupidity and connivance of the exploiters, it ruins every genuinely dramatic situation; it cannot tell the simplest story, point the shallowest moral, or portray the most commonplace sentiment without transforming it into complicated and glittering horrors.

We must, however, apply a higher and more philosophical test to the movie to appreciate how fully it has arrived at the true significance of art. As a reflex of life it has no parallel, nor has the creative labour of any past period—the sculpture of the Greeks, the painting of the Renaissance, the drama of Elizabethan England—approached it in ability to reach the hearts of the people. It is an art which actually works; it travels to the four corners of the earth bearing a message within the scope of housemaids and children. I do not insist that it represents contemporary manners with absolute fidelity, or that its western heroes or drawing-room characters have their counterparts in real life; it is not so literal as that, but transcending nature, as art should, it symbolizes the hopes and aspirations of the unfortunates. Hence the vast popularity of the "society film." These orgiastic conceptions of high life whet the social appetite of scheming, restless femininity the world over. The modern industrial slave, given money and leisure, would model his life after the frivolous debauchery and lavish amativeness depicted by the movies; and the producers, having been slaves themselves—not so long ago—are thoroughly alive to the fact and play upon it. It is an advertised fact that one of the most celebrated actresses of to-day, and a producer in her own right, after the completion of a film, tries it on her retinue of servants before releasing it : if the lackeys approve, the success of the film is taken for granted.

The above paragraph will help to explain the remark of a leading manufacturer to the effect that the business caters mainly to women and depends upon them for its immense profits. Throughout the entire organization the spirit of effeminacy prevails. Except in directing, which, it would seem, demands not brains but the physical stamina necessary to goad and control the mummers, women are predominant. They have no false impressions about their work or about other women; they understand precisely the dreams and desires of their sisters in the audience, and set about fulfilling them; they write the *scenarios,* continuities, and titles; and the cutting of the films—an exceedingly important process—is entrusted to young girls. In addition, women are the best critics of the movies. Their writing, for the most part, is trivial, but it is none the less pertinent. They know what the game is about, which cannot be said of male scribes. Latterly, a number of our young Hazlitts have veered into movie criticism with the expectations of princely rewards, but how ludicrously they have floundered about seeking a point of view! I need not dwell on the effeminacy of the actors. I know that it is difficult to make an actor look like a man, but in the movies the idea is to make him look like a woman. In German and Scandinavian pictures I have seen actors who managed to retain their masculinity —they were not disfigured with hideous make-up, and they were only moderately "temperamental."

For the success or failure of a film the director is held responsible, and rightly, since he is invested with autocratic powers. He is usually a "ham-actor" who entered the movies when competition was less strenuous, and who had the aggressiveness to advance himself to a commanding position. The director is a peculiar fellow. He can be, and often is, illiterate; he need have no knowledge of plastic, graphic, literary, or dramatic art; but he must have unbounded confidence, great forensic strength, and the ability to lord it over the actors with Napoleonic fearlessness. His work begins when the preliminary constructive details are finished—the best-seller bought and retold, the *scenario* prepared by the women experts, the cast selected, the costumes gathered, and the elaborate settings designed. He has no plan of action and proceeds entirely by impulse. Considering his qualifications, is it not wonderful what he accomplishes? The answer is that he has unlimited funds at his disposal, and that he is surrounded by assistants more capable than himself. If, perchance, he must "picturize" a masterpiece, say a novel by Balzac, he instructs one of his servants to find out who Balzac was, hires a woman to read the book and relate the story to him, hires another woman to improve upon it and to "adapt it to the screen," and then packs his troupe off to France for local colour. If he capriciously desires to throw a million dollars away, there is no one to stop him; if he calls for the United States Naval Academy, the Coliseum, or the city of Versailles, his employers are convinced that he is a prodigy of imagination, and arrangements are forthwith concluded. But why a man like Mr Zukor, a master furrier who would not have permitted his cutters to fashion a single garment without guarding every stroke and seam, should not investigate the progress of his pictures and curb the extravagances of his directors, is a mystery I cannot fathom. Of course, if the director turns out a series of failures, he is himself turned out, but the mischief has been done. From the charges of the Federal Trade Commission it would appear that the big producers have a different and more summary method of preventing failures: they would, by virtue of a complete monopoly of all branches of the industry, force the small exhibitor to accept their films, or close his doors.

On the whole the distinctions between the autocrats of the studio are of no great consequence. The subtlest is Ernst Lubitsch whose pictures are admirably put together, coherent from start to finish, and devoid of wasted space. Rex Ingram has the best taste in sets and backgrounds, and Erich von Stroheim is the least frivolous. Von Stroheim, with a Germanic passion for detailed accuracy, has more than once demonstrated the impossibility of rendering the emotional effects of literature by pictorial methods. In Greed he exerted a truly heroic effort to capture the epic quality of MacTeague, spending years on the job, duplicating the scenes and following the geography of the novel with the utmost patience and exactitude. The result? An ineffably dreary performance containing not a single flash of the genius of Frank Norris. D. W. Griffith, the "master of the movies," has done nothing in recent years to justify the title. We must thank him for the "super-film," the "close-up," the "long-shot," and the "fade-out," and for the excruciating Way Down East. His latest pictures are the usual trash. I quote from his address to the American Motion Picture Advertisers: "What a tremendous instrument for truth! . . . This is no business to joke about, to speak covertly about, to be ashamed of. It is as beautiful and sweet and decent and clean as any business or any profession has ever been in the history of the world." The one lonely exception, not only among directors but among actors, is Charlie Chaplin of whom I shall have more to say presently.

The movie, as I have pointed out, is the only art which cannot, or will not, use intelligence. In the business are a number of subordinate functionaries who have grown up in the studios, and who must undoubtedly have practicable ideas for improving the films, but as yet they have been unable to subdue the commercial instincts of their employers. The present tendency of the producers is to make a show of outside talent and to trade on the publicity of best-selling novels; and greedy authors have heeded the call expecting to conquer the new medium without effort and to repeat their popular successes instantly. But the literary folk have fared badly. Clayton Hamilton, as a critical adviser, was a total loss; Rex Beach failed to grasp the mechanics of the art; Mary Roberts Rinehart was shipwrecked; Fannie Hurst, after deprecating the butchery of her masterpieces—which she had sold to the movies for tidy sums—now condescends to write prize-winning trash; and the versatile Hergesheimer, composing directly for the screen, has done nothing to be proud of; the great Maeterlinck's only script was thrown into the scrap-heap; and Michael Arlen, who had no sooner disembarked than Mr Jesse Lasky begged him to accept fifty thousand dollars for the promise of a *scenario* or two, is on probation. The idol of Mayfair is a canny purveyor and should have no difficulty in supplying Hollywood with amoristic morsels. I cannot do justice to the solitary eminence of Director Rupert Hughes, the only man of letters who has found himself in the movies—you will have to see his picture.

It is not surprising, when we remember that about seven hundred feature-films were put in circulation last year, that the producers should be desperate for material. They

will buy anything at any price. If a popular novel or play
has no pictorial value, it is consigned to the *scenario* staff
for treatment; if, as sometimes happens, it is a work of
honest purpose, it will probably have to be rewritten any-
how in order to pass the vice-fiends of the various States.
(In Massachusetts, for instance, a movie baby may be
born out of wedlock on week-days but not on the Sab-
bath!) The absurdly inflated prices paid for raw material have had a debasing effect on literature, and latterly,
men and women of more than ordinary ability have sold
themselves to the sensational movie stuff. On the other
hand we have the proud, irrelevant whining of certain
authors against the filmed versions of their books. What
do they expect? The better the book the worse the movie.
Isolated cases like Greed or Anna Christie in which the
director has conscientiously striven to preserve the spirit
of the original, have no relation to literature, and little or
no validity as pictures.

In the aesthetics of the movie we are confronted with
several interesting problems. Those who have followed
the films—and who has not?—must long ago have lost
patience with the ambition of the directors to re-create
works of fiction. Characterization in the novel is an intricate and laborious process, fundamentally a psycholog-
ical development. Slowly, through devices varying with
the temperament of the author, a figure is set in motion,
begins to move and breathe, and to attain a life of its own.
Exactly how a character acquires stature and reality is a
debatable issue—the author himself is unable to analyse
his talent and is as likely to fail as not—but one thing is
certain: the novelist must have power over his medium,
which is verbal, must have a feeling for words and the
ability to convert them into living instruments of expression. But I doubt if the most acute and sympathetic reader

ever visualizes a character: he responds to that part of a created figure which is also himself, but he does not actually see his hero. (Ask a dozen readers to describe the physical appearance of Hardy's Tess, and note the results.) For this reason all illustrations are disappointing. I am pretty familiar with Don Quixote, but I cannot somehow project him into the external world; I have seen many drawings of the old knight, but none of them agrees with my own conception which, having been shaped by words, is not graphically clear. The painter, if he is more than a mechanical copyist, in creating a character, infuses himself into the work, thus constructing a Don Quixote utterly at variance with all the Don Quixotes in the world.

And yet the moving-picture companies persist in trying to reproduce literature, and will spend millions of dollars on a single venture. The most that can possibly be extracted from a piece of fiction is the bald outline of action, and the plots of distinguished novels, as the movies have conclusively shown, are melodramatic. Nor will the directors get it into their heads that the backgrounds of novels are also literary creations, and that the camera cannot, by transcribing "on location" the hills and vales of Dorset, convey the scenic atmosphere of Thomas Hardy. When the stars are assembled and smeared with grease paint, the director lashes them into action, and the one-eyed camera obediently registers their grotesque contortions, catching only the externals of form, and giving us, instead of reality, a negative world of silhouettes. The movie bears as much relation to literary characterization as photography does to mural painting. Its trials in this direction may be attributed, first, to the energetic ignorance of directors who esteem themselves artists, and second, to the avarice of producers who, as I have already pointed out, have learned the value of pandering to the appetites of women.

It has remained for a man of genius to discover the obvious province of the movies, and to employ the "silent drama" as an original vehicle. Charlie Chaplin has never had any delusions about the "high art of the screen"; with him it has always been a low and earthy art, and he has proceeded to perfect it on that basis. A born actor trained in the Keystone Comedy school where *scenarios* were unnecessary and plots superfluous, he had the wit to see that the essence of the movie (does not the word itself suggest it?) is pantomime, and that it must create its own effects, and supply its own material, independent of the other arts. Chaplin has sensibly avoided the emotional values of literature; his films are practically empty of narrative; and his plots, if they can be so called, are only wandering chains of comic situations in which his genius for clowning is allowed full play. He is content to be himself, not once, to my knowledge, having attempted to disguise his personality in the character of another, or to interpret a *rôle* which, without words, simply does not exist. Like all great comedians he is not above coarseness; the humour of his pictures cannot be translated into words, and his curious antics, when described, are childish and nonsensical. But to see him at his best—in parts of The Pilgrim—is to enjoy the most intelligent entertainment the movies have yet provided. The recent apotheosis of Chaplin was to be expected. Dilettantes and critics joined in the hymn of sanctification, and the ablest of our clowns became a conquering god. In The Gold Rush there are signs that Chaplin is beginning to feel the burden of his greatness and to listen to the praise which designates him as "a man of sorrows whose pathetic feet express the eternal suffering of mankind." Let us hope that he will stick to his coarseness and not be persuaded by the quack aesthetes to produce Euripides.

The fact that the movie has achieved its most interesting results in comedy does not imply that it is limited to this field. The Last Laugh, a German film shown in New York last spring, though egregiously sentimental, was an excellent piece of pantomime, and could not have been conceived in any other form. On a larger scale we have the spectacular picture, the movement of crowds, pageantry, and historical episodes, all of which might be very pleasing to the eye but for the directors. The average director's imagination runs to the three-ring circus. Incapable of inventing a sequence of events, or exposing consistently and without deviation the ideas of others, he drags in everything that is queer and costly. What an edifying spectacle could be evolved from certain phases of American history, if the director could be made to understand their significance, and to tell the truth in orderly pantomime! But he would probably resort to trick effects and to the miracles of photography. The technical sleights of the movies are legitimate and amusing, but as imagination they are on the same plane as the magic of Houdini.

In its present state of criminal extravagance the moving-picture industry will not get anywhere. Of the annual harvest of feature-films, how many will ever be seen again? If the experiment of The International Film Arts Guild, in reviving old pictures, has been of any service, it has proved that the movies, in the last ten years, have made little or no progress. True, the photography has gained in clarity and mechanical finish, but it has lost some of its original honesty, just as the slippery modern print has departed from the dignity of the old daguerreotype. Let us compare The Birth of a Nation with The Big

Parade, two pictures of the same *genre*. Technically the latter is the better picture, but it employs the same conventional sentiment and the same pictorial devices as its prototype, accomplishing in a more expert fashion the discoveries of Mr Griffith. It is undeniable that the war material in The Big Parade is, if not more moving, inestimably more accurate than the carnage of The Birth of a Nation. This is because Mr Laurence Stallings, the author of the *scenario,* wrote from experience, and experience bitterly remembered, and used his whole intelligence to impart the hideous realism of the modern shambles. The scenes, I take it, are identical with those in France, and the attacks manoeuvred in conformity with military science, but the horrors of war do not come out. Photography is far too thin a medium to carry such horrors, and one leaves the theatre remembering, not the agonies of the combatants, but beautiful flashes of pantomime and odd scraps of comedy.

Nor is there a vast aesthetic difference between The Cabinet of Dr Caligari and The Beggar on Horseback, to name two pictures of the most eccentric type. Both seek to arouse bizarre emotional effects by means of complex technical machinery, and both are freak pictures. The Caligari film is more striking in its sets which are arranged in broken planes in the manner of the Cubists, and which give an inkling of what a real artist might do if allowed to co-operate with a director.

The truth is that the movie of to-day is intrinsically the same old ten, twenty, and thirty cent show, and will increase in sumptuous prosperity as long as the public is willing to finance the mad expenditures of the producers. Not until actors, directors, and all concerned are paid in proportion to their worth, and intelligence is displayed in the selection and manipulation of materials, shall we behold any progress.

TRAVELLING INTELLIGENTLY IN AMERICA *

By Henry Seidel Canby

THE war ended, perhaps for good and all, the golden age
of travel. There was a brief, happy period when the young
American could put a few hundred dollars in his pocket
and irresponsibly see all that he never saw at home. No one
born after 1900, perhaps no one born after 1890, can understand what Europe was to an American in those naïve
days, now as far off as the Grand Tour or Italy of the
Renaissance. Normandy was what Normandy is still, a
country of delicious villages, there are inns in Somer-
set yet, hill towns in Italy, and churches in Rome, but the
American can no longer be irresponsible in Europe unless
the irresponsibility is congenial. The French, Italians,
English, Germans are individuals now who have opinions;
who fight, suffer, think, have personalities of which we
know more than we ever expected.

In that age of innocence, of which the turn of the century was perhaps the prime, Americans wandered abroad
like Anglo-Saxons in ancient Rome, amazed, delighted,
reverential, taking everything seriously but the inhabitants, and seeing them as part of the background. Europe
was quaint, Europe was cheap, Europe touched our world
—our left-behind problems of rivalry, progress, and a living—only as an escape. If democracy in politics was to be
found at home, democracy in pleasure was abroad, for one

* Reprinted from *Scribner's Magazine* by permission of the author
and of the editors.

drank wine at a franc a bottle, had ready service for coppers, and saw the greatest museum on earth for the price of shoe leather or a bicycle. War was a romance of monuments and crop-grown battle-fields; boundary lines a subject for ridicule; arrogant officers or marching troops like seeing the antiquities of history on a stage.

We sang our college songs in cafés sacred to the *beau monde,* good-natured rowdies too innocent to be really offensive. We herded through art-galleries, memorizing the unessentials that distinguish one great painter from another—white horses, high lights, lips with a double twist. We drank Munich beer and played the toy ponies and climbed easy mountains and saw shameless vaudeville, always with the feeling that this was the Land of Cockaigne, which for us had no reality outside of the pleasanter emotions. The past of Europe stirred us immensely; its present not at all, except in women, wine, and song, and the delights of easy travel. On Monday we did Shakespeare's birthplace and were duly thrilled, on Tuesday in a chance-found canoe went whooping down the Thames with two suit-cases and a hat-box between the thwarts. Poverty in Europe was picturesque, temper in Europe was merely amusing, people in Europe were like the stage mob that gesticulates, sobs, shouts, passes off, and is forgotten. It was not our world—that is why we loved it.

And if by chance we came upon the familiar—saw steel towns in Germany, suburbs in London, modern universities not like Oxford and Cambridge—we passed on quickly. For, with tremendous vitality and an incredible freshness, we undergraduates and schoolmarms and bank clerks and professors, who in France or Germany would have been bending over a desk, were privileged to buy for our tiny price what no millionaire could have at home.

Blue water and ancient beauty, sophisticated amusement and enlargement of every sense and faculty in a strange world spiriutally familiar, all were ours for a little saving. No travellers were ever so blest.

II

Most of it is gone to-day. The Great Museum is still there, but an uncomfortable sense of the problems that lurk behind the show-cases has penetrated the idlest intelligence. I fancy that one has to get drunk in Paris now to achieve complete irresponsibility. Nineteen Fourteen and Nineteen Eighteen tore away veils of illusion and made Europe hard reality. It is not the isolationists who most regret the harsh circumstances which now unite America and Europe in the bonds of industrialism. It is those travellers who felt the curious power of Europe over the American mind when there was real isolation in all the bread-and-butter affairs of life. Then twenty centuries were focussed at once upon an imagination which owed less allegiance to the foreign present than to Shakespeare, Dante, St. Louis, and Rome. It is those travellers who are the first to take up the new relationships because they know that old detachment is hopelessly gone forever.

III

Travel for the American must be less gay in the future; let it then be more intelligent.

That travel is not often intelligent, even among professionals, the hundred or so travel books and thousand or so travel articles published annually are voluble witnesses.

There are, as I see them, four prevailing modes of travel books, and if they were arranged in a pyramid the successive cross-sections would indicate their relative numbers.

Most numerous is the kind of book for which some worthy but unimportant person crams up on Brittany, or Scotland, or Siena, like an undergraduate cramming for an examination, and then empties his notes into a manuscript. It seems a harmless way of paying for travel, but the results are not honest. The land he describes must have a lure, and so he sentimentalizes it. Everything, from the results of economic tyranny to the habits of the prostitutes is picturesque, and there is an uncritical piling up of legend and anecdote all in one plane that would perplex a historian. Reading one of these books is like taking a cocktail or an injection before each experience to be sure of an exaltation of mood. You cannot see Europe plain for the Oh's! and Ah's! and Is not antiquity wonderful! This is the decadence of the romance of travel.

The second variety of travel book is less fervid and much more honest. Oil or big game or mere restlessness has tossed the author into some out-of-the-way corner of the globe, whence he returns full of surprising information and is readily persuaded to write a book. It is not usually a very good book, for a book depends not upon things seen but the writer thereof, and it is not often that circumstance brings the born observer and the rare experience together. Yet if the natives were queer enough, the adventures surprising, the country little known, such a travel book is worth publishing—if the pictures are good.

The third variety is an English specialty, although any race can produce it, given importance in the individual, opportunity, and an itch for autobiography. It is the anecdotal travel book which proceeds from the Austria of Francis Joseph to the India of rajah entertainment and back by way of Wild Western adventure to dinners with celebrities in London or Paris. This may be a good book if the man who writes it is good for more than the money it costs him to travel. He must have a personality that draws personality to it, and he must have luck. Notables must speak out in his presence. He must be on the edge of wars, or in the swirl of rapid events. He must, in fact, have sensational goods in his windows, or be sensational himself, else his book is worthless. Great books of this variety there are—but they are as rare as epics. Vasari did one of a kind. Boswell's "Journal of a Tour to the Hebrides" is another. But once these books verge toward real excellence, the travel sinks into unimportance and they become memoirs—ambulatory memoirs, not travel books at all.

Then, of course, there is the book of solid information—unliterary, unimaginative, dependable, a repository of facts. If more writers of travel books would stick to this kind of writing we should have fewer and better books. For clearly, if the romantic, or the anecdotal, or the mildly adventurous travel book should be evaporated to its facts, only a dozen pages or so would be left. I find solid facts of travel good reading; they stir my imagination sometimes when romantic vaporing leaves me cold. The diaries of some Arctic adventurers—Scott, for example—are thrilling; there is worse reading than a Baedeker, and Xenophon is still a classic.

And yet the relation of such a book to the living world it records is usually photographic. The facts are all there, but the facts themselves may mean nothing, else we should be content ourselves never to travel. A Doughty was not necessary to tell us that Arabia was desert, nor a Rockwell Kent to note the tempests of the Horn. The right and best travel book will have facts enough, and adventure if it happened, and anecdotes if they are relevant, and romance if romance there was, but it will be written for none of these things. It will be an achievement, because good travel should be an achievement; it will be an exhibition of the art of geography.

IV

I am aware, naturally, that geography is a science— so, I believe, is history, in the opinion of many; yet history undeniably has its aspect of art, and so has geography. The study of the influence of earth's surfaces upon life is the ample definition I find for geography. Now, travellers must follow earth's surfaces and they go to see life as well as bring it with them. If they consider not merely the cause and effect of what they see but also the emotional and intellectual values, then they may remain scientific but have certainly verged on literature. That, it seems, is the way of good travel and good travel books.

It would be easy to cite good books as an example, but let me take a more difficult means and cite a subject, the homely example of Connecticut, which has not been properly studied for the art of geography since the elder Dwight drove his buggy (if it was a buggy) up its central valley.

Now Connecticut is a land, a *terra,* as different from the rest of New England as Somersetshire from Devon, as different from New York or New Jersey or Pennsylvania as Yorkshire from Kent. Distinctions have been better drawn in England than here, because the folk have lived closer to the land, and there has been more time for the native to synchronize with his environment; that is why I use as contrasts these English counties whose characteristics have been made familiar in literature. Only

Thoreau and Muir, among the great American artists in words, have known a country as well as have a hundred lesser British contemporaries.

Connecticut is a land of scrubby ranges, not high but broad, with sunny pastures set among their crests, and valleys not deep but narrow. It is a country where wildness is never far away and open country always close at hand; a land of great variety, where the scale is small, the proportions excellent, the scenery never grandiose and never mean. There is always a range beyond the range to suggest infinity, but no peaks to set one dreaming; always the rocky frame of earth pushing through the soil to remind one of Connecticut and hard common sense.

In three hundred years civilization has done little or nothing to the ranges. They are as primitive as the English downs except that their pelt of forest has grown scrawny from too much fire and cutting. The rivers follow and seldom break through them, running north and south, though crookedly, while men in Connecticut since the earliest settlements have wanted to go east and west. Since they could not find "gaps," as in the softer, higher hills of Pennsylvania, nor go round, as in the broad, sleepy valleys of New York, they have cut over the ridges, piercing the woods to get to the open valleys.

It is therefore a State singularly adapted to the breeding of men, even as Iowa is perfect for the growing of corn and the Dakotas for wheat. As a breeder of men it has had no equal in North America. Most of them, to be sure, have left Connecticut! But that is natural. Either they stayed in the hill towns or the valleys—or they began crossing the ranges westward, and kept on.

It has been a breeder of men because it is a country of alternates, of centres of civilization made self-dependent by the no man's land of the hills rising beyond each populated valley. This made for isolation, isolation caused self-sufficiency, and out of self-sufficiency came the lovely Connecticut village which perfectly expressed its inhabitants—a capital in miniature, following the elms both ways along the street to the church, which was in its centre; looking both ways under the elms to the boundary ranges. It was a village state, decorous, proportioned, complete, with its hinterland about it.

The essence of Connecticut is in the hill towns, of which Cornwall is typical, a community as self-sufficient as a rabbit-warren and once as energetic as a coal-mine. In its tiny fold of the Appalachians the first missionary school was founded and the Christianizing of China and the South Seas begun. Hawaii got its first white rulers here; this is where Indians were educated, and the first teaching of scientific agriculture attempted. Intellectual and spiritual impulses that universities and churches might envy took their rise in this little area. Cornwall Old Home Day begins with a panegyric like Pericles's Funeral Speech, where more dead heroes are celebrated than there are live voters in the town.

Natural selection, I suppose, did its part in sending to the borders of the Stockbridge Indians an unusually prepotent breed. But that is not all. The strong families in Cornwall stay strong; the poor whites have been poor whites since the settlement. It has been by geographical necessity a self-dependent community, where, in politics, finance, human relationships, religion, and education, each man had to take his part and could see from his own hill pasture the boundaries of the community where he was responsible. Connecticut towns like Cornwall saved the Constitution, giving the senatorial system to the United States, which was essentially a method by which a small population could keep its self-dependence in a continent.

V

Indeed the country moulds the man, whatever else may be influential in his making. In the cities this geographical influence is overlaid by other factors. Modern industrial cities so greatly resemble one another that a city type of man has been developed who in many respects is more like the other city dwellers than the products of his own region. How much of this resemblance is superficial it is still hard to say, but in any case it complicates but does not change the problem. Already many American cities have established an individuality which is due far more than they realize to natural environment—New York eminently so; San Francisco, I should say, next; then Boston, Charleston, Chicago, Philadelphia. Yet only in long-settled rural communities, like the Connecticut towns or Sussex, can one readily distinguish those qualities of the country which may have affected man. In man himself the results are too subtle for complete analysis.

Complete analysis, however, is not the job of the traveller, who may leave that to the ethnologist and sociologist. He should know that the aspect of a land does mean something, that the ultimate effect of the bit of earth into which he has wandered is significant in terms of humanity as well as æsthetics, and capture its peculiar flavor and quality if he can. It will prove to be like style in literature, the most imponderable quality, never to be defined and never to be neglected, which when found or felt is a new clew not merely to beauty, but to subject, significance, mood, and result.

This Cornwall, for example: the final problem I should

set myself there would not be to detail its self-sufficient
history, but to capture the subtle distinctions of the land
itself—how its grassy valleys wind always just beyond
the eye, how pine meets oak, how white birch and low
huckleberry march upon the pastures, how hawthorn and
gray dogwood æsthetically arrange themselves in old fields
so that beauty is not lost in ruggedness, how every open
hill carries its view rolling upward to the west or down-
ward toward the sea, how the nights, even in summer,
sparkle with northern vigor and clarity.

I fail, of course, to be more than suggestive, but I fail
in part because I am not bent upon describing rural Connecticut. For that one should wade in careful phrases like
Thoreau in spring in his Massachusetts swamps. There
should be mention of white boulders carved from the
glaciers, of the great-shafted pasture elms, of the shrewd
crows the Indians left in their place, of self-respecting
houses that scorn easy living, of melancholy cow-bells, of
autumn garnet and gold, of wild rains, and the nights
when even in the villages we go back to wilderness. And
afterward the inhabitants. . . .

VI

And yet it is not the quality only of a country that a
traveller must catch, but his own mood also that reflects
it, and his mood is compounded of what he brings with
him and what he observes. It will be his own mood that
ultimately he describes for us, and his zeal in interpret-
ing his own reactions will determine whether his account
is to be a guide-book or literature.

Therefore an entrance examination set for those about
to travel would exclude from the bookmakers all who lack
a recording mind. A recording mind is a sensitive mind,

with a rich subconsciousness that takes abundant impressions easily and returns the best to the memory. It is amazing what an individual can fail to see. Most of the westward pioneers rode through the Appalachian belt without distinguishing, in the finest forest in the world, more than evergreen from deciduous. John Woolman, the Quaker saint, was so intent on ethical meditation that when he crossed the Great Pocono in the early seventeen-hundreds he saw no more than that it was terribly steep on the northern side. Audubon, who followed him fifty and odd years later, wrote a chapter on the Great Pine Swamp which still stirs the imagination. Borrow had the traveller's mind in perfection, which is best tested by little things—a dingle, a door-moulding, a cloud, or the words of a peasant met by the road.

Travellers' and poets' minds, then, should be alike in this, that they can recollect emotional impressions as vividly as facts. Tennyson was an ideal poet-traveller. Poe, who travelled much for an American, was a good poet but a bad traveller, for his turbid imagination beat his recollections into a romantic froth that seldom suggested anything in this world. Byron was too grandiose to travel well. He founded the railway-poster style of description. Artists and natural scientists travel intelligently. When the eye has had some training the impressions stored away are not likely to be so vague that they have to be worked up with rhetoric in order to make an effect. Ruskin, so tiresome elsewhere, is a magnificent recorder of travel. His study of the arts taught his senses to keep line and color. Hudson and Thoreau had a like advantage. They saw more in nature than other men and so had more to draw upon. Darwin was a good traveller. Kinglake's "Eothen" is one of the best travel books, not because it is history, but because its author was a born historian. Rockwell Kent's remarkable twin *tours de force* at the two ends of the Western Hemisphere—Alaska and Tierra del Fuego—are sharpened in the text as well as in the pictures by an artist's discipline. Tomlinson's exquisite travel narrative has profited by a journalist's cunning. If you are going to write a travel book get experience in looking at something, even if it is only bugs, or stones, or men's noses. See one thing clearly, and you will see more.

Yet the good traveller's mind differs from the poet's in that he must interpret what he sees for different purposes. He is, as I have said, a geographer. He moves in space primarily, a poet in space and time. Granted he brings a real mind with him, and personality, he must nevertheless use both to the furthering of knowledge as well as pleasure, and the knowledge cannot be from his inner consciousness, else he could better write from home. He must feel the effect of a land upon its people, and if he has not done this he has not written a book.

This standard, applied severely, would eliminate most of the travel books now being written, with excellent results. We should have large editions of the remaining ones, and the writers of future travels would be forced to do some real work. What opportunities were lost in this country when the greatest movement of peoples since the fifth century was under way, only the student of pioneer literature knows. The travel-minded writers who took their job seriously (Harriet Martineau and a few others excepted) were doing grand tours, or following Byron to the Orient, while the chance for the great travel books of the nineteenth century passed. If Irving had spent as much time on the prairies as in the Alhambra or England, his fame would now be much brighter. As it is, his Western chapters begin to make his romance of Moorish Spain seem a pastiche.

VII

It is questioned as to whether travel books are literature at all. The very suggestion implies a contempt for
the genre which the majority of specimens, for reasons
given, justify. But the question is absurd. If the term is
loosely used, some of the great books of all time come
into the category—"The Canterbury Tales," "The Divine
Comedy," "Gulliver's Travels," "A Sentimental Journey," "Paradise Lost" in many cantos, "The Faerie
Queene." These are, to be sure, loans from a convenient
format, but it is to be noticed that in every instance the
author made real use of travel.

That is all one asks of travel in the more prosaic world
of actual geography—where indeed another list of famous
books could readily be compiled. The map of the world
is made now, and there are few brand-new sections of the
globe where the mere facts of a journey are news. Big-
game trails in Africa are more written up than Broadway; Mr. Stefansson has copyrighted the Arctic for
trade purposes; South America is not likely to yield new
phenomena except underground. What we want is the not
too familiar scene made significant; not a new book on
Cambodia, but a study of Nebraska as meaty as "A Week
on the Concord and Merrimack Rivers"; not another visit
to the New Guinea savages so much as an account of that
new genus, the Californian, and the California that is
making him; not a map of the Antarctic Continent, but
the art of geography applied to the city of New York.

We live in a curious rootless state in this industrial
civilization, far more conscious of the morning paper,
which may come from a hundred miles away, than of the
atmospheric pressure which affects our mood, and per-
vaded with the dangerous fallacy that because New York,

Berlin, Tokyo are educated in the same sciences, eat much the same food, make money in the same general fashions, and believe in the same general principles, they will feel alike and, under stress, act alike. Any geographer knows that this is not true, but who will listen to any geographer! Literature has always been the middleman for science—for theology in the Middle Ages, philosophy in the eighteenth century, biology in the nineteenth. Literature must suck from geography now, and that means more and better travel books. It is quite possible that travel, geographically considered, and interpreted with knowledge, emotion, insight, and art, will make the best books that can be drawn just now from the shift and whirl of these United States.

A HOUSE IN THE COUNTRY *

By John Erskine

In a recent book on the future of the United States an Englishman prophesies that we shall all be living in apartment-houses before long. There will be no servants, he says, and a house in the city will therefore be impracticable —and what American could be persuaded to live in the country? The answer, of course, is almost any American who has lived in the city. At least, an increasing number of us who earn our living in town want to spend a good part of the year on the soil, and on soil which is our own. We did leave the farms and move to the great centers, at one stage of our economic development. Now he knows little about us who overlooks our buying up of deserted farms and converting them into a refuge from something or other—from the city heat in summer, from city rents all year round, or from spiritual discomfort and loss, more serious than high temperature or monthly bills. We find it no longer desirable to live in an unrooted condition. As soon as we have bought the farm, the small piece of land for the children in vacation, we begin to think of it as home. The city apartment becomes frankly what it always was, a high shelf to rest on between working-days.

The American return to the land is not a return to farm life; it is not a reversion to former economic systems; in

* Reprinted from *The Century Magazine* by permission of the author and of the editors, and from *Prohibition and Christianity*, copyright 1927, by special permission of The Bobbs-Merrill Company, Indianapolis.

fact, economic considerations have little to do with it. More often than not, when we balance our books we discover that the simple months close to nature are quite a luxury. But we always tell ourselves the money is well spent; we have recovered something beyond money. In a dim way we know what we mean. We may be rather feeble in the philosophy of man's place in nature, but we have got back the feel of the soil, the smell of earth and rain, the dramatic contact with the seasons, the companionship of the elements. After too many miles of city pavements, after too many hours of city dirt, a mere stain to be washed off, we have learned again to be conscious of wisdom and beauty through our feet and our hands. To walk on grass, to cross the meadow through all the grades of softness between May and September, to know you are near a spring or a brook, when the ground feels spongy; or to plant a garden and weed it, and to learn from your fingers whether the earth is thirsty or satisfied—is to get back what is perhaps man's oldest sense, the sense of the soil. Our predecessors who made our farm out of the wilderness had a richer and more varied sense. They must have had the feel of rocks and stones by the time they collected and lifted these walls, miles of them between the fields, and sometimes a yard thick. Their fingers must have known wood—not only the bark on the tree, but the grain of the boards they cut and framed for their houses —our houses now. But we doubt if they could be more sensitive than we are to the smell of earth and the smell of rain. With little or no practice we know the difference between a night in June and a night in October, such rich change of perfume follows the months; and in early June the rain is cold, yet not like the chilly rain in early November, and in July the showers meet the earth-warmth half-way. In the city all these distinctions can be wiped out with one umbrella. The very seasons are annihilated in town. There we make an even temperature stretch the year round, except for the two awkward joints when the steam heat is turned off or on. The electric lights hide the stars, and what is more important, the moon; coal-dust sometimes hides the sun. But when we go to our farm for the week-end, we are suddenly interested in the fact that the moon is full, we discover a remarkable sympathy between the temperature outside the house and the comfort within, and we are grateful for the sun. To be sure, we may install an automatic oil-heater, which, as we assure our visitors, maintains a city evenness of temperature, at the cost of a curious noise in the cellar every once in so often. The visitor, putting together the noise and his idea of oil, asks if we are not afraid the thing will blow up. We say it hasn't blown up yet. But with all our confidence in the oil-heater, we still are thankful when spring arrives to stay, and we understand why the ancient world, closer to nature than we care to be, used to dance and sing when the sun got high, and poetry was invented, to welcome the sweet season. We understand air and earth now, and fire and water become personal and friendly—the flame on our own hearth, the rain from the clouds for our vegetables, our flowers, our lawns, the water we boast of, for us, from our own well. The farmer who sold us the house had probably closed the fireplace and put in a stove, but that was only because his soul was on the way to the city. We know what we need; we restore the hearth and feast our eyes on fire. Even the farmer who first closes his hearth, and then wants to sell it, knows the worth of a clear spring.

To recover all this, to have again our place in nature, we buy a house in the country.

II

In the first paragraph of "Marius," his great romance of the sensitive spirit, Walter Pater reminds us that the word pagan means countryman, and that the pagan religion is simply the religion of the country. After Rome became Christian the worship of the old gods lingered on the farms. But when the old gods were still worshiped in Rome, there had been another pagan religion, an earlier faith. The country keeps its habits longer than the town, and even within the same church the landworker is of an older theology than the merchant. There is always a pagan religion.

And a pagan system of ethics. We are glad to reënter it when we establish our house in the country. If we should examine all the religions which the countrymen in Italy or elsewhere have held for thousands of years, we should find a quiet evolution in theology but little change in ethics, for pagan ethics is learned as much from nature as from tradition. Life close to the soil teaches certain virtues peculiar to no religion, but necessary to them all.

In the first place, man's needs do not correspond to the seasons. Nature supplies food and heat, but only during a limited period, yet we must eat and keep warm all the year round. Industry is a city virtue as well as a pagan, but in the country it must be industry at the right moment, and coupled with foresight. Nature forces us to have ideas larger than our experience, since everything here is for a season, but eternity is in our hearts. This is the fire from heaven, which Prometheus, or Foresight, brings in the hour when nature is cold. It is not less divine, though we city folk ridicule it in the humble form of thrift. The short-sighted countryman, we say, has little courage; he won't take a bold chance with life. We forget that in the prime matter of food no one can take a chance; we can eat only what we provide.

Perhaps it is in this primitive discipline that we learn first to appreciate the beasts, the birds, and the trees. It is odd that the farmer who rejects the idea of evolution, because it seems to contradict his pagan theology as to our physical origin, will at the same time accept with satisfaction all that his infallible book says about the moral superiority of the animal world. He is akin spiritually to these companions of his toil, and when he has observed their sagacity, he does not feel they are beneath him. "Go to the ant," he tells his children; he reminds them that "the ants are a people not strong, yet they prepare their meat in the summer"; and he says a word, too, for the conies, the locusts, and the spider. But in the country we learn a deeper lesson than mere prudence: we come to value animals, birds, and trees as friends. The horse, the dog, the cow, the apple-tree, the great elm or the oak, our favorite malicious squirrel, even that pest the old woodchuck, touch our hearts subtly; should we lose one, we should feel the loss—though the passing of the woodchuck could be borne with patience.

With the sense of the precarious terms on which we are here, comes a just vision of the dignity of life and death. In the presence of death the country seems to pause. Perhaps we should not learn our destiny in advance, or be able to frame any clear picture of human life in all its stages, if we had not the animals around us, the arc of whose life is so much shorter than ours. They dramatize for us in a few years birth, youth, age, and death, and they play their parts with enviable dignity—probably because they are not encumbered with speech. If they have any theories about themselves, at least they don't tell them, and they are able to offer for our study what could hardly be found among men, a wise life without comment.

Some deep wisdom of the pagan world we are not likely to acquire; we have still the city in us, even though we return to the soil, and we probably do not intend to support life exclusively by the product of our land. We shall therefore miss the point of view toward money for which the countryman is often blamed. Looking at him from the town, we say he is stingy. But as a matter of fact, he has reason to know, what we have forgotten, that every piece of silver represents so much life. If he gives it, he knows what he is giving—as we often do not. And for that very reason his hospitality is a direct sharing of life, in a sense we city men hardly understand, though our own etiquette of hospitality derives from ancestors who were close to the soil. The stranger who comes to the door must have food. He may not deserve it, he may be a lazy vagabond, but give him the food first and ask after his morals later. In very ancient times they would not have asked his name until he was fed, for fear he might be an enemy, and the sacrament of hospitality would be difficult. Even if the stranger is already fed, you offer food—in the city called refreshments. The habit goes back to man's first knowledge that in the food he stored up he had life; and who could refuse to share life, if it were asked or needed? The bread and wine, or their parallels, are the symbols of divine hospitality in many religions, exalted emblems of fruitful labor and generous love, yet still akin to the fare set out for family and guests in every country home.

But hospitality covers more than this central gift. I ask my neighbor in the country to let me use his saw or his mower; he never refuses, nor should I think of saying no to anything he wanted. Least of all do we keep back the desired article until the need for it is greater. If he asked me to lend him some butter, and I explained that my butter was on ice, to be delivered in the off season when he would have to pay high for it, my moral reputation with him and the other neighbors would be low. In the city cold storage does not offend us; we even explain the benefits of the system. Perhaps there are benefits—but not to human character. An economic theory enables us to do things which in the presence of nature seem a little mean.

There is an old doctrine that our moral strength comes from the country. Not that all farmers are angels, but that the pagan virtues are the basis of any social goodness in us. Where the countryman is dulled to the deep wisdom of his fields, his weather, his cattle, his seasons, his sun and moon and stars, you may be sure he has heard that civilization is found in cities. There is no one to tell him he already has the secret of sound culture, and the thing he is beginning to long for may be a disease. But those of us who have lived in the midst of civilization, and find it a spiritual anemia, are grateful for the farm he leaves behind as he goes to his bright danger.

III

The problems of marriage, incompatibility, divorce, flirtation, sentimentality, are common to the race everywhere, but they are emphasized in cities. We sometimes explain the comparative peace of family life near the soil by saying that the poor woman is too tired even to criticize her husband, or that she does criticize him in her heart, but lacks the opportunity to free herself. Most novels dealing with the soil—written of course by city people—make the point that the wife has had the soul crushed out of her, and the children are just waiting for a chance to run away. So far as I know, this picture may be true, on the whole. I have met it in so many books that when I first saw the homes of farmers in my neighborhood, and discovered that the families were affectionate and cheerful, I feared that the district was not quite genuine.

But though I cannot say dogmatically that marriage is happier near to the soil than in the city, I think it ought to be, and I suspect it is. If you cite instances of domestic tragedy, such as have occurred in many an old farm-house, I will·shift my ground and say that city folk who fall deep in love, and have a noble vision of comradeship between men and women, can realize that dream best in the country. Nothing, not even the church's blessing, so sanctifies marriage as continuity of the hearth, from generation to generation. To be born in the same house as your fathers, to see your children playing in the fields of your own boyhood, to enjoy the shade of trees planted by men now long dead, to set out young saplings with some confidence that they will benefit those of your blood after you are gone—this raises your private love-affair to a dignity above city romance; it makes your wedding of some importance to the stream of human fate; it helps you to guess that you and your beloved are less original than you supposed, and your passion less personal—nature having included you in her program.

We must blame the city, and the modern civilization which the city begot, for the exaggerated importance we attach to falling in love, and for the desperate attempt we have made to invent a kind of marriage which would be to the end of life a youthful love-affair. If you object that the importance of falling in love could not possibly be exaggerated, you probably disagree with Francis Bacon, when he says that the stage owes more to love than life does, since love furnishes the dramatist with a plot, but while you are in love you are of no use to general society. You probably dislike the way Walter Scott, wise man, portrays love-affairs in his novels, letting us feel that they are in the air, so to speak, but never devoting to them more than a quarter or a third of his pages. You cannot approve, it would seem, of the ancient world, as you read of it in the Greek writers or the Hebrew; they put love-making, with all respect, somewhat in the background, incidental to more important business. It is we who have created for ourselves insoluble problems by trying to prolong indefinitely the psychology and the sensation proper to youth, making them an end in themselves, and consequently forgetting the great purposes they are fitted to serve.

Close to the soil man learns another version of romance. Unless he is blind, he sees every year the vast creating force which continues life in the beasts, in the vegetable world, for all he knows, in the whole solar system. He will say, with the rest of us, that in him the mighty impulse takes its noblest form, but he is more likely than the city man to realize that if it is nobler, it is because man resolves it shall be so. Otherwise the universal passion is impartial and indiscriminate. In a field across the road there is a cow which seems to be getting sentimental. It is not for me to say that her emotions are not profound and adequate to the occasion. So far as I know she will be equally concerned later to look after her calf and supply the world with milk. If we differ from such an animal, surely it is because we possess other faculties in addition to the capacity for sharing in the creative principle of nature. Successful marriage ought to attend to the development of those other faculties.

But we cannot attend to them until we have got our minds off ourselves, and perhaps our best chance for such salutary distraction is in the contemplation of nature and her doings. Nature provides as it were a scale against which we can measure ourselves, a detachment from which we can see the part we play in the whole. If you watch the city traffic from a high building you are impressed with the formal patterns the ant-like procession traces; it is the very picture, down there, of a mechanic destiny. You may have imagination enough to recall how free and individual you felt when you were one of the crowd; or later when you hurry along that same sidewalk on your particular errand, you may remember how small, lost, and fated you seemed from above. Some such wisdom can be learned in the constant presence of nature. Our souls are important, yes; but there seems to be a good deal of soul in nature too. If you value man's power, wait till you have seen the lightning strike one of your trees. If love has profoundly moved you, and you have told yourself that for such divine ecstasy the world is well lost, wait till you have watched day and night come and go in the heavens, and have caught a glimpse of the love that moves the sun and the other stars.

Near the soil we can imagine a happy marriage, a pagan marriage, of two souls disciplined by the recurring drama of the seasons, and none the less kindled by the creative impulse to live constantly toward greater heights and greater depths. After the moment of romance passes, the season of partnership remains, a sharing in the happy task of building the home; then comes the season of rooted friendship, with the works of our hands about us, and the life we put forth and cherished—our gardens, our trees, our children; last comes the rich time of remembrance, affection, and wisdom. Shall we be lovers then? The word seems inadequate. We need a word which includes comradeship, long habits together, and so much illumination as to nature's ways that we can think of our falling in love as her wholesale device for bringing men and women together. Yet that it was we who met, will not seem accidental after all.

IS MAN A MACHINE?*

By Will Durant

DETERMINISM is the oldest of philosophies, as animism is the oldest of religions. The simplest faith sees whimsical will in everything, and the earliest speculation reacts against that vivid creed by asserting the helplessness of the individual in the face of omnipresent law. From these diverse beginnings religion and philosophy may reach one goal: the universal will may be divested of its whims and become identical with the inviolable order of the world.

In the ancient Orient, where the feverish fertility of man has outrun the patient bounty of the soil, and the soul is broken with hardship and dwarfed by the engulfing crowd, the primitive belief in will tends to disappear from religion as well as from philosophy; happiness is conceived as the cessation of desire and the bliss of surrendered personality, and a somber fatalism envelops priest and sage. In those seething cauldrons of humanity the individual can have no fundamental value or significance; against this background of an endless and tragic past he sees himself a futile atom projected unasked, out of nothing, struggling pretentiously for a while, and then drawn down irresistibly into the dark as by some unreasoning enemy.

But in active and progressive civilizations, where the mysterious flame of thought burns brightly in the face of

---

* Reprinted from *The Century Magazine* by permission of the author and of the editors.

fate, achieving some transient mastery of the environment, and rearing fair temples to divinity and proud structures of philosophy, the individual finds better reason for believing in his own creative personality; he feels in himself a spark of spontaneity, and fashions on his own model even the Olympian deities. So the Greeks saw growth and evolution in the universe; everywhere there were gods, and in the midst of contraries, harmonies appeared; it seemed to Plato and Aristotle that all the world moved toward some beautiful purpose as if drawn by a lover's eyes. Yet that exuberant culture was only a happy interlude born of wealth and victory. When Spartan arms destroyed the Athens of Pericles, and Alexander leveled Thebes, men seemed no longer so akin to the immortals; and philosophy, in the Oriental Zeno, reached the conclusion announced by Sophocles many generations before, that *Moira,* dark fate, held power over gods and men.

Tired civilizations, like senile souls, are apt to be deterministic; unable to overcome the forces of death, they dignify their fatigue as fatality, and their defeat as destiny. It was in the black soil of this despair that Christianity grew, a slender flower of hope in a disintegrating world. And always in the heart of the new religion (where it was not richly overgrown with pagan rites and joys) lay the pessimism out of which it came; the other side of faith in heaven was distrust and fear of life. That gloomy faithlessness reached its nadir in the predestinarianism of the melancholy Calvin; God had foreseen all things, and therefore also the final lot of every man; the eternal selection or damnation of each soul was determined before its birth, for the future would not dare to violate the infinite prescience of God. Christianity, which had sought to comfort the bereaved and to solace the oppressed, fell apart for a while into creeds more cruel and more bitter than any earthly fortune.

It remained for modern minds to phrase this merciless theology in the new infallibility of science. Galileo, enamored of the mathematical regularity which he discovered in the stars, laid it down as the goal of every science that it should reduce its field of knowledge to mathematical and quantitative law. The high repute of Newton, and the transient perfection of his work in mechanics, cast a spell upon every student; physiologists and psychologists hungered for mechanical explanations and mathematical formulæ for the growth of the cell and the perturbations of desire. For a time philosophy was drunk with mathematics; Descartes suggested, with a cautious obscurity, that all the world was a machine, a geometry in motion; and Spinoza emulated the rigor of the universe in the Euclidean structure of his thought. It pleased the rebels of the enlightenment to learn that man was made not in the image and likeness of God, but rather on the model of the machines that in that age had begun to replace the work of human hands and wills.

It was the industrial revolution that destroyed the old philosophy of freedom. For first, it accustomed the mind to dealing with machines, and induced it more and more to think of causes as mechanical. The worker immured within factory walls, seeing all the throbbing life about him slip by on pulleys and revolve on wheels, forgot that older agricultural existence, in which life had seemed a matter of seeds miraculously sprouting from the soil, responding eagerly to every encouragement, and multiplying with a spontaneous and bountiful fertility. The world, which had once been a field of growing plants and wilful children, of loving mothers and ambitious men, became for the modern mind a vast array of mechanisms, from the planets that mechanically circled 'round the sun, to the microscopic life that mechanically congregated about a ray of light. Science was sure that it had at last been permitted behind the curtain of the cosmic drama; it marveled at the unsuspected machinery that had created delusions and shifted a thousand scenes; it concluded, in modest admiration, that the property-man was the real dramatist, and that the wires were the play.

But again, the industrial revolution made cities, and cities made crowds, and crowds unmade men. Once more in the modern metropolis those conditions appeared which in the Orient had shorn the individual of personality and meaning. In this teeming welter of population, one became a number or at best a "hand," the mind an instrument for measuring and counting; and man became part of the machines he fed. Democracy, which had proposed to liberate the individual, became itself a mechanism, a chain of "machines," automatically leading mindless masses to the ballot-box. It was as useless for the individual to rebel against this system of wires, pushes and pulls, as it had been for him to indulge in self-assertion against the crushing crowds and conformities of the distant East. Even the "leaders" became half-inanimate parts of the new contraption, as dull and will-less as the deluded herds whose noses were counted (or not counted), quadrennially, at the polls.

If the slaves rebelled against this mechanism it was with a philosophy that acknowledged the supremacy and divinity of machines. Socialism unhesitatingly allied itself with determinism and mechanistic science; it fed its recruits on Büchner and Haeckel, Spencer and Marx. Not only was the world a machine, but history was a machine, in which every move was caused by the price of bread, and a good economist sufficiently cognizant of present and past could predict with fatal certainty every turn and destiny of the future. Man was now a creature composed of heredity and environment; whatever he did was the result of ancestral or physical causes over which he had had no control; he was merely a marvelous, superfluously-animated automaton. Therefore he was "not guilty": if he committed crimes, society was to blame; if he were a fool, it was the fault of the machine which had slipped a cog in generating him; he should not be deprived of his right to vote, or be president for that reason. What the world needed was a bigger and better machine, a nationalized machine; one hundred million mechanisms managed by one executive machine, pressing a presidential button mechanically.

In an aristocratic age the leaders might have allowed a monopoly of this narcotic philosophy to the oppressed masses. But in a democratic century the loftiest thinkers felt themselves called on to share patriotically in the metaphysics of the mob. It became unfashionable and antediluvian to doubt the omnipresent and omnipotent machine. Great writers hastened to announce that they too were machines, whose thoughts had been put into them, with a time-attachment, a million millenia before. Taine acknowledged the new god, and created a theory of criticism in his honor; Zola wrote interminable tragedies to show that one must pay a price for having ancestors; Thomas Hardy presented man as helpless in the fell clutch of circumstance; Anatole France mourned with immaculate elegance the slavery of the soul and the futility of life, and d'Annunzio saw everywhere the triumph and mockery of death.

Doubtless the loss of our childhood faith has saddened us; and the double bereavement of every mature soul, which must lose the theological ideals of its childhood and then the social ideals of its youth, leaves the heart a little heavier with the weary weight of this unintelligible world. But something of the somber undertone that runs beneath our superficial gayety is the result of the jejune precipitancy of our thought. It was not demanded of us that we should fly from a theology that scorned the natural basis of existence, to a philosophy that ignored the creativeness of life and the initiative of mind, neither was it demanded of us that we should cast away, along with the garments of our old faith, the body of truth and beauty which they had transiently clothed. It was not asked of us that having abandoned our puerile pretense at being the center and summit of universal history, we should humble ourselves before the machines in our factories, and accept them as the Platonic ideas on whose august models fortuitous variation had fashioned our souls. We were not called on to give up our share in the vitality of the world, in the resilient expansiveness of life, in the persistent constructiveness of thought. But defeated on one part of the battle-front, we fled from the field in cowardly surrender and despair.

Was it necessary to yield so utterly? Is determinism inescapable? Is human behavior of the same order as the erosion of the hills, or the flight of the wind, or the tides of the restless sea? Is the inexhaustible solicitude of motherhood, or the eager ambition of youth, or the quiet tenderness of love, merely a mechanical redistribution of physical force and chemical elements? Is the undiscourageable pertinacity of life an appearance only, and the passionate striving for perfection but a blind compulsion, and the efficacy of thought a delusion, and the reality of will no more than a dream? Is man a machine?

Consider locomotion. Let us imagine a mechanism, some toy automobile that will run resolutely enough when its spring has been wound and released by a living hand. At its head we attach a square of rubber as a sensitive proboscis. We set the toy down upon a smooth floor, directly facing a slightly distant wall. We wind the spring, and then release it. We shall suppose that the alignment of wall, floor and toy are as perfect as in mathematical and mechanical theory. Under such conditions the car will rebound from the wall in the same line by which it came, and will approach the wall in that same line again. In theory it will do this repeatedly, always in a straight line against the wall, until its artificial energy is completely spent.

Now fill a rectangular glass bowl with water. Across the center place a transparent glass partition, as much shorter than the width of the bowl as will leave a narrow passage at each side. Into one side of the bowl drop a piece of food; into the other side, some lowly organism, as simple as possible,—say *Paramecium*. Observe it under the microscope. It moves directly toward the food; it strikes the glass partition; it retreats in a straight line; apparently it is a machine. But suddenly it veers slightly about, to the right or left; it sets out again, and once more it strikes the glass, rebounds and veers and strikes again. . . . It rebounds and veers and passes through the opening to the food.

Consider digestion. Some sensitive plants, such as the *Dionæa* or the *Drosera,* close upon and absorb particles of food placed on their surfaces; to inedible substances similarly placed they make no response at all. The *Amœba* normally rejects what cannot serve for its nourishment. The little swan-animalcule, *Dileptus anser,* thrusts out a neck swollen with trichocysts (coiled stinging threads), which it discharges only upon fitting prey. The cells of the human intestine are selective in their action, each class of cells acting on certain foods and on no others. Every cell in the human body chooses from the blood-stream the specific substances that it needs; it ignores the rest, and pours into the blood the products of its own metabolic waste. It breaks down into parts the materials it chooses, and reunites their elements into the compounds required for its support and activity. It breathes, and eats, and excretes, and grows, and reproduces, and dies, as if it were an organism with an individuality of its own. Says that better physicist than psychologist, Le Bon: "That which these cells accomplish in every instance of our existence soars far above all that the most advanced science can realize. The scholar capable of solving by his intelligence the problems solved every moment by the cells of the lowest creature, would be so much higher than other men, he might be considered by them as a god."

Consider growth. How could a machine grow? Why should it care to grow? Was there ever a mechanism so marvelous that it might offer analogy to the astounding expansiveness of life? Behold the lilies of the field; what enchanting power is it that draws them from their prison in the soil, and lifts them slowly and gently toward the sun?

Here is a child; why does it hunger and thirst for nourishment, and reach out with its soft fingers to possess the world? See it grow; it needs but one food to make from it dimples and curls and laughing eyes. See it raising itself for the first time, fearfully and bravely, to a vertical dignity; why should it long to stand and walk? Why should it tremble with perpetual, perilous curiosity, touching and tasting, watching and listening, manipulating and experimenting, observing and pondering,—till it weighs the earth, and charts and measures the stars? What mysterious transfiguration of puberty is this, that takes the boy and quiets and broadens him into a man, that takes the girl and fashions her into a gentle beauty fairer than any art?

Consider regeneration. Cut off any ray of a starfish, and the ray will be regrown; cut them all away, and the center will regenerate them; cut away the center, and the rays will grow it again. A machine out of order does not repair its parts; it stands senselessly still waiting for the touch of a living hand to re-order its parts into meaning and efficacy. But these larger phenomena, which Bergson has unsurpassably described, are not the most significant; the simplest healing of the slightest wound is unmechanical and marvelous enough. With what artistry the new cells are laid over the injured flesh, as if some cellular intelligence were guiding the beneficent work! We offer mechanical or chemical aids to these vital processes, but we know that they have the same relation to Nature's healing power as marble or clay to the artist's hand. We know that in some way which mechanism will never illuminate, the energy and impetus of life will bear us on through a thousand battles and a thousand injuries, till that divine vitality is spent, and finds for itself another form.

Consider reproduction. Here is a little egg, invisible to the eye; here is a restless sperm, moving about in worlds unrealized. Each of these microscopic cells is infinitely rich with hereditary characters bearing the memory of a thousand generations; each carries within it unique and subtle qualities of body and mind, impulses, dispositions and aptitudes, hunger, eagerness and love; perhaps in their plasm already lie the passion and patience of genius. Well, let sperm and egg unite; suddenly those possibilities become realities, and the miracle of a new life begins. By some internal urgency, nourished with placental blood, the fertile cell divides into two cells, into four cells, into eight, into a hundred million cells that seem to grow in unity even as their number mounts. A heart forms and begins to beat; a brain forms and begins to feel; tiny hands and feet bud forth and stir in the womb, and then the little marvel enters the world; air and cold and sound and light impinge upon it; its eyes and lips and ears open, and all its nerves tingle with sensation. Life has broken through death again, and pours itself lavishly into its new mould, joyful and strong and young once more!

Is it mechanical? Jacques Loeb discovered that he could fertilize the egg of a sea-urchin with a salt solution or the prick of a pin; he concluded, hilariously, that he had proved the mechanical nature of reproduction. In truth he had merely shown that in certain cases the female organism can of itself generate offspring without even the casual assistance to which nature limits the male; he had rediscovered that peculiar parthenogenesis which biologists had known for a few thousand years. That the female herself was hardly as mechanical as the pin, or as simply chemical as the salt, might go without saying; indeed the performance of the unaided female seems a little more marvelous than that of her more fortunate sisters. It is also more ominous, and indicates that the emancipation of the female sex will in our century proceed to unpleasant extremes.

Far more revealing than these experiments of Loeb were the allied discoveries of Hans Driesch. Driesch had been brought up in the laboratory of Ernst Haeckel at Jena; he had every inducement to be a mechanist of the purest dye, but he found phenomena undreamed of in his master's philosophy. He cut a fertilized egg in half, and nevertheless it developed normally. He haphazardly disarranged the cells after the second division, and nevertheless the organism developed normally. He disarranged the cells after the third division, with the same result.

Now let us imagine, first, the cohabitation of two machines for the generation of a third machine. Let us imagine that each part of each machine is also endowed with the power and habit of reproduction, and continually divides and grows. Let us imagine, further, that certain parts of the parent-machines coalesce to form the model of the new one; that the model produces the complete machine by spontaneously dividing into two, into four, into eight, and that the more it divides, the more it becomes one. Let us imagine some Brobdingnagian Driesch appears, who cuts the coalesced machine into halves, or disturbs its parts into a deliberate chaos, and let us imagine, finally, that the machine proceeds normally and successfully with its work, as if nothing whatever had happened. Was there ever a jollier hoax in science or philosophy? Is there any miracle in any religion, ancient, medieval or American, that could compare with this magnificent and monstrous myth?

But the mechanist will tell us that we are unfair, that we have taken his term too literally and have attacked a position he has not offered to defend. We may conceive his reply.

"What we mean," he says, "is not so much the machine-like character of human behavior, as the inviolable sequence of cause and effect in the mental as well as in the physical world. Man is a part of Nature, and is presumably subject to her laws. It is highly improbable that there should be a break in the causal chain; such a break would involve the destruction and the creation of energy. But the continuity and conservation of energy stand out visibly everywhere. Cease to feed a man, and soon his reactions stop. Feed him properly, and he becomes virtuous and patriotic; feed him wrongly, and you can make him an invalid, a criminal, a pessimist, an idiot, a believer in freewill. Measure a man's activity from birth to death; it will correspond almost precisely with the energy in the nourishment he has received. Obviously mental energy in man is a product of the energy contained in the organic substances which he uses as his food. But these substances are ultimately derived, through plant metabolism, from inorganic materials in the soil and air. To admit a rigid causal chain in the inorganic world is therefore to accept it for even the subtlest processes of human life or human thought.

"Again, it appears that the more we know of human behavior the more successfully we can predict it. Presumably, if we knew all the conditions affecting the actions of our friends, we could foretell their responses with the same accuracy with which we predict the phases and eclipses of the moon. But if determinism were untrue, if human actions did not follow invariable laws, it would be impossible to develop the prediction and control of human behavior by increasing our knowledge of man.

"Above all, a man's conduct is clearly the result of his character and the circumstances that surround his action. His character is the product of his past environment (back to his conception) and his heredity. 'We are,' as Mark Twain said, 'the tail-end of a tapeworm of ancestry.' We originate nothing, and we decide nothing; we are moved, directed, and compelled by forces ultimately external to us, and over which, in the last analysis, we have no control. Choice is a delusion; it is only a composition of determining forces. 'Men think themselves free,' said Spinoza, 'because they are conscious of their volitions and desires, but are ignorant of the causes by which they are led to wish and desire.' In truth our behavior is as rigidly determined by the forces that produce and encompass us, as the fall of a stone is fixed in time and space by its mass, velocity and direction. It is in this sense that man is a machine."

Let us see.

First of all, let the determinist honestly envisage the implications of his philosophy. If every action is necessarily the result of pre-existing and ultimately physical conditions, we must conclude, first that determinism and mechanism are identical, and that Michelangelo's piety and Shakespere's passion, Socrates' nose and Cleopatra's smile were due to the mechanical and chemical structure of the primeval nebula. It is a large order; one wonders at the readiness with which professional skeptics like Renan and Anatole France swallowed this deterministic camel. But even doubters are believers; their proudly scientific rejection of one faith is soon followed by their blindly human acceptance of another.

It remains a marvel that this tremendous nebula never choked the gullet of credulity. What hypnotism was it that made us for a generation accept the transient categories of physics as the laws and symbols of our lives? Which of us really believed that he was a machine, and acted honestly on that humorous hypothesis? Or did we secretly know, beneath this Byronic pretense, that sense and mind are active as well as passive things, and that we are in our little ways creative centers in the flux of force? How could we honestly conceive in terms of mechanism and determinism the vast variety and fertility of life, its endless experiments and forms, its inexhaustible ingenuity, its patient transformation of the world nearer to the heart's desire?

Our determinism came of Locke's conception of the mind as a clean slate on which sensations wrote, a passive wax, shaped and reshaped helplessly by external things.

But we are being taught to-day a different psychology. At the bottom of our souls we find desire, desire which is "the very essence of man"; and we can trace in a thousand ways the selective and formative action of desire on our sensations, perceptions, memories and ideas. Life has divided its great hunger into specialized instincts and capacities; it is these that determine our actions, our attitudes, and the orientation of our senses; we are unconscious of innumerable stimuli that vainly try to send their messages to us; we ignore vast realms of sensible reality because we select through our purposes the sensations we need. We hear certain sounds that interest us, and are deaf to a thousand others; we look at some temporarily meaningless object and see straight through it to some goal that fills our minds and therefore guides our eyes. It is our purposes that interpret sensations into perceptions, unify perceptions into ideas, and co-ordinate ideas into thoughts. It is purpose, and not recency nor frequency nor vividness, that explains the association of ideas. You are told to add given pairs of numbers; soon the "mental set" of addition "determines" without effort the association of stimulus and response; and hearing "7 and 7" you answer "14." But if you had been told to multiply, you would have reacted with "49" to that identical sensation. You are not, then, the helpless recipient and victim of whatever stimuli may chance to impinge upon your flesh. You are an agent of selection. Education is not, as Spencer led the world to believe, a scheme for adapting you completely to your environment; it is the far more subtle art of developing in you the powers through which you may adapt your environment to your own purposes, and the susceptibilities through which you may receive the meaning and beauty of the world.

In this process of active adaptation we perform mental

prodigies which only a fanatic could conceive as mechanical: we analyze wholes into parts, and recombine parts into new wholes; we dissociate ideas in perception, and reassociate them in reasoning; we consider purposes, measure values, imagine results and invent ways and means for our innermost desire. We recall the issue of past responses, vision their like again in these surroundings and judge them in the light of our purposes. Knowledge is the memory of the results of various modes of action; the more our knowledge, the greater our foresight can be; the greater our foresight the wider our freedom. Consciousness is the rehearsal of imagined responses; through memory, imagination and reason we eliminate unwise reactions, and express with some success our final aim. Freedom, like reason, is delayed response leading to total response; our freedom grows as by delay we permit a complex situation to arouse in us all relevant impulses, and as by imagination, we combine these partial impulses into a total reaction that expresses our complete and maturest self.

Mechanism is secondary; what we see as primary, fundamental, and immediate, what we take for granted in the actual and honest philosophy of our lives, is that every organism, in proportion to the flexibility of its structure, is a center of redirected force, and (in some measure) of spontaneous initiation. Life is creative, not because it makes new force from nothing, but because it adds its own remoulding force to the powers that enter from without. And will is free only in so far as the life of which it is the form, actively reshapes the world.

Can this conception of freedom withstand the assaults of the determinist? He will remind us that "will" is an abstract term (he will forget that "force" is not less so). To which we should reply that by will we mean no metaphysical entity, but the propulsive and expansive behavior of life itself. What life is, another page must try to tell; but let us not turn a fact into a mystery, or the determinist will recall the conservation of energy; the organism cannot emit more energy than it has received. Which is to forget that life itself is energy, visibly transforming the forces and materials brought to it into combinations that aim at the mastery of environment by thought, and occasionally succeed. What issues from action may be no more in quantity than what entered in sensation; but how potently different in quality! This transforming power of life is the highest energy we know; it is known to us more directly and surely than any other energy in the world, and is synonymous with freedom.

The determinist supposes that freedom is illusory because the "stronger" motive always wins. Of course this is a vain tautology: the motive that is strong enough to win is stronger than the one that fails. But what made it stronger if not its harmony with the will, with the desire and essence of the soul? "But there cannot be any uncaused actions." Verily; but the will is part of the cause; the circumstances of an action must include the forward urgency of life. Each "state" of mind follows naturally from the total preceding state of all reality; but that state and this include the transforming energy of life and will. "The same effect always follows the same cause." But the cause is never the same, for the self involved is always in flux, and circumstances are forever changing. "But if I knew all your past and present I could infallibly predict your response." You could if you knew also the nature and power of the life-force within me; you could, perhaps, if you abandoned mechanistic principles and asked yourself, for your guidance, what you—that is, life—would do in this complex of circumstance. Probably you could not predict successfully even then; probably there is in life an element of incalculability and spontaneity which does not accord with our categories and our "laws," and which gives peculiar zest and character to organic evolution and human affairs. Let us pray that we shall never have to live in a totally predictable world. Does not the picture of such a world seem ridiculously incongruous with life?

"But all action is the result of heredity and environment." Not quite; the determinist modestly fails to take account of himself. He supposes once more that life is the passive product of external forces; he neglects (if we may use a pleonasm) the very vitality and liveliness of life. We are not merely our ancestors and our circumstances; we are also a well of transforming energy; we are part of that stream of creative force, of capacity for adaptive choice and thought, in which our forefathers also moved and had their being. These ancestors are in truth living and acting within us; but the will and the life that were once in them is in each of us now, creating the "spontaneous me." Freedom is narrower and wider than as conceived of old; it is subject, no doubt, to ancestral and environing limitations of a thousand kinds; nevertheless it is as deep as life, and as broad as consciousness; it grows in scope and power with the variety of experience and the clarity of thought. Will is free in so far as life is creative, in so far as it enters, with its fluent energy, as one of the determining conditions of choice and action. There is no violation of "natural law" in such a freedom, because life itself is a natural factor and process, not a force outside the varied realm of Nature. Nature itself, as its fine name implies, is that living power through which all things are begotten; perhaps throughout the world this spontaneity and urgency, which we have claimed for life, lurk. To say that our character determines our actions is true. But we *are* our character; it is we then that choose. To say with Huxley that we may be free to act out our desire, but are never free to choose what our desire shall be, is also true, and also tautological; for we are our desires; desire is life itself, and in realizing our desires we realize ourselves. It is not enough to say that external and hereditary forces compel and conquer us; the other half of the truth is that life itself is a force of its own, with its own direction and power, cruelly limited and constrained, but effecting its will in an amazing degree, rising from the lowliest organisms to the lonely heights of genius, and covering the world with its forms and its victories.

This realization of our fundamental freedom restores to us our responsibility and our personality, and challenges us to create. There was something cowardly in determinism, with its shifting of guilt to heredity and society, those poor abstract scapegoats of our vice and our sloth. It reflected not only the domination of the individual by the vast industrial machinery of our times, but also the overshadowing of personality by the ever-growing city and the rapacious democratic state; in a mob it is difficult to retain initiative and individuality. Determinism was a result of the intoxication of physics with its own external glory, so that it thought to include the universe of mind, art and love in its partial and precarious formulæ. But slowly we are passing out of the age of physics into the age of biology. We shall learn to see, behind the superficial mechanisms of the world, the pulsing life beneath. We shall understand that in our modest measure we participate in the "procreant urge" of the world, and that if we wish, we may write some lines of the rôle we play in the drama of Creation.

Let us note before we end, how the mechanical approach is breaking down in biology, in psychology, in physiology and even in physics itself. "To-day," says Lucien Poincaré, "the idea that all phenomena are capable of mechanical explanations, is generally abandoned." "In modern physics," says Cassirer, "the mechanical view of the world has been more and more superseded and replaced by the electro-dynamic view." "In spite of the efforts of thousands of workers," says Le Bon, "physiology has been able to tell us nothing of the nature of these forces that produce the phenomena of life. They have no analogy with those that are studied in physics." As chemistry needs the concept of quality in addition to that concept of quantity with which physics tries to be content, so physiology needs, in addition to quantity and quality, the concept of organism. Physics and chemistry are the study of parts which determine the behavior of their wholes; biology is the study of wholes which determine the behavior of their parts.

Among the biologists themselves the rejection of mechanism has become a common thing: Driesch and Pavlow and Haldane are names that might make any mechanist take thought. And it is significant that Schopenhauer and Nietzsche, with all their hostility to traditional theology, rejected mechanism scornfully.

Perhaps biology will rebel soon against its domination by the methods and concepts of physics; perhaps it will discover that the life which it is privileged to study reaches nearer to the bases of reality than the "matter" of natural science. And when biology is at last freed from the dead hand of the mechanistic method, it will come out of the laboratory into the world; it will begin to transform human purposes as physics changed the face of the earth;

and it will end the brutal tyranny of machinery over man-kind. It will reveal even to philosophers, who for two hundred years have been the slaves of mathematicians and physicists, the directive unity, the abounding resource-fulness, and the creative spontaneity of life.

CLASSICS ON THE FARM *

By Walter Peirce

THE period was the late 'eighties, and the farm was in southern Ohio. The victims flung to the classics were aged twelve and fourteen, and they went to their martyrdom with no enthusiasm whatever. In those days education was administered without anæsthetics, and college implied Latin and Greek. However, college also implied four years of living in a seething centre of population, our college town boasting ten thousand inhabitants if you took the census in term time, and four years of blessed relief from farm tasks. We accepted the Latin and Greek therefore along with other incomprehensible evils, all of which were to lead to the magic city.

I do not remember that our first year of Latin stirred our imaginations in any way. We hated declensions and conjugations as thoroughly as two young barbarians ever hated them, and they incited us to no histrionics. But Cæsar was different; here was war, here was action, here was bloodshed. Some years before this the Zulu war had stimulated us to try the effect of spears and shields in bush warfare, and then a visit to Buffalo Bill's Wild West Show turned our attention exclusively to bows and arrows and scalping knives. When we reached Cæsar, we were already seasoned veterans.

Do not misunderstand me; we were not inspired by the

* Reprinted from *The Yale Review* by permission of the author and of the editors.

beauty of the classics, and we loathed constructions and indirect discourse with the normal loathing of the young male. But we detected a story. As early as October of that year, every tree and bush in the yard had been baptized by the name of some *oppidum,* and the house itself served as Cæsar's camp. Subsequent acquaintance with France has led me to believe that Cæsar changed his camp as often as Queen Elizabeth changed her sleeping quarters, and the French village which cannot boast a Cæsar's camp is as hopelessly undistinguished as the English town which cannot produce at least one bed in which the Virgin Queen at some time reposed. But our imaginations pictured Cæsar as occupying the same camp throughout the Commentaries, or at least the four books required for college entrance, with the various *oppida* placed about it within convenient marching distance.

My brother, being the elder, naturally chose the best rôle for himself, which was invariably that of the conqueror. I, the younger, passed my life in fleeing from an ever victorious pursuer. As the stage-coach, I had fled from the onslaught of the redskins, only to become a redskin myself and flee in turn before General Custer or Buffalo Bill. As the Gauls, however, I had my share of the limelight, and while it was not inspiring to be burned as Orgetorix, the rôle of Vercingetorix was not unattractive, and the earlier part of his history involved chasing the Romans into their camp. Our weapons were archæologically correct, for were not our Cæsars illustrated, in the hope of inspiring interest in the classics? In our case the editor's faith was justified, and our swords had parallel edges coming to an unexpected point. These were not only in accord with the most authentic models, but were very easy to whittle out of a lath, and a cross-piece nailed on for a guard did the rest. Our shields might have been mistaken for boards, but for the two leather straps nailed on the inside, and the conventionalized thunderbolt painted on the obverse. We had even a standard, which we called a "spookwar," this being our interpretation of the S. P. Q. R. on the board at the top of a pole—which was supposed to incite the Roman soldier to victory. Since, however, the contending forces were limited to one Gaul and one Roman, and those both generals, the spookwar was usually stuck into the ground and forgotten, and if the legions were victorious the Roman Senate and People could claim no credit for the slaughter.

While we were reading Cæsar we began Greek, and we were soon to discover that depths of horror lurked in classical learning of which Latin had given us the merest hint. Not that we minded the Greek alphabet; on the contrary, we considered it to be a sort of cryptogram, such as we had long been familiar with, and we made ourselves unnecessarily offensive to the rest of the class by exchanging elaborate notes in these cabalistic characters, adopting the simple expedient of transliterating English words. No, it was not the alphabet that terrorized us in Greek, it was the grammatical complications; and as if three numbers and three voices were not enough, there was a catalogue of tenses as long as the catalogue of ships, and six years of familiarity with the Greek verb bred no contempt in us.

In the summer following Cæsar, somebody spurred our love for the classics by a gift of "The Last Days of Pompeii." Here was a revelation. Then the Romans really did live, and spoke Latin? It seemed improbable, but according to Lord Lytton they not only lived but had a very exciting time of it, with something doing every minute. I cannot say that we wasted much time over Nydia's love or misfortunes, and I am sure that we skipped many pages of improving archaeology; but the arena scenes—here was blood in its most entertaining form. There was no point in the Roman games that we missed, and no variety that we did not attempt. Our Roman and Gallic weapons did very well for the ordinary gladiatorial contests—were not Gallic prisoners of war used for exhibition purposes? But this was too much like playing Cæsar; we longed for something distinctly Pompeian. Christian martyrdom seemed to have been well thought of as a form of entertainment, and we had an amiable setter who was willing to assume any part assigned to him. Further acquaintance with the drama convinces me that his one really brilliant part would have been the lion in "Androcles," for his sole accomplishment was fawning on his victims. When the victim showed fight, the Numidian lion or Hyrcanian tiger rolled over on his back and held up four supplicating paws. On the other hand, if the Christian died early in the game, the destroyer displayed a glee that might have been considered ghoulish, and worried and mouthed his prostrate victim with a conviction that would have won him a place in any community cast of "A Midsummer Night's Dream."

An audience was provided by two cousins, whose sex debarred them from the sterner joys of the arena. They impersonated the Vestal Virgins in the imperial box, and blood-thirstily turned down their thumbs in hope of seeing murder done. They were further trained to call for fresh victims, and we tolerated none but the purest Pompeian accent, as we had learned it according to what was known as the Roman method of pronunciation, though I am sure it would have been unintelligible to any Roman that ever lived. The rules of this pronunciation were very rigid, and we allowed no slurring over of short vowels. When, therefore, the Vestals wished to see Glaucus brought forth to be dismembered by the lion, they yelled something that sounded like "Glowcoos ate layo."

The success of the Christian massacres led us to stage a still more difficult sport, the combat between the gladiator and the retiarius. We knew how this was to be done, for there was a most exciting picture about it, but the costume of the net-and-trident bearer stood in the way of a public performance. Not that this costume was too elaborate for our means—on the contrary. One hot Sunday afternoon came, however, when the older members of the family went for a drive, and we had the stage to ourselves. My brother was attired in the conventional costume of the gladiator, sword and shield and stew-pan helmet; I had a pitchfork and a tennis net, and beyond these implements only the slightest concession to propriety. The game proceeded; the Ural bear barked and frisked about the combatants, and the Vestals kept their thumbs directed permanently towards the nadir. The pitchfork being, like the pen, mightier than the sword, as well as considerably longer, the game was going rather well for the retiarius, who had finally succeeded in snaring his adversary in the tennis net and was prodding him vigorously, while the virgins, laying aside all vestal dignity, leaned far out from the box and shrieked for blood. At this moment the family returned from the drive, with company for supper. The trident-bearer, not having even his net in which to drape himself, suddenly realized that not only was he unsuitably clothed to appear in society, but that his costume was inadequate for the scene that was likely to follow, and fled from the arena. The Vestals left their drapery trailing over the edge of the balcony and disappeared through the window, and there remained on the scene of carnage only a highly pleased bear and a very much embarrassed gladiator, upon whom the burden of explanation devolved.

Autumn came—the third of our excursion into the classics—and we sustained a simultaneous attack from Virgil and Xenophon. The Anabasis proved to be more or less a second edition of the Commentaries, but the arms were different, and sufficient excuse for inventing a new game. Swords were abandoned for spears, and the rectangular shield gave way to the round targe. There were no pictures in the back of our Xenophons, so that our weapons were not so archæologically correct as they had been the year before, but we had abundant material on the Trojan war, and our arms were modelled after the equipment of the heroes of that conflict. One detail which we adopted enthusiastically was the horsehair plume to the helmet. Horses were plenty, and their tails were not docked; by taking a little here and a little there the horses didn't miss it, and we got two variegated plumes that any of the Seven against Thebes might have worn with pride. There was some difficulty about affixing horsehair to stew-pans, but much can be done with tar and twine. My brother, who was of course the Greeks, claimed that the barbarians had no right to horsehair, but I answered logically that the Greek and Trojan heroes dressed exactly alike in the pictures, and therefore why not the Greeks and Persians? This was unanswerable, and I wore my black-and-white plume as long as the game lasted. As for the game itself, the very opening lines of the Anabasis laid down a situation singularly adapted to our case, to Darius and Parysatis two sons being born, the elder indeed Artaxerxes, the younger on the other hand Cyrus. By every law of justice and equity I should have been

Cyrus indeed and my brother on the other hand Artaxerxes, but the law of primogeniture held, and I had to
be the Persians. In general, the expedition of the Ten
Thousand was identical with the Gallic war of the winter
before, except that we were now provided with a war-
cry: with total disregard for comparative theology Greeks
and barbarians rushed to battle yelling "Zeus Soter kai
Nike." Moreover, the fine drama of Cyrus's shout when
he made for his brother in battle, "Ton andra horo," did
not escape us, and in the heat of combat we shrieked it
at each other indiscriminately. It must not be supposed
that our uttering war-cries in Greek had any savor of
pedantry. It was local color we sought, and we whooped
Zeus Soter exactly as in the Zulu days we had rushed
from ambush with the shout: "Beel me coola longee
whitee fellow," culled from a story then appearing in a
periodical for the young. Between the dramatic episodes
of battle and sudden death, however, there were weary
parasangs to march through cities, inhabited and otherwise, and a desolate waste where we marked time while
Xenophon addressed the mercenaries. On the whole, none
of the Ten Thousand shouted "Thalassa, thalassa" with
more enthusiasm than we did when from a lonely height
we descried the end of the fourth book.

We began Virgil in the autumn, but I do not remember
that the histrionic possibilities of the story manifested
themselves until spring. About the time the brook began
to flow, we built a small Carthage on the bank, and Aeneas's fleet sailed majestically up to it. I refused cate-
gorically to be Dido, and was relegated to the most ungrateful rôle of romance, that of Faithful Achates. One
of the Vestal Virgins consented to be Dido if she might
wear a towel for long hair and a skirt that dragged, but
the other declined to be Anna Soror on any terms; Juno

or Venus if we wished, but not that silly Anna. The hunting scene proved a dismal failure, for the long skirt got caught on the blackberry bushes; and the funeral games in honor of the venerable Anchises only half came off. The one real Virgilian success was Dido's incineration, for just as we came to that tragic episode we found a hen that had died a natural death—at a more or less remote period. A magnificent pyre was at once erected, Dido was laid upon it with all funeral pomp, and the fire was lit. Pious Aeneas and Faithful Achates—though neither piety nor fidelity seemed to be particularly manifest on this occasion—sailed stonily away, the Vestals in the guise of Carthaginian matrons beat their breasts and tore their short hair, and the odor of burnt feathers and other things rose acridly in the spring air. An investigating committee issued from the kitchen door, and if Iris arrived in time to clip the fatal lock before the fire was extinguished she must have tobogganed down the rainbow. On the whole, Virgil rather palled, and we remained as unimpressed by Dido's passion as by Aeneas's filial piety. We thought, and I still think, that Aeneas was a pious bore, given to doing exactly as he pleased and referring the responsibility to the gods.

The Wooden Horse had possibilities, but was beyond the mechanical ability of the stage carpenter, and somehow Laocoön missed his effect, even when aided by half-a-mile of hay ropes. I think perhaps one reason why Virgil failed to hold us was that before we had finished him we had found the real thing, for we were reading Homer. Greek did not get easier as time went on, but even when wrenched out of the original line by line, not to say word by word, the potency of the Iliad carried. We wasted no time on preliminaries; Calchas might walk by the many-sounding sea as long as he wished, we were not affected.

We craved action, and immediately assumed the rôles of Achilles and Hector. For the sake of form I protested against being the Trojan, but I was secretly pleased, for I had read ahead in Bryant's translation, and I thought Hector by far the more admirable character of the two. Moreover, in the parlor hung a beautiful steel engraving of the best Victorian period, labelled: "Les Adieux d'Hector et d'Andromaque," and I used to stand before it and practise Hector's graceful attitude. The spears and targes and horsehair helmets that had served the Ten Thousand earlier in the year were furbished up, the house became Troy, and the yard in every direction was the plains of Xanthus and Scamander. Every evening between school and dusk these plains were the scene of carnage, and sometimes the Trojans found time for a sally in the early morning. The fortunes of war shifted; sometimes the Trojans were driven behind their walls, sometimes they carried fire to the Greek ships beached along the shore. The combats were not always bloodless; a stout ash sapling well aimed will sometimes glance from a barrel-head shield, and our mother, now as Thetis, now as Hecuba, bound up bleeding knuckles and rasped shins, and sent us back into the fray.

Some time before this, a book had come our way which was admirably calculated to round out our classical studies. A young aunt had preceded us to college, and among her scholastic baggage was a small blue Behrens's Mythology, with most entertaining accounts of celestial activities, and half a dozen capital tales at the end bearing such titles as the Story of Troy, the Story of Thebes, the House of Atreus, and the Argonauts. These we knew by heart, and were on speaking terms with the gods. When we learned the Greek alphabet, one of my first essays was to write the names of the gods in this new and fascinating crypto-

gram. When the list of gods gave out, I went on to the
heroes, and then to those entrancing groups of three, the
Graces, the Furies, the Fates, and the Gorgons, and finally
to the nine Muses. Not the least of my debts to Behrens
is the habit I acquired of thinking of the immortals by
their Greek names, and to this day Venus is a staid and
respectable matron compared with Aphrodite, and Artemis
ranges enchanted forests while Diana, when she walks,
treads on the ground. For a month I went around with a
piece of charcoal in my pocket, writing on barn doors and
other convenient surfaces cabalistic *graffiti* which usually
fell into three lines, and which being interpreted read:
Aglaia, Euphrosyne, Thalia; Stheno, Euryale, Medusa;
Clotho, Lachesis, Atropos. My brother had no patience
with this form of erudition, but was willing enough to
dramatize the stories. As Jason he sailed through the
Clashing Rocks and as all the seven chiefs against Thebes
he made determined assaults on the walls of that notorious
city, to find the seven gates stoutly defended. And since
success in arms depended on the propitiation of the deities, we erected in the back yard a temple after the model
of the Parthenon. It is true that the columns were rectangular, being bricks stood on end, but the effect was spa-
cious and imposing. In the naos stood an awe-inspiring
figure which in Christian times had been a china doll, and
across the brick that served as architrave was charcoaled
in capitals: ARCHILOCHE.

Before the temple stood the altar, half-a-brick on end,
"and on this altar sacrifices were offered to the dread
goddess." Not that we ever really killed anything to offer
up, however essential it may have been to win a victory,
but on a farm a certain mortality in young animals can
always be counted on. Very small chickens in particular
had a way of succumbing to the rigors of an Ohio spring,

and their downy bodies were promptly laid on a neatly arranged pyre of pine sticks, and the deity's nostrils were refreshed by the odors of burnt offerings. Mice that came to a violent end in snap-traps were well thought of as sacrificial beasts, though the cat regarded this disposal of them as sinful waste. When we read Homer we were impressed by the gory possibilities of a hecatomb, and we started to make a collection to that end. But a hundred animals of any kind, even small ones, are a good many, and as the weather suddenly turned warm we were obliged to abandon the idea, and to propitiate the goddess *en détail*.

After Homer and Virgil, I do not remember much of our play. Cicero was hustled through in a hot summer, as a final spurt of four years' preparation done in three, and we were tumbled into college still breathless from the fourth Catilinarian. In any case, however, I cannot think that we would have been inspired to dramatize these philippics, principally because the murders planned by Catiline never came off.

It was not until many years afterward that I realized that we had stumbled on the most approved principle of pedagogy. The motto of Dotheboys Hall: "When they knows 'em they goes and does 'em," is now appreciated at its proper worth, and Squeers may still form a trio with Pestalozzi and Fröbel. Our games began, as they should, at the earliest culture-period—and stayed there. If we had known we were adding to our apperceptive mass, we would have dropped our games like hot pokers. We played them because we were two, and it takes eighteen to play base-ball, and we dramatized those stories because we were too busy to read any others. Our efforts were entirely undirected; our parents never knew what form the game was taking, and we were not communicative.

As for our instructors, I cannot remember that there was so much as a map of Gaul or Greece in the school-room, certainly no effort was made to vitalize what we were reading. Not long ago it came to me as a pleasant shock, as I was riding in the train from Lyons to Geneva, that this valley of the Rhone must have been the very one chosen by the Helvetians for their exit when they burned their crops behind them and started on their historic trek.

They do these things better nowadays. I have a niece who is preparing to enter college, and is reading Virgil to that end. The other day she came home and announced that she had that morning attended a moving picture performance at the school showing Æneas's descent into hell, and his encounter with heroes dead and heroes yet to be born. "Ah," thought I, "we are certainly living in an age of progress. Æneas in visible shape descending into Hades—'facilis descensus Averno' indeed. What an inducement to study, what an aid to the memory, what an inspiration to the imagination! If we had but gone to school in these days!" Presently Jane got down her Virgil and we started to do a little reviewing in the fourth book. Dido, about to be forsaken, goes around as one distraught. "Bereft of her reason she rages," read Jane, "and burned with consuming fever in her blood she ranges the city, even as a Bacchante when he hears the name of Bacchus shouted and the nocturnal revels call him to Cithæron."

"Even as a what?"

"Even as a Bacchante when he hears the name of Bacchus . . ."

"What is a Bacchante?"

"Why, isn't he a man that worships Bacchus?"

It is, to employ Jane's own idiom, up to modern education.

THE ART OF THE BULLFIGHT *

By Waldo Frank

THE bullfight is as old as Spain; but the art of the bullfight has little more than a hundred years of history.
Perhaps Crete, which gave El Greco to Toledo, gave the
bull worship to Tartessos, the ancient Andalusian Tar-
shish whose silver wealth glittered so wide in the eighth
century before Christ that it drew the thunder of Isaiah
and the desire of Jonah. Doubtless the Romans served
to turn the bull-rite into a spectacle. The Visigoths assuredly had bullfights: and the mediaeval lords of Spain
jousted with bulls as Amadis with dragons. The Spanish
modern kingdom became firm; and the bullfight crystal-
lized as a play of prowess for men of noble blood. The
toreo was held in the public squares of towns, alternating
possibly with *autos-da-fé* of the Inquisition. In the one
sport, the actors were nobles and the victims were bulls.
In the other officiated captains of the Church and the
victims were Jews. In both, the religious basis was more
or less lost sight of, in the spectacular appeal; but no
aesthetic norm had been evolved to take its place. The
bullfight was a daredevil game to which these young
bloods of the Court—in their lack of Moors to slay—became addicted after the Reconquest. It was dangerous
sport, and it cost the kings of Spain many good horses

* Reprinted from *The Dial* by permission of the author and of
the editors. In slightly altered form the essay constitutes a chapter
of Mr. Frank's *Virgin Spain*, copyright 1926 by Boni & Liveright,
New York City.

and not a few good soldiers. Still, it throve until in 1700 a puritan, Felipe V, ascended to the throne. Felipe disliked the bullfight. It lost caste among the nobles. But its usage was too deeply, too immemorially engrained. The gentleman *toreador* went out : the professional *torero* and *banderillero* came in.

From 1789 to 1805 the first brilliant phase of professional bullfighting drew the urban crowds of Spain. When Napoleon came south, French culture deemed it incumbent upon itself to do away with so barbarous a sport. The bullfight lapsed. And when with the wild surge of the War of Independence it arose once more, it had become an art.

Francisco Goya has recorded in genial sketches and engravings the nature of the early classic bullfight. It was still chiefly a game of prowess. If an art, it was more allied to the art of the clown and acrobat than to the dance or the drama. The professional *torero* was a gymnast. He had to risk his skin in elaborate ways : and skill was primarily confined to his grace in going unhurt. He fought the bull, sitting hobbled on a table, or lashed to a chair, or riding a fore-runner in a coach, or saddled to another bull.

This was still the pre-Napoleonic mood. After the war against the French uprose Spain's popular tragedy, the modern, profound *corrida*. Its birthday was the same as that of the *jota* of Aragon which sprang directly from the incitement against the French. And like the *jota,* it was new only as an integration of old elements. Like the ancient bull-rite of Tartessos it reached its climax in Andalusia : more particularly in the Province of Seville.

The *plaza de toros* is of course the Roman circus. Rome created no more powerful form for an aesthetic action than this rounded, human mass concentred on sand and blood. With its arena, the bullfight wins a first vantage over such western spectacles as cricket, baseball, even the theatre. In all of these, the audience is a partial, unbalanced unit: it is not around the play, but beside it. The arena of the bullfight is a pith of action, wholly fleshed by the passionate human wills about it.

The *plaza* is too sure of its essential virtue to expend energy in architectural display. Here it wins a point over the modern theatre whose plush and murals and tapestries and candelabras so often overbear the paleness of the drama. The *plaza* has tiers of backless seats terracing up to balcony and boxes. The seats are stone: the upper reaches are a series of plain arcades. The *plaza* is grim and silent. It is stripped for action. It is prepared to receive intensity. The human mass that fills it takes from the sand of the arena, glowing in the sun, a colour of rapt anticipation. These thousands of men and women, since the moment when they have bought their tickets, have lived in a sweet excitement. Hours before the bugle, they are on their way. They examine the great brutes whose deaths they are to witness. They march up and down the sand which will soon glow with blood. When they are signalled to their places, the grey round pile is stark with their spirit.

Bright shawls are flung on the *palcos*. Women's voices vein in bright nervousness the murmur of the men. A bugle sounds, and there is silence. The crimson and gold *mantones* stand like fixed fires in this firmament of attention. The multitudinous eyes are rods holding in diapason the sky and the arena. Two horsemen (*alguaciles*) prance forward through the gates. Black velvet capes fold above their doublets. From their black hats wave red and yellow plumes.

They salute the royal or presidential box; circle the ring in opposite directions and return to the gate. The music flares. They proceed once more on their proud stallions, and behind them file the actors in the drama. The *toreros* are first: four of them: they wear gold-laid jackets, gold-fronted breeches, backed in blue, rose-coloured stockings. The *banderilleros* in silver drape their pied *capas* across their arms. The *picadores* follow. They are heavy brutish men, with chamois leggings and trousers drawn like gloves over their wooden armour. They are astride pitiful nags, each of which is a portrait of Rocinante. The shoes are encased in stirrups of steel; the spurs are savage against the pitiful flanks. Behind the *picadores* are the red-bloused grooms, costumed like villains. It is their task to clean up entrails and gore. And the procession closes with two trios of mules, festooned and belled, who draw the drag to which the bodies of slaughtered bulls and horses will be attached.

The cavalcade crosses and salutes. *Toreros, banderilleros, picadores* on nervous nags, scatter along the barriers. The rest retire. Again, the bugle sounds. Doors open on the interior passage which two high barriers hold as a protective cordon between the audience and the arena. A bull leaps into the glare.

His massive body is a form for the emotion of rage and for the act of plunging. The forelegs are slight beneath the heft of his shoulders whence he tapers down, so that the shoulders and head are like a swinging turret. All the brute is this infuriated flesh pivoting the ferocity of horns. They are exquisitely curved, needle-sharp, lance-long: and they turn about for an objective. The bull stands, aware of the strange ten-thousand-headed creature that shouts at him and drives its will upon him. He understands that the mob is his foe. He bellows, circles, plunges at last to reach it. The barrier jerks him up, splintering with his onslaught. He is bewildered and poised, pawing the sand, while the mob prepares to send its single emissaries to engage him.

The first act of the drama is a loose form of farce. *Toreros* and *banderilleros* toy with the bull. They fling capes, side-step, dawdle with him. But gradually they withdraw the brute's first fury from the indeterminate mob ringing him round, to the accessible lives in the arena. The bull sees a horse, capering before him in a blind presentiment of death. The ears are tied, the eye is bandaged. The *picador* who rides levels an enormous pike, steel-pointed. The bull charges and a horn sinks in the soft belly. Horse and rider rise and are flung in a clatter of bone, in a drench of flesh against the barrier. The bull draws out his ensanguined horn and charges a *banderillero* whose cape is there protecting the *picador*.

The crowd roars. The horse is whipped to its feet by grooms. The *picador* is hoisted back. The old nag's entrails hang in a coiled horror within a foot of the ground.

The horse supplies the laughter of the drama. The bull tosses him. He lies on his back and his four anguished legs beat like drumsticks on the barrier. Or, losing his saddle, he plunges mad and blind around the ring, kicking his own intestines, until death stills him. Or the bull mangles him at once, and he disappears in a swirl of flesh. This is farce; and this is also the sense of the immanence of danger. The bull is drunken with his victory. The crowd, beholding the fate of a horse, laughs with a tinge of terror. For what has happened there may happen to a man.

Enough horses have been slaughtered, and their poor flesh shredded into the gleaming unconquerable sands. A bugle summons the second act of the play.

This is the scene of the *banderilleros*. They are the critics, the epigrammatists, the *graciosos* of the accelerant drama. They bespeak the bull. They test him. They show off his subtle points—and their own. If he has faults— clumsiness, cowardice, lethargy—they correct him. They call forth his finest rage; and as he plunges on them, they leave gay ribboned darts within his flesh. If he is slow to anger, they will serve him darts that explode beneath the skin of their victim. They enrage him. But all the while, they sober him as well, making him realize that the holiday of the horses is no more: a harder enemy is on the field.

Often the bull is put into a meditative mood. He halts, panting in the centre of the arena. Blood drips from his mouth. His horns are carmine and the laced *banderillas* dance on the scruff of his shoulders, biting, nagging. He wants to understand what his life has become. The fields of Salamanca—the good grass, the warm care—have been wiped out in this blare of terror. That background of pleasaunce merely serves to sharp the tense present—this delirium of men and sun. A *banderillero* dances up. The bull faces him, asking a question. But the man will not tell. His smile is false; that swing of his cape is treachery. There is nothing to do but plunge—whatever it means. The cape of red and blue folds over the eyes of the bull and vanishes like a cloud: a dart bites his flesh. The crowd roars. The good life behind and the peace beyond are mist: life is this glare and this roar and this goad of steel.

The second act is over: the bull is chastened. He has been cleansed for the tragedy, after his brief triumph. Once again, the bugle: the *torero* to whose lot this bull has fallen selects his slender sword and his red *muleta:* he steps forward for the ultimate tragic scene.

Toreros are of many kinds. This one is called Belmonte

and he is one of two great *espadas* of recent years in Spain. He is a small man, smaller than the average and more swarthy. His body moves rhythmic and slight into the hard glitter of the sand.

The elemental glare of Spanish sunlight makes that body, striding so quiet toward the bull, seem frail and helpless. Could this man run away, as do so many? Could he, if need be, vault the high barrier to safety just as the horns splintered the wood beneath him? The head is heavy. The nose is large and sharp; the mouth wide; the lower jaw thrust out. But the brow is sensitive and smooth. Close by, this is the face of a neurotic. The arena's flame bakes it into a brooding gloom above the body so ironically decked in gold and silk.

Belmonte in this instant has already awakened in the crowd the troubling emotion of pity mixed with fear. He salutes the bull and spreads his red mantle (the *muleta*) across the fragile sword. He steps in close; and while the arena hardens into silence, he lifts the *muleta* toward the eyes of the brute.

Within an instant, breathless save for the breathing of the bull, something goes forth from Belmonte to the beast and marries them into a perfect fusion of hostility. The bull is the enemy, and they are joined more close, more terribly than by love. He plunges. Belmonte, motionless, swings the *muleta* to his side and the bull, as if attached to it, grazes the frail body. The *muleta* lifts. The bull lifts and turns, as if ligated by the mantle to Belmonte's will. The cloth thrusts to the other side. The bull along. Back and forth they go, in rigorous dance. The *torero's* body does not break from its repose. He is as cool as sculpture; he is as fluid as music. The bloody beast is attuned by a will, hard and subtle as Belmonte's sword. His clumsy movements are moulded into grace: his rage is refined into these exquisite feints. He, too, like the *torero,* leaves the plane of nature, and becomes a symbol.

As the *torero* stepped out to the sand, his *rôle* was god-like. His minions had played with the great innocent victim: fed him victory and blood: taunted him: taught him. Now he, to enact the ultimate rite of life . . . the ultimate gift of the gods . . . the only gift which they give unstintingly . . . death.

But this dance has transfigured the *torero.* Meeting the brute upon the plane of danger, he becomes a man. Those hypnotized horns graze human flesh: if they find they will rend. That gold-lined body is a sheath, holding the blood of a man. The bull could plunge through it . . . plunging so near, so rhythmically near . . . as if it were indeed the mist and dream of mortal life.

And now another change in the beauty of their locked encounter. The man becomes the woman. This dance of human will and brutish power is the dance of death no longer. It is the dance of life. It is a profound and terrible symbol of the sexual act. The bull is male; the exquisite *torero,* stirring and unstirred, with hidden ecstasy controlling the plunges of the bull, is female.

The crowd acts its *rôle.* The little man is but a gleam, the bull but a shadow of Dionysian act within this dark womb of ten thousand souls. From them come forth dream and desire and memory of sense: and concentrate upon this spot of drama: and merge with it and make it a symbol of themselves. At every pass of the bull from side to side of Belmonte, the crowd is released in a terrific roar. So silent the dance of the two coupled dancers: so vast the response of the crowd. Now, the red *muleta* comes even closer: it wipes the furious bloody head, making the horns plunge diagonally athwart the *torero's* breast. *Verónica* is the name of this classic gesture. And the allusion is to the handkerchief which smoothed the forehead of the Christ. So the ancient orgy of Dionysus and Priapus is tinged with Christian pity. The commingled symbolisms of many Spains meet in the passionate dance: become restrained and abstracted. The whole is harmony; is the silent balance of all the wills of Spain.

The bugle signals for the final action. Belmonte, who has knelt before the bull's last plunges, rises, withdraws the *muleta* from the slender sword. It is a flexible two-edged steel, dipped at the end. He stands still before the brute whose sweat rolls red from the heaving rugose flanks. He stands with heels clicked together, holding the brute with his eye, and raises the blade deliberately forward. The steel points not at the head, but slightly above it. In that mountain of flesh beyond the deadly horns there is an unmarked spot which the sword must pierce. It is the tiny crutch formed by the bones of the shoulder. Within that aperture the blade can go, unimpeded, to the heart. Anywhere else, the blade will not bring death but a mere plunging rage.

Belmonte stands. He is frail and erect. His shoulders are flexed and his head is slightly forward. Grace becomes subtly rigour. He has chosen the more dangerous of the two classical solutions. The bull pants and obeys Belmonte's will. He leaps. The blade sinks to its gemmed hilt. A wave of blood gushes from his mouth, as the dead bull sinks.

This is the essence and the archetype of the Spanish bullfight. This is a description of a masterpiece performed by an artist who has consummated many. It is not the usual *corrida*. In an art so profound and so dangerous, masterworks are rare even as in other aesthetic fields.

The elements which go to the making of a great *corrida*

in Madrid, Seville, Barcelona, Zaragoza, San Sebastián, are intricate and varied. If any of them fails, the consummation will suffer. The rearing of perfect bulls is a science in Spain. Only a few pre-eminent ranches—*ganaderías de toros bravos*—are equipped to supply them. They are either in the province of Salamanca or in Andalusia. The *toreros* study the bulls in the field, co-operating in their upbring. Experts breed and train them, and prepare them for their supreme moment in the sun of the arena. And before the conflict, they are examined by veterinary surgeons. If they are one jot less than perfect, they may not enter the ring of a true *corrida*. They are then consigned to the *corridas de novilleros:* the innumerable encounters of the apprentice fighters who must go through several seasons and win the applause of the most exacting critics ere they are admitted to the rank of *espada*.

Yet despite this care, imperfect bulls (bulls who refuse to fight, who fight erratically, who flinch at crucial moments) do enter the best *corrida* and blot out the artistry of the most expert *matador*. Indeed, the skill of the *torero* lies in great measure in his ability to control the bull. The genuine artist must possess hypnotic power. He must compel him in the instant of confrontation to forget the multitude, the flashing *capas,* the *banderillas* that bite his flesh : to concentrate upon his own frail grace all the bull's hate and all the bull's vigour. He must be able to compel a brute to be the partner of an exquisite dancer.

He must control his own body as perfectly as any artist on a stage. Utter purity of form and pace must be preserved within this threat of death and in conjunction with a frantic beast. There is no virtuosity like this in all the world. Beyond is the crowd, not at all loath to seeing him undone : before him, *his colleague,* is a maddened bull whose horns are more terrible than swords. He must control the crowd; he must model the lunges of the brute into the design of an essential dance. And all this he must do, in utter diapason of coolness.

The *torero* who can achieve this, not one time in a career but with reasonable frequency, and before the most savagely critical audience in the world, comes not often in a decade's passing. The art of most *toreros* is at the mercy of the bull. If he behaves, they acquit themselves with credit. If he baulks, they must trust to luck—to the saving *capas* of the *banderilleros*—even to their heels. Hisses are more frequent in the *plaza* than cheers. The great artist rises here as rarely from the ruck of honourable craftsmen as does the great actor from the mob of the Rialto.

Indeed all artists must labour against the inclement will of their materials. The temper of the bull, the action of the *cuadro de banderilleros,* the mood of the crowd, present the common problem of technique. What distinguishes the art of the *torero* is the immediacy of death. If the dancer slips, he fails and that is all; if the acrobat misses, he lands in a net; if the actor forgets his line, he hears the prompter. If the *torero* makes a false step, he is dead.

And the *corrida* will go on without him! for he is never alone. But he is alone with his skill and with his nerve. The slightest trace of haste or sign of fear will spoil the pure line of his style. If for an instant he breaks from the perfection of his pose to save his life, he loses his art. And if in that moment he elects rather to hold to his art, he may not live to reap its glory.

It is this marriage of art and blood that distinguishes the bullfight and gives to its flashes of poesy and plastic form the mystery of human drama. Man here is writing his fleet poem with his blood: carving a statue from his flesh.

In recent years, two *toreros* of genius have arisen in Spain. One, Joselito, died on the horns of the bull:[1] and the *corrida* went on despite the mourning of the nation. Joselito shared with Belmonte the summit of his art. He was an Apollonian classicist. Chance and inspiration were reduced to a minimum. He had control over the brute: but it appeared to be less of hypnosis than of reason. He operated on the bull with so cool an accuracy that the infuriated beast was soothed into an obedient opposition to the *torero*. Joselito was exact, unostentatious. But when he had coupled with his enemy, his art became ornate. He moved facilely, he gave delicate steps. When he was killed in Valencia, Spain lost the most exquisite if not the profoundest of her tragic dancers.

Nature has aided Belmonte with its abstruse law of compensation for inferiorities. In this abnormally frail body live titanic courage, great rhythmic articulation, a genius for Dionysian gesture. When Belmonte steps out to meet his bull the mind falls into heroic channels. For the head is brooding. And when, as once when I saw him, there is a white bandage across the brow with a touch of blood upon it, the effect is magic.

Belmonte at his worst is an ugly boy vaguely at odds with an unwieldy task. At his best, he is the propounder of rapture. He does not abstract the individuality of the bull like Joselito, and then perform his cold objective art. He measures the foe. He accepts him as he is. He plunges into the bull's fury. And thence, he rises to his high victory. There is always a moment in Belmonte's act when he is lost. The crowd gasps. Gone altogether beneath the fury of the brute, he emerges, dominant. His body sways in the

[1] Another victim, killed in the arena of Madrid, was Granero, who promised to go far. Granero had given up the career of a violin virtuoso to become a *matador*. His work was unemphatic, aloof, with a gracious romantic note.

prepossessive grace of one who has come through death. His art is perhaps greater than that of Joselito because its content is greater. Joselito excluded from his victory the reality of defeat. Psychologically, he crushed his foe first, and then worked on him at ease. Belmonte begins by submitting to the bull's might. And then, from this submission of the man, from this faltering of the god, he creates a form sculpturally superb.

But although great *toreros* are rare, one actor in the bullfight is always masterful. The crowd of Spain, against intellectual and Church, has held to the bullfight because it is so deep a symbol of the Spanish drama. It goes to the *corrida* as to a feast. All of its locked desires which history has bred and then robbed of an issue find here an aesthetic complement. Conflict is the stratified substance of the Spanish soul. For too many centuries has the Spaniard lived on war to be able to do without it. War for him has always been a full expression of his life. The lusts of the world and the glory of religion became one in war. And so, in this dumb show of man and bull do they conjoin in an essential form. In the bullfight there is the gross comedy of blood: crippled horses and clownish *picadores* rise and fall in a shower of gore and clapping bones. There is the sexual symbol, direct, sadistic, Dionysian. There is the associative shred of ancient rites and of eternal fate. Finally, there is the image of *stability,* of the closed fusion of warring elements into one, which is the ultimate form of Spain. Though everything may happen here, nothing happens. Blood, passion, circus, dance, and death are equated to a rigid nullity. Like life, this spectacle is self-sufficient without issue. . . .

TO YOUNGSTERS OF EASY MEANS *

By Albert Jay Nock

When I was a boy the American millionaire and his impulsive prodigality were already good stage-properties; his generosity towards everything he believed in was as great, as easily touched, and often as spectacular as it is now. Nor was he behindhand in patronizing the fine arts, at least for the embellishment of his own surroundings. He built elaborate houses, some of which it is safe to say were in certain respects truly remarkable, and he ornamented them with pictures bought at inflated prices which he paid without wincing—and concerning a good many of these, too, it is becoming to speak with like indefiniteness and reserve. These ventures often, perhaps, reflected the easy indulgence of feminine fancies and foibles which early became proverbial of him, but in many cases—I believe in most—they came out of the more admirable sentiment that while pretty much anything would do first-rate for him, nothing could be too good for the folks; and the thicker the folks chose to lay it on, the grimmer his satisfaction in seeing them do it. This satisfaction was sometimes about all the poor man got; he was often oppressed by his surroundings, and found it hard to expand his simpler tastes to meet their demands. Mr. Howells sketched his type well in "The Rise of Silas Lapham," and in an earlier day Mr. Curtis also sketched it well in "The Potiphar Papers."

* Reprinted from *The American Mercury* by permission of the author and of the editors.

235

The primeval millionaire's interest in the arts, however, reached no further than this. He would do anything in reason or out of reason by way of providing gimcrackery to satisfy the notions of his wife and daughters, but he did not regard art in itself as something incumbent on him to reverence and to promote. *L'art pour l'art* was distinctly out of his line. Perhaps the arts were all very well for women, who were strange creatures anyway, and hardly to be understood. In his practical view of women (he being a Victorian of deepest dye) some were superhuman, others sub-human, but none human. Yet even for women, devotion to the arts could be overdone, and the effect sometimes was to make things devilishly uncomfortable. Like Silas Lapham, he remembered his earlier surroundings, the rag carpets that his mother made, the bric-à-brac and chromos, the stout rush-bottomed chairs, and so on, and he thought a little rebelliously of how much easier they all were to get along with. For one thing, then, and perhaps primarily, the promotion of the arts meant pushing all the real comforts of personal environment into yet more hopeless inaccessibility, and he instinctively resented the idea. One can criticise this sentiment in the abstract, probably, but all things considered, it is not easy to disparage those who had it. In them, on the contrary, considering all their circumstances, it seemed pretty sound and natural, and its conservatism savored of a wholesome simplicity. After all, the arts were exotic to America, and these men behaved extremely well towards a rather busy and importunate obtrusion of them upon their intimate life. If unselfishness be the first instinct of a gentleman, probably the unpretentious figures of Mr Potiphar and Silas Lapham will stand pretty well up in the category with Roland's and Sir Philip Sidney's.

Our typical rich man regarded the arts, moreover, as

essentially European, and a devotion to them as not only negatively un-American, but as a positive and culpable hankering after the insignia of an alien civilization. This was not the worst; he regarded this civilization as effete, decadent, effeminate. Even that was not the worst. Aside from the nationalist view, artistic pursuits and interests related themselves directly in his mind with a distinct possibility of personal peril and humiliation. Too deep a feeling for the arts might easily open the way for the fetid fascinations of European social life to assert themselves upon his wife and children. His boys might suffer undermining of their sturdy American morale. Most undesirable of all, his girls might find a bond of sentimental communion with some utterly impracticable and objectionable foreign man of title, eager to feather his nest. The Marquis de Vautrien, the Duca del Scioccone and the Viscount Dedbroke stood continually before his mind's eye as sinister figures, suave, ingratiating, impecunious, immoral, deceitful and desperately wicked. When he thought of the arts, he thought of them; and when he thought of them, he ground his teeth, and expressed his emotions of the moment in a flow of spirited profanity.

Perhaps it was the Marquis, the Duca, the Viscount and the deportmental exactions of the new house that carried the rich man of my boyhood a little beyond his predecessors in an impatient wariness of the arts. The prosperous American of earlier days, especially in New England, had a little different attitude towards art, at least when art assailed him in the guise of a domestic issue. Once in a generation or so, one of the God-fearing, whale-catching, rum-distilling, close-fisted Puritan families of the New England coast would produce a black sheep who did not want to go to sea, and cared nothing for rum and whales, but instead had a passion for beauty and harmony. He

wanted to paint pictures or sing, learn the violin, study
architecture or write books. It was a fearful blow to the
family's pride. The neighbors, hearing of this appalling
calamity, would look at one another with blank faces,
and say "Isn't it awful?" But the stricken family would
swallow the disgrace, and if they found their erring son
actually obdurate and beyond entreaty, they would grimly
and prayerfully stake him. They would send him to Europe to study, devoutly hoping he might soon get it all out
of his system, come home, and go before the mast in the
honorable tradition of his ancestors. Thus it happened
that in those days America showed some well-developed
ability and talent; not much, perhaps, but more than one
would expect, I think, considering the circumstances of
the country.

II

But in my childhood, there was nothing like this in the
life of the fine old buccaneering type of millionaire who
went mostly in his shirt-sleeves in the Summertime, and
worked fourteen hours every day until Satan foreclosed
on his flagitious enterprise of cabbaging everything that
was not spiked down. He distinctly did not regard sub-
sidizing a promising youth, whether his own or somebody else's, to learn to paint pictures or play the fiddle, as
a good investment. Propose it to him, and before you got
the words out of your mouth he would be jumping three
feet high. I speak with authority, for I knew several very
rich men of this type. My father was a clergyman who
had a parish for twelve years in a virgin lumber-country,
and his congregation comprised a dozen such, maybe
more. I studied their ways with immense amusement and
considerable admiration. They were the only very rich

men I ever knew, and I rather regret the disappearance of
their type. Perhaps our modern man of wealth has as
vivid, distinct and forceful a personality as theirs, but I
doubt it. Looking over the contemporary rich man at long
range, I question whether Satan would think him much of
an acquisition, or be in any particular hurry to gather him
in. There was no discount on those earlier brethren, however. They were lurid personages, who could be counted
on to make their surroundings extremely lively wherever
they found themselves, and each one who dropped off
was just so much clear gain to the social life of the
lower regions.

So, if it were a question of setting up an art-gallery,
endowing a conservatory of music, boosting the theatre
or opera, doing a good turn for literature, or staking individual talent on its way to an exiguous self-support, the
millionaire of my early days would count himself out with
emphasis. But curiously, at this same period a great deal
was being done with the arts in an amateur way. In the
town that I have been speaking of, for instance, where my
father's parish was, there was a most extraordinary development of amateur music. In particular, I have never
since then seen the coincidence of so many really fine male
voices in a town of its size, and all with fine amateur cultivation. There were many good woman singers too, and
one woman, I remember rather vividly, the wife of a
local shoe-dealer, got marvellous and beautiful effects out
of whistling. We were a lake town, sixty miles from a rail-
way, and when an old-fashioned Michigan Winter closed
down on us, we were completely isolated, and thrown on
our own resources for entertainment, for a good long six
months. All these people worked hard at music then, individually and in a sort of loosely organized choral society, and they did some excellent things with it.

The country was at this time, moreover, just on the fag-end of the period when young men at large were rather gingerly encouraged to have an "accomplishment," and well-to-do young women had one or more as matter-of-course. There was a good deal about this that was afflictive, and a later generation recalls it with merited raillery. Mark Twain speaks of the beribboned guitar standing in a corner of the Southern parlor—a guitar capable, he says, of playing the Spanish Fandango by itself, if you gave it a start. As I remember, however, most of the acute distress caused me by the amateur musicians of that day was due to the répertoires. Young ladies who played the piano were likely to spread themselves on a considerable line of "descriptive music," like "The Battle of Prague," or to exude sentiment over the ilk of Leybach's Fifth Nocturne. The vocalist's range of choice was even more poverty-stricken, being ninety-eight per cent bilgewater English ballads, and the remaining two per cent Scotch and Irish, with an occasional variant of early American, such as "Home, Sweet Home," and "The Swanee River." I have heard many glorious voices and many very decent musical instincts wasted evening after evening on things like "In the Gloaming," "The Blue Alsatian Mountains," "O Fair Dove, O Fond Dove," and "Alice, Where Art Thou?"

As much can be said of the common run of china-painting, work in crayon, charcoal, oil and water-color, leather-burning, hammering metals, and so on, that prevailed in that period. I am quite of my young contemporaries' mind in deriding the puniness of artistic aspiration represented by all this. I know more about it than they do, indeed, for I have suffered under it, and they have not. Poetry, too—amateur poetry—I have fit, bled and died over reams of lushy poetry. So I am not dwelling regretfully upon the disappearance of that epoch, nor do I seriously wish it back again. Far from it. I am merely remarking the fact that in a day when it was impossible to get money to promote the practice of the arts in a competent way, and to make sound taste prevail, a great many people were actually practicing them as best they could in a misdirected and hamstrung way, and employing sometimes a very fine talent to make bad taste prevail.

At the present time, I seem to see an interesting reversal of this state of things. My observations may be superficial and inaccurate, for I have been for years entirely out of any kind of social life in America, and all manner of things that I know nothing about may be going on here. Quite obviously, however, the arts are lavishly patronized—patronized, I mean in the sense of direct subsidy. Every few days, it seems, one hears of some great gift or endowment to promote them. Sir Thomas Beecham was lately quoted as saying that one American friend of his spent as much money annually to keep up an orchestra in his town as all England put together raised for like purposes. I do not doubt it. When one reads publications devoted to the various arts, as curiosity has led me to do for some time as regularly as I could get my hands on them, one is impressed by the enormous amount of money laid out in these ways.

III

I should say, too, that there would be relatively little difficulty in finding subsidies to almost any extent for promising individuals, although it is true, I think, that our rich men do not as yet go in as much for this form of patronage, which is the oldest, and still seems to get the best results, as they do for the institutional form. For my part I wish they would do more with it. I fully agree with Miss Suzanne La Follette's excellent idea, which she expressed so cogently in THE AMERICAN MERCURY for June, 1925, that they would find it the most satisfactory disposition of their money they could make. I know that if I were a rich man, I would do precious little with endowing institutions, and content myself with nosing out individuals of the right sort, and endowing them. But aside from method, in so far as national progress in the arts can be measured by the gross of money given to promote it, America is stepping faster than any country on the earth has ever stepped.

At the same time, I notice that relatively much less amateur work is being done in any of the arts except one —literature—than was done under the old régime when I was a boy. The arts have come to be a matter concerning two classes only: a professional class and a non-participating public. Most of the immense amount of writing that is being done has a professional or semi-professional turn, being done in some kind of forlorn hope of some day making money by it. The amateur "accomplishment" in the arts has largely disappeared, except in dancing. Nearly all young Americans dance, and most of them extremely well. The youngster of my day, especially the young woman, had, as a rule, a preposterously imperfect idea of what an accomplishment was, and what it was for; but their successors, instead of retaining and valuing the accomplishment, straightening out its theory and improving its practice, have tended rather, I think, to drop it altogether.

Thus it is that while people today know far more about really good music, good pictures, good sculpture, than the people of my time, and are possibly more interested in them, their knowledge and interest are pretty strictly of a non-participating kind. They themselves do not sing, play, daub or gouge. They patronize staunchly, look and listen attentively, applaud enthusiastically, All credit to them for this. But a non-participating interest can never quite attain to the quality of a participating interest, and is almost always something quite different and much less satisfying. No amount of time spent in sitting on the grand-stand will get one into the innards of a ball-game, and give one the gratifying feel of the skill involved in certain plays, like a little practical apprenticeship out on the sand-lots in Mr. Briggs's "days of real sport." I played ball for eleven years myself, and speak whereof I know.

Similarly, no one gets the instinctive appraisal, the true and exhilarating *feel* of fine points in tone-production and in breath-control, in line and color, like him who has ever so little perhaps, but with love and intelligence, done his bit at warbling and smearing. No listener can appreciate the "inside play" in a suite of Bach, like one who has tried to drum it out himself. Therefore it follows, I think, that the general climate of opinion and feeling which prevails in a participating public is higher in quality, and much more conducive to the true and effective promotion of art, than that which prevails in a non-participating public. It stands to reason that the real status of musical art in a community is to be estimated by the number of people who practice it, and not by the box-office returns from concerts and the opera; just as the status of cleanliness is not estimated by the amount of plumbing sold, but by the number of people who wash.

IV

But whether so or not, there can be no doubt that participation is more fun, and this is the only point that I mean to dwell on. I have no thought of making a plea for

the future of the arts in America. What really started me
out on writing this article was the news lately conveyed
to me in a private letter, that in one of our Western cities
several business men, well along in years and of large
wealth, have secretly, clandestinely, surreptitiously and
insidiously banded themselves together to study drawing
and painting—practically, I mean, by doggedly plugging
away with brush and pencil, under a teacher. Here, I
thought at once, is the real thing! Here is America in
earnest! It is commendable to have learned how to give
money prodigally for the support of the arts, but the
genuine fun begins when the same people who give the
money make up their minds to jump in themselves, tackle
the actual practice of some art, and make what they can
of it strictly "on the side." Incidentally, it is good for
art; it is the one thing needful, really, because, as I said,
it helps most to engender a congenial atmosphere, and it
also puts into effect the best insurance against waste of
money.

This handful of Western business men are really in
the best way to protect their investments. When some
one tells them cock-and-bull stories about the colossal in-
novations of Schmierpinsel in Vienna, and the revolutionary ideas of Barbenfeu in Paris, and how these have completely effaced all traditions, and sent Rembrandt and
Frans Hals back to the woodpile, they will be in a position
to look the matter over intelligently for themselves—an
advantage which some of our contemporary private col-
lectors appear to have missed most lamentably. But apart
from this, they are laying up a resource of incalculable
delight for themselves, and that is the great thing.

In the new social order, the leisured class—those, that
is, who can command leisure if they wish it—stand towards art in somewhat the relation of the old aristocracy;

and in Europe one sees the extraordinary leavening power of the talents which were cultivated by such of the aristocracy as had them. As talents, they may have been unpretentious, rather pleasant than robust, but they tended powerfully towards the diffusion of an agreeable and amiable life; and because they did this, one cannot help thinking that they made life amiable primarily for those who exercised them. The poetry of the Grand Duke Constantine connotes a more agreeable life than that which (without pretending to know) one instinctively associates with the thought of Judge Gary, for example. Seeing in Brussels the beautiful paintings and sculpture done by the Count de Lalaing—not great, I think, but very lovely—one thinks of him as a happy man, and one would like to have known him. *Noblesse oblige*—men like these seem really to have made something of their position and opportunities *all around,* and there is no happiness to match what one gets out of doing that.

There is much room in America for the exercise of a merely *pleasant talent,* if it be exercised in true taste and for no motive but the love of it, for money and leisure are so abundant—one has to be in Europe to realize how relatively abundant they are, and to understand how much happiness a little intelligent self-direction could produce from them. I know a solicitor in London, as pure a type as the one that Gilbert and Sullivan put on the stage in "Patience," who plays Bach for an hour every evening when he comes home from his office. In talking about Flemish folkways lately with a Belgian engineer, a man busy with his profession from dawn to dark, mention was made of a couple of interesting old Flemish songs. He sat down at the piano, rattled off a rather intricate accompaniment, and sang them for me most agreeably, and with the unmistakable taste of the cultivated amateur. The

Royal Opera would never put him on for his singing, or the Conservatory for his playing, and he would not have the least wish to go on for either. He simply had the view of the arts, so general in Europe, so uncommon in America, as something for any one to take a hand in, naturally and easily, because one loves them, because they are familiar and domestic assets for making life agreeable and amiable for oneself—with no thought of using them on the chance of money or fame, or for any one's pleasure but one's own, and least of all with any repulsive delirium of vanity about "self-expression."

Americans are inclined to be a little impatient of a critic who does not offer what they call "practical proposals"; one, that is, who does not pretend to do all their thinking for them, furnish all their initiative, and diagram all their actions, thus imposing on them no harder task than the rather mechanical one of putting one foot before the other. For certain reasons hardly worth recounting here, I have always been a little diffident about making practical proposals. Still, if it helps to show that one is in earnest, one might perhaps venture a little way with them. To the men who now give money so liberally to promote the arts, the men who might be thought, perhaps, to be looking at the arts a little wistfully—men like the late Mr. Munsey, for example—I would say, if you wish really to promote the arts, keep on with the money, but also sell one of your motor-cars, buy a second-hand piano or some paint or crayons or modelling-clay, and get somebody to show you what to do with it.

You will have a great deal of fun, more fun than ever you had in your life, and you may incidentally turn up some aptitude inside yourself that you never suspected of lurking there.

V

But there is another class of candidates for my magisterial attentions, and with them I shall be even more specific. These are the young men and women who are not doing much at the moment but amuse themselves, who feel some faint stirrings of a desire to do something a little more important, who think they may possibly have some small ability in some department of art, and who also have enough money—or may have it for the asking—to see them through pretty much anything that they wish to attempt. America is full of just such youngsters. Their surroundings are rather against their doing more with themselves than they are doing, yet a good many of them are vaguely dissatisfied and would like a job, if they could find one that they felt really counted. Naturally, they do not want something that keeps them merely marking time, or that will show no particular achievement when it is done; but they are ready to look disinterestedly at something that is an actual challenge, and if they liked it, they would be willing to put their backs into tackling it.

Well, the fields of art are full of jobs—great jobs—that ought to be done, that would bring endless satisfaction to those who did them, but that can never be done except by people who can afford to do them, because there is no money in them and never will be. Here, it has always seemed to me, is the leisured young American's chance, and I cannot understand how he has managed to miss it for so long. In the sciences, I notice, he has long ago caught on in precisely the same adventurous way he might catch on in the arts. He is in the laboratories, he is on all sorts of scientific expeditions, toiling away at his own expense in enterprises that he knows will never bring him the worth of a copper cent in anything but the exhilarating sense of a great job greatly done. Exactly the same chance is waiting for him in the arts.

Take it in the one department of art with which I am, perhaps, a little acquainted. There is not a publisher in America worth his salt who does not know of at least a dozen great and distinguished pieces of literary work waiting to be done, which can never be done until some one comes along who can afford to do them. I could myself name offhand a dozen such. In my casual talks with publishers about various pieces of work that needed doing, the first question has always been, Who can do it? and the next one was, How will he keep himself going meanwhile? My conviction is that the only procedure that will get this kind of work satisfactorily produced is the one that produced the great Flemish pictures, or the one that now gets analogous results in science, *i. e.,* training people to produce it; and because there is no money in such work when it is produced, the only people eligible to be trained are the ones I am addressing.

This procedure is as follows—and here I hope I shall be specific enough to meet fully the American yearning for practical proposals. Suppose these paragraphs that I am writing fall into the hands of a young man or woman, such as I have described, who takes stock of himself and decides he wishes to try his edge on a real job in literature. Let him go to some publisher with this magazine in his hand, and say, "You see what this article says. Well, now, my general training is so-and-so; my leanings, as far as I can make them out, are so-and-so; and I have so-many dollars a year to live on while I am on one of these jobs that this magazine-article says are going begging. What about it?"

Then the publisher, if, as I say, he be worth his salt, as

none too many of them are—tell it not in Gath!—will bring forth a line of subjects that will make the young person's mouth water. They will agree on one, and the publisher will say, "Now, the thing to do is for you to go to So-and so, just as Rubens went in his youth to van Noort and van Veen. He is quite a fellow in that line, so go to him and stand him up on the carpet, get him to talk it over with you, put an eye on your work once in a while, stiffen up your backbone, and in a general way hold the bull-whip over you until you get your gait."

The other arts hold as many and as great possibilities, and they are to be developed by the same line of procedure. I myself happen to know of one most spicy adventure in the line of the graphic arts, which calls for just the resourcefulness and quickness of mind that Americans are supposed to have. It might turn out to be a dud, but how many exploratory and experimental scientific undertakings turn out that way! Any really competent expert in that line knows of others; any really competent musician knows of a dozen lying here and there in the theory, history or practice of music; and so on. The thing is to get these experts to stand and deliver, as they will do if they are put under reasonable conviction of the young person's seriousness of purpose, and to convince them of this is a good preliminary test of the enthusiasm and pertinacity of American youth.

THE SHORT BALLOT IN LITERATURE *

By Henry Morton Robinson

"I HAVE read all the books," sighed Baudelaire; and if he meant by books the undiluted race-plasm of great men, he might have added, "And they were not numerous either."

All that is published is not Book. There is not enough energy in the world to produce more than three Books in a century. A Book is the gist of an epoch, the archive of an era. "The Lusiads" of Camoens *is* the maritime glory that was Portugal; the "Summa Theologiæ" of Aquinas *is* the culmination of Christian theology, thirteen centuries in the making. A Book drives its tap-root into the granite strata of race thought and aspiration; and it is the fate of any grubbier weed to be choked down by contemporary tares before a decade passes—witness the last end of Tupper, Paley and N. P. Willis. Who reads to-day "Evidences of Christianity," "Vignettes of Manhattan" or even "If Winter Comes"? The half-million volumes published in Europe and America last year will furnish half a million exhibits to the collector of cynical statistics; the books and the snows of yesteryear are to be found in exactly the same place.

Competent opinion differs as to the publication date of the last Book. A few academic stalwarts believe that the Folio of 1623, carelessly and lovingly edited by Heming and Condell seven years after Shakspere's death, was

* Reprinted from *The Century Magazine* by permission of the author and of the editors.

the great divide in English letters, and that since that
time our literature has been tumbling downhill. A handful
of revolutionists cry out for Rousseau's "Le contrat social." Others testify that nothing has been written since
Karl Marx corrected the proofs of "Das Kapital." The
scientist with a flare for polemics will say that 1859, the
year of Darwin's "Origin of Species," is the last great
date in English literature. And occasionally we encounter a Grecian who believes that Aristotle was the first
Neoplatonist, and that since 399 B.C. everything has been
mere comment and repetition. But wherever the decision
rests, whether with the synoptic gospels or Lyell's "Geo-
logical Evidences," it does not affect the contention of
this paragraph that a great Book visits these lunar
glimpses about as frequently as Olbers's meteor.

The paucity of human ideas has a cheerful corollary:
one idea will suffice for a Book. Jesus developed one text
only; Horace sang one song. Carlyle, Epicurus, and Mon-
taigne had a theme each. Yet though the thoughts of men
be few, they are deep hidden among stagnant swamps of
commentary, plagiarism and gloss. To trace the germinal
ideas of literature through jungle-bogs of exegesis and
abridgment to their purest source, to read again the
words of Dante, Lucretius and Cervantes—even in translation—and to hale the democratic herd up to the clear-
gushing rock, seems to be the simple task of the guardian
of literary morals, be he teacher, critic or dictator.

As a humorless and prematurely gnarled baiter of college youth, sitting day after day on the infallible side of
the class-room desk, I have been more than casually entertained by the contemplation of the great Books of the
world. Out of the surplus of an instructor's salary I have
bought them all, one at a time, and there they stand on a
short shelf—the noblest library a man could wish to own.

And doubtless they will continue to stand there until the president of the Tremendous University drives up to my door in a taxi, leaps out and cries aloud:

"I want you to revise all my reading courses. What is your program?"

Whereat I shall look up from my book (I hope it will be Plato) and, to the astonishment of boggle-eyed academicians, roar:

"The short ballot in literature!"

What do I mean by the short ballot in literature? I mean, quite literally, that there are in the world less than one hundred books that can seriously engage the attention of the mature reader. That there are other books of value and interest I do not deny—jolly books, pretty books, tender books. But I am concerned here with nothing but the quintessential oil of literature, attarized and triple-distilled. And I contend that any man of favorable predisposition can read these books with pleasure and inestimable profit in less than five years; that by so doing he will acquaint himself with the best that has been thought and said in the world, acquire a finer palate for truth, establish trustworthy bases of departure for his own contemplative life and, in short, render himself immune from the miserable plagues of popularizers, outliners and book-a-month mongers that infest the day.

To understand further what I mean by the short ballot, pick up its antithesis, the catalogue of the Great University. Heft the article. It weighs from one to three pounds, contains about two hundred pages and offers more than a thousand courses. Disregard the extension courses devoted to brass-crafting, tuba-pumping and home-budgeting. Persons who take these courses are incapable of being harmed anyway. But turn to the college section and view the extraordinary jumble of electives permitted the undergraduate. After satisfying a major and a minor sequence (a sequence is a consecutive series of courses in the same subject), he is allowed to wander at his own discretion among the specialized courses in eighteenth-century diarists, commercial geography and histories of esthetics. At the beginning of his second year the student begins to stock up on preprofessional courses leading to business, law or medicine. After the third year he is admitted to the professional school, sticks his nose into text-books and is forever lost to the humanities. Hundreds of students enter professional school without a single course in philosophy or literature beyond the scanty and compulsory introduction of the freshman year. I have sat at college tables with dozens of these men, none of whom happened to be working toward a baccalaureate degree. They were using two years of college as a spring-board, from which they jack-knifed into the specialized pond of some professional school. Very well—each to his own. But what did we talk of? Did we share a common body of traditional knowledge, the superb inheritance of the English race? Did we stand on the hill of Western culture, surveying civilizations, languages and philosophies in the perspective of twenty-five centuries? We did not. My friends were interested in torts, office management and Spanish with which to net the South American trade. Lacking better subjects, we talked always of comparative football scores or trailed off into the lethal patter of fraternity politics and personalities. Since we had no ideas to broach and no arguments to settle, we met on what ground we could. Or, finding no ground at all, we turned on the graphophone exclaiming, one after the other: "Hot mama! . . . Dickety-dog! . . . Eva, burn my shoes!"

But during my own junior year John Erskine conceived the bewildering idea of the short ballot in education, and jammed it through a skeptical Committee of Instruction. In effect his idea was to stock a small room with great books and to expose a selected number of upper-classmen to their naked influence. That was our only *ratio studiorum*. From Homer to William James we read a Book every week, and discussed that Book around a table at a single weekly meeting. How or where we spent our week did not matter, the only requirement being that we *read the Book!* The carnage was awful. About twenty of us fell to reading the Greek dramatists, historians, and philosophers so avidly that we entirely disappeared from the campus and came out only to rage in debate with each other over midnight sandwiches and matutinal coffee. We pernoctated with Plato and with Boethius outwatched the Bear. We read Lucretius and were Epicureans; we read Marcus Aurelius and straightway became Stoics. We had discovered the heritage that was rightfully ours. Within two years we had wrestled and been thrown by nearly one hundred of the giants of Western literature. We familiarized ourselves with the noblest, the most delightful and the most difficult thoughts of man. We read Goethe for twenty-two hours at a stretch and boiled mystically over the "Enneads" of Plotinus. Boring passionately through the outer kernel of appearance, we arrived somehow at an intimation of our immortality. I think we were the luckiest score of youths that ever attended a college since the days of the Academy.

I predict that the university of the future will give its entering students a list of not more than one hundred books; that it will say: "You who are entering upon life are saluted by those who were the lords of life. Read these books over and over until their furious and exalted language has inflamed you with the flame of desperate beauty. Let them immerse you in the blood and tears of

a thousand invasions, martyrdoms, visions and prophe-
cies. When you feel that you have absorbed as much of
their energies as your youthful fibers will bear, come back
and tell us about these books. If you speak of them elo-
quently or penetratingly or even with stammering intensity, we will confer upon you the only honor we are able
to bestow : in a world of brass pretension and vain noise
we will extend to you the assurance of our esteem and
high friendship."

And these young men, having been admitted to the
esteem and high fellowship of the university, will step
out into the public square and on the morning of the first
day will pull the greasy and disorderly togas off the limbs
of a noxious hack-quack literati. Undraped, this gentry
will be seen in all their blue puffiness and will be ridiculous
at last in the eyes of those who have been reading their
daily column. Next, the young stalwarts from the Academy will erect a huge oak measuring-post in front of the
Public Library, flanking it with a steel seismograph and
a gold spirit-level. All books from all publishing houses
will be measured, leveled and attuned to the vibrations of
the earth. If they fail in any test, they will be consigned
to mean fires amid the rejoicing of the multitudes. And
the terse motto on the oak measuring-post will run,
"When a new book is published, read an old one."

What are these mystical old Books on the short ballot
of literature? They are the indubitable world books, the
Kalevalas, the Faustiads, the Njala Sagas, the *niemals aus
der Mode* books, the compacted archives of cultures past
and present. They are the Best Books of a planetary dis-
pensation, the spiritualized experiences of the human race.
They are few, huge and unmistakable. And I believe they
can be selected quite arbitrarily. Let any ten persons,
whose only qualification be that they have read all the

world books at least six times, each compile a complete list of great works. On comparison the lists will be found to be almost identical. How could it be otherwise? Who, having read Sophocles, could possibly leave him off such a list? Or Euripides or Shakspere or Thucydides? Actually it will not be necessary to consult ten opinions. Any man who has spent his days in the presence of the masters will be the Aristotelian "just man," the measure of all good and bad. And after debating briefly with him concerning a few doubtful members of the list—Adam Smith, Bernard of Clairvaux, Henry David Thoreau—(do you wrangle with me here?) I should willingly accept his list as my own. If he rated Hegel greater than Kant, or Corneille of more importance than Racine, I could readily assimilate his suggestions and doubtless be nourished thereby. For I believe that humility is the abiding mark of the world reader and that his first emotion on discovering a new work is wonderfully close to gratitude. To read the words of any hero is to become his violent champion; his rock, Peter; or John, his first and best loved disciple.

But if I prescribe these books to physic the rankness of a costive age (and I do), it will be objected: "On what tablets of gold is recorded the virtue of these classics in correcting the humors and inflations of men? Why should flaming youth and crabbed age be dieted on Homer, or suffer Virgil's epic leech to tug at their swollen veins?"

It is a long time since any one has written a defense of classical culture, and a restatement of the grand position is ripely overdue. George Edward Woodberry's "New Defense of Poetry" is probably the last sonorous peal from the deserted battlements of a great tradition. His utterance is lucid, sanguine. He believes that the race mind, being the warder of the best that anywhere comes into being, clings with the grip of fate to anything of beauty, wisdom or eloquence emanating from the heart of man. With a preternatural selective economy the race preserves every syllable of its greatness:

> "One accent of the Holy Ghost
> The heedless world has never lost."

The ornate, the trivial, has been purged away by the pitiless erosion of centuries. The remainder is best *quia* Best, if that superlative means only the highest comparative of the Good. And contact with this chaste superlative beauty is a swift abrasive, potent in scraping away the barnacles of our brackish mortality.

"The thing's restorative i' the touch and sight," cries Browning, tossing in the air his great "Yellow Book"—

> "A book in shape, but really pure crude fact
> Secreted from man's life when hearts beat hard
> And brains, high-blooded, ticked two centuries hence."

"Give it me back; I need the vigor of its blood-stream pulsing through my own," he added. He knew the energy of a living document. In the feel and flavor of a veteran book there is a lean muscularity that shames all flabbier ware. It is the cardiac muscle of a generation. Though it has run far, you need only to touch its resilient pulse to know that it will again outrun a million broken-winded glanderous nags with blurbish jackets and bishoped brown teeth.

It may seem rash and ill-considered to expose a citizenry bred on slops to the close-fibered loaf of a grand book. But I know of no other expedient to correct the shocking lack of taste and nutriment in the annual troughful of literary pap sanctioned by the critics and consumed by the readers of the United States. My jeremiads are concerned not so much with colleges, for there at least the great tomes are silently exuding their energies, *volo nolo,* into the skull-pans of teacher and pupil. But my lamentations are loudest when I seek for one honest man in Newspaper Row. The newspaper critics—what a microcephalous race! No ephemera is too wispish, no trash too trifling, for their conflagratory superlative and fudge signet of approval. "Most significant book of the decade"; "centered on the axle of profound genius"; "worthy of a place beside Balzac and Melville and Fielding"; "tremendously *total*"—are some of the log-rolling, backscratching, cent-a-word dithyrambics over a tawdry plot-jobber or Mayfair Priapus. With neither perspective nor common honesty, these "critics" (is it Swift who suggests that critic means, etymologically, *mirror of brass?*) ring the old changes in present-day journals better known for their rotogravure sections than for their literary good taste.

But this is not the worst affliction of a harassed and gullible people. In an age of frantic compression and tabloid culture, there has arisen a crew of popularizers and outliners and cogging hacks who will for a penny hire (a pretty penny too) dismember, chop, season and stuff into handy-sized skins a sausage-like mixture of pseudo-learning and greasy sciolism. Outlines of History, Religion and Science, Mankind, Womankind, Love, Marriage and the Seven Arts are baled up like cut fodder and marketed by the ton. But in this chopped straw there is no juice, no healthy vitamine, no intellectual roughage. Chaucer and Puvis de Chavannes are ticketed with orange labels; the Logos is made into a story; and Louis Untermeyer is proved kin of Beowulf! "Before I read your 'Story of Philosophy,'" writes Mr. Heywood Broun, "Plato and Aristotle were mere names to me." Well, we are getting on. At the age of thirty-eight Mr. Broun realizes that there is a Book called "The Republic." Possibly he may review it some day in his column.

If the bristling bustle of modern life has made the tabloid a necessity and has driven a poetry-hungry, beauty-starved nation into the corners of the lending library and upon the spikes of the outliners, then the short ballot in literature should receive the joyous suffrage of a people. For I think that a kind of compression and exclusion not hitherto practised in our lives is the solution of many evils. Only by the exclusion of all that is cheap and ephemeral can a race grow substantial in truth. Only by a rigorous economy can the few hours we devote to reading be made at once a delight and a tonic stimulant. And whatever *progress* may mean, I am sure it cannot be attained by gulping down frantic digests, nor by dosing the intelligence with mystery novels and shoddy romances. By taking thought the individual *can* increase, by the much-to-be-desired cubit, the stature of society. And only by affectionate knowledge of the good, the courageous and the durable can he protect himself against the vicious, the transient, the trivial. Under a little heap of great literature lies the double-edged Theseus sword of personal liberty and cultivated taste—the only objects worthy of the free man's worship.

EDUCATION AND BUSINESS *

By Raphael Demos

SOME time ago I read in the daily papers the news of an interesting statistical survey among the graduates of a noted university. The report showed that the earnings of the graduates who were members of the Phi Beta Kappa Society were considerably less than those of most of the other graduates. The papers drew what to them seemed the clear moral of the tale: it is a mistake to concentrate on the things of the mind while in college. Was this really the moral? The reply suggests itself that the Phi Beta Kappa men had been successful in the light of what they had sought in education, which was a knowledge not of how to make money, but of how to make something of themselves. Is the function of college to equip the young for a specific occupation or for life? Many students incline towards the former of the two alternatives, and while in college choose their courses accordingly; if they intend to enter business, they concentrate on courses in economics, if medicine, they study chemistry and biology, and so forth. And these same youths, when well on their way to a business or a professional career, find that once through with their work, they have nothing to fall back upon; they have formed no habits of reading, and cannot keep their minds long enough on an open book; they lack any cultural interests

---

* Reprinted from *The Yale Review* by permission of the author and of the editors.

with which to refresh the mind, and so resort to the "movies" or the radio to fill their spare time; and what is more important still, they have constructed no general philosophy of life with which to face the world and see their own occupation in its proper perspective. So gradually their work engulfs them; whether in or out of the office, their minds are never off its problems, till business ceasing to be mere business becomes life itself.

College is a preparation for life, and life is infinitely wider than work. Life is also leisure and thought and family relationships; it is play and art and religion; it is sleep and waking and death itself. Not only is life wider than work, it is the only thing that justifies work. If you absorb life into work, you find that there is nothing to work for. Work must always lead beyond itself to a life of the mind by which the fruits of work may be enjoyed. To work is to make a tool of oneself; and man should be not only the tool, but also the craftsman behind the tool. All too often, the calls of action are so insistent that one has no time for the repose and thoughtfulness that enter in the building up of an inner life; one comes to live altogether outside oneself. And here is the opportunity of education. College should fill, to some extent, the rôle of the mediaeval monasteries in which man may take an inventory of his vital resources, away from the bustle of the world, and determine his place in the general scheme of things. It is impossible to complete this task in college, but it is possible to begin it. Education should be the process of forming a personality which may function in the world of work and yet be out of it, of cultivating those intellectual and spiritual interests by reference to which only has work or life any importance.

How should one go about preparing for life? To at-

tempt to master individually all the details of the process
of living would be futile; there are too many things to
learn—a modern university offers as many as a thousand
courses—and you might find you have spent so much time
preparing for life that you have no time left in which to
live it. Why indeed try to learn all the facts? They are
duly recorded in the books, and it is sheer duplication to
record them in the mind as well. Life is not only complex;
it is also unpredictable. No matter how earnestly one tried
to cover the field, one would always be exposed to sur-
prises. Man is in the position of an embattled army which
does not quite know from what direction the attack may
come; the best he can do is to occupy the strategic positions from which he may dominate the assault of the
enemy.

The function of education is not to stuff the mind with
facts, but to teach one how to handle them; not to make
one into an expert, but to show one how to choose an expert; not to give one a ready-made solution for specific
problems, but to make one so resourceful that one may be
ready for any contingency. Not memory but intelligence,
not knowledge but power—this is the objective in college.
Clearly, the means by which education seeks to achieve its
end are roundabout; while taking this or that course, one
is not just trying to learn all about a given field; one
is rather acquiring a method of thinking, a conception
of cause and effect, and a feeling of law and the systematic character of things; one is cultivating an intellectual
imagination that sees beyond the immediate. But mere
training of the mind is cleverness, and this is not enough.
The student must develop an appreciation of ideals and
learn to distinguish the genuine from the counterfeit in
the fields of ideas and of art, among persons and causes.
Far more important than knowledge of the technique of

life is wisdom, which is knowledge of the ends of life. How is this quality of wisdom to be imparted to the student? Certainly not by word of mouth or by any intellectual instruction. Contagion is the only way, that is to say, the influence of example in history, biography, art, in personal contacts with great minds and great men. We must admit that our colleges have not attached to this phase of education the importance which it merits.

The methods of standardization, of mass production, and of the division of labor have been so magnificently successful in the development of the resources of the country that it was very natural to suppose that they would work with equal success in the field of education. As a matter of fact, what makes for efficiency in business, makes for inefficiency in education. Take the demand for results. In business you know what you want and you know when you have got it. Not so with education; there, we cannot ask for immediate results, or results that can be measured in any definite way. We can test whether the student has learned his lesson, not whether his mind has grown. Intelligence is too elusive to be pinned down in such an obvious manner. Only a lifetime can measure the success of an education, and sometimes even that is not enough, for ideas may not bear fruit until a generation or two have elapsed. I suspect that something of the kind is true of business—that the reason one has the impression of being able to measure results accurately in industry is because one limits oneself to the immediate means and forgets the ultimate purpose. The real ends of work are leisure, of course, and comfort, and the ability to pursue the life of the spirit unembarrassed by material considerations. Having these ends in mind, can the prosperous business man affirm for a certainty that he has got what he wanted?

You cannot draw any sound analogy between the production of knowledge and the production of goods; education deals with persons while industry deals with things. As soon as you standardize the educational procedure, you lose what is so absolutely essential—individuality in the product. Knowledge is not a piece of merchandise to be transmitted across the counter to the student consumer; it is an achievement for oneself, as personal as the color of the eyes. The success of modern industry comes from its state of perfect organization, and the public is apt to draw the conclusion that learning, too, consists of a systematic arrangement of information. So we get the type of mind in which thought has been nicely arranged into a pattern, with each idea referred to its proper place. For such a mind to think is to classify, to fit into an outline. Now, this is neat, but it is not thought; it is rather a mechanical moving of counters into their squares. Instead of dwelling on the substance of the question, one settles it by simply relating it to predetermined categories. Thought becomes formal—a shuffling of symbols. In reality, thought is a dynamic impulse which may never be tamed into submission to formulæ; it is a movement, a transition, and therefore essentially unfinished and overflowing all outlines. To organize thought too perfectly is to kill this impulse and this movement. The man of wisdom is above everything the man with open horizons, eschewing all finality because he has a sense of the mystery of things. We tend to overestimate the merely clear mind, I mean the mind which is clear because it is not tortured by the subtleties of ideas. Such a mind shines when called upon to make comments on other people's theories; but it is not creative itself. Sometimes, much more creative may be the mind that seems to be slow and muddled; for its lack of facility may arise from the fact that ideas are germinating within it, and its slowness may mean that it is struggling with obstinate facts. Often such a mind is confused because it would rather retain the truth of its fresh intuitions, in their unblushing contradictoriness, than tone down their differences in order to produce the effect of a neat but artificial pattern.

The teacher cannot disclaim all responsibility in this matter. His method in the class-room is sometimes too exclusively one of presenting the subject in the shape of a rigid outline, with a complete set of headings and sub-headings under which all the various details of the idea are exhibited. The student is thus presented with a finished product, and all that he may do with it is to receive it and file it in his mind. Yet the business of the teacher is not to do the work for the student but to give him suggestions on the basis of which he may work out the problem for himself; not to instruct the student but to release the impetus of thought in his mind. And movement in the mind of the student can be generated only by a parallel movement of thought in the mind of the teacher actually thinking out the problem in the presence of the student, wrestling with its difficulties, and reaching out for a solution.

We should guard against applying the test of success to education too narrowly. It may happen, for example, that at a given period intellectual or artistic production receives no appreciation from the world; at such a period it may well be that academic instruction is a definite hindrance to success. Does it follow that education under those circumstances is a failure? No, because such a world would be not worth succeeding in; the state of affairs would be an indictment of life itself, not of the school. The reader will say that this is too utopian, and not practical. In reply, I would point out that the view of education as a preparation for life is only half true. Education not only prepares for life, it makes life; it is life. The world is not something fixed and immutable, to take or to leave. Education is always moulding the world by moulding those who live in it; it is the workshop of life, in which humanity thinks and works out new standards and ideals for itself. If life happens to be below the requisite intellectual and cultural level, then, rather than compromise with the world and seek to turn out potential business successes, education should endeavor to lift the level of life. Education must be adequate to life, and life must be adequate to education.

Occasionally, we hear complaints from good citizens of the community concerning doctrines expounded in this or that college. Sometimes, even, attempts are made by the public to interfere with the procedure of the college and stop what seems to them the teaching of pernicious ideas. Such efforts, though well-intentioned, arise from a fundamental misconception. It has just been pointed out that colleges are the laboratories in which the world tries out novel ideas; and unless the experiments are carried out in the fullest freedom, they are worthless. Since it is dangerous to experiment with novelties in real life, all the more reason why we should experiment in the colleges where the risks of immediate application do not exist. If the students seem to be talking wildly, one should realize that they are only sowing their intellectual wild oats, and the earlier they do this the better. And, if the professors seem to be expounding unorthodox doctrines, one should realize that the university is the leader rather than the servant of the public—or rather that the university serves the public by way of leading it—and that it is for the public to respect its efforts to make new conquests in the realm of truth. Education is the edge of life pushing into the unknown; how natural, therefore, that university opinion should be ahead of contemporary popular opinion.

For these reasons, it is advisable that the government of academic institutions be entrusted to the members of the institutions themselves. To put their government into the hands of business men and of outsiders generally is not only to violate the principle of self-government, not only to vest control with those who lack expert qualification, it is to put individuals in charge whose mentality and values and methods are foreign to the spirit of the educational process. I am not overlooking the great debt which education owes to business; undeniably, the progress of education in this country is, to a great extent, based on the material prosperity for which business is responsible. I am only urging that it is foolish to elect a leader and then try to advise him what to do. Education must be granted the right to cut out its own path. Though its purpose is to serve the community, it must formulate its social obligations in the light of its own insight.

What we procure in college is very little—hardly a sketch of knowledge—and unless gone over later, it drops from memory. Indeed, how many of us grown-ups can recall our zoölogy and the formulæ of chemistry and the theorems of geometry that we learned in college? Very few. Moreover, education always comes too early; a person of college age is too immature to enter into the depth of meaning of the great classical authors. Often have I heard graduates say that in the light of their later studies, their college work seemed childish. They felt they had not really begun to understand the authors studied in college until they took them up again later. It seems true that a certain fulness of experience is requisite for a proper understanding of the work of great minds. Does it follow that college work is not worth while? Not in the least. College education may not provide actual knowledge, but it provides a map of knowledge to guide the mind in its maturer studies. College education is a useful preliminary for the maturer education of life; without it, we would find it very difficult to direct and organize our intellectual life in the years of middle age and after. But it is also evident that, unless we do continue it in our years of maturity, college education remains of very little value. Here life must help; the world of affairs must be so organized as to permit the mind to continue its education. Business must never be so engrossing that one has no time to reread the classics or pursue one's intellectual interests. But it is not merely a matter of having the time for such pursuits, outside of one's work; what is needful is that work itself should be mentally cultivating, that life should include thought and artistic interests, so that the individual may participate in these activities naturally as part of the process of living, without having to say to himself: now I must cultivate my mind. Clearly, life has its part to play in the task of education, and to be adequate to this part, it must sustain itself at a certain spiritual level.

In actual practice we fall far short of this ideal. We are in the habit of regarding education as something to be confined within the four walls of the college campus, and once out, we abandon all study and plunge headlong into the problems of practical living. We feel that we have done our bit of thinking and that now we must act. So the mind is atrophied, and action suffers also, for unless action be continually exposed to the scrutiny of thought, it becomes mechanical and stagnant. It is wrong to regard education as a transitional stage in life. Education is the mood of self-consciousness—it is life turning upon itself and taking stock of its resources; it is a mood which must therefore extend throughout the entire length of life.

Just as action must not exclude thought, so must thought not remain apart from action. The scholar has sometimes isolated himself from the world of affairs and erected knowledge as an end in itself. But intellect cannot function in a void; life is its laboratory, and action its natural consummation. Through action, one obtains a certain type of education which no amount of purely academic instruction can afford. In any concrete problem of life, one gets the feeling of being up against it, of being confronted with something absolute, of coming to grips with reality—and of all experiences this is the most essential to the growth of the mind. Much odium has been cast upon work from all sorts of sources; philosophers have condemned it as degrading and poets as uninspiring, the Bible speaks of it as a curse laid upon man, and the socialists picture Utopia as a state in which work has been reduced to a minimum. Yet one of the marks which distinguish a civilized from a savage race is that the former has a routine of work while the latter has not.

Work is nothing but systematic productive activity, in which the personality finds an opportunity for concrete self-expression. Through work, the more ethereal substance of the spirit is mixed with the coarser grains of the earth and is thereby strengthened and rendered more solid. To work is to walk out of oneself into the fresh air of the common world; it is to abandon the privacy of introspection for the publicity of action. And by thus turning oneself inside out, one discovers oneself. Unfortunately, for many people to-day work has become so extremely organized that all spontaneity has gone out of it; it is mere mechanical routine affording no outlet to the personality. So the mind is driven to look elsewhere for channels of self-expression—in amusements which are as strenuous as work. It would be a short-sighted policy to accept the actual character of work as final and then try to diminish its amount as much as possible; the desire for action is an instinct which must be satisfied somehow, and it is best satisfied through productive labor. The energies of civilization should be marshalled to the task of humanizing work, that is, of connecting work with the springs of personality, and making it more imaginative. When thought and action are divorced, we get the pedant on the one hand and the intellectually tired business man on the other; to join the two is to give vitality to thought and vision to work. Hence the importance of incorporating business schools into the university. If business is not a profession, here is an opportunity for our educational institutions to help it become one, by welcoming it into the fellowship of the arts and sciences and exposing it to the winds of academic tradition.

Our universities are being invited to assist this process and to help business become a more scientific and a more humane enterprise. But it would be almost criminal were they to accept the current conception of business as a means of private profit and to engage in teaching their students how to make money as quickly as possible. What the universities should do is to present the conception of business as an instrument of social service, and by thus presenting it to help translate the conception into a reality.

CONCERNING ENDOWMENTS *

By Hanford Henderson

EVERY man, however original and independent he may think himself, is in reality the beneficiary of a tremendous endowment. He is the direct heir of that universal experience which we call Civilization. We are all of us the possessors of marvellous wealth. We have our wonderful bodies, the product of an evolutionary process stretching back so far that the most speculative among us hesitate to hazard any guess as to its duration. We have our still more wonderful intellects, creating a world much larger, much more intricate, much more subtle, than the vast world of visible Nature. Most beneficent of all, we have the spiritual life, with its conquest of space and time, and its irrepressible claim to immortality.

No one, not even the apostles of equality, would insist for one moment that this vast inheritance is the same for all, that the heirs of civilization are the recipients of like portions. We have only to compare bodies and minds and souls to realize how endlessly unequal are these human legacies. Even our individual share varies, and we are aware of periods of drought and plenty. We do not bring to the succeeding adventures of life the same body, the same mind, the same soul. These vary so amazingly that after some great emotional experience we rightly speak of a changed man, and of being born again.

* Reprinted from *The North American Review* by permission of the author and of the editors.

In our ordinary moods, and in the midst of our daily preoccupations, we are not greatly impressed by this tremendous gift of the past, for it represents our accustomed environment. We are prone to take it for granted and to offer no thanks. We seldom stop to think how good the gods have been to us. In spite of all our frailties, it is a marvellous thing just to be a man! But in taking so much for granted, we commonly take too much and assume a human average which does not exist, and apply a generalized standard which labels without really evaluating. There seems objectively to be one world, but in effect there are as many worlds as there are people in it.

And then, in addition to this personal endowment, this legacy wrapped up in the organism itself, in body, mind and soul, there is a seemingly capricious external legacy which must never be forgotten, since it plays so important a part in human destiny. This outer aspect of civilization represents a skilful adaptation of the raw materials of Nature to human uses. It constitutes a universal contributory endowment which we too little take cognizance of, —the cleared field, the dwelling-house, the public building, the road, bridge, tunnel, the vehicles of transportation, the lines of communication, the stupendous mechanical equipment of industry, all the clever discoveries and inventions, all the lovely creations of art. This vast accumulated wealth is the product of a multitude of dead workers, driven some by want, some by ambition, some by curiosity, some by reverence, some fortunate ones by the sheer love of beauty. And we, the men of today, inherit collectively this immeasurable wealth. Part of our inheritance is personal, our individual share of houses and lands, and the multiform tools and achievements of civilized life. But the larger part is impersonal, the marvellous beauty and convenience of that outer world to which we, late comers among the toilers, have for the moment succeeded. And it is worth remarking that while man, in thinking of his wealth, commonly has in mind his personal share in our colossal joint heritage, this is not necessarily or even generally the more important. A "poor" man, living in the rich environment of an active, intelligent community, may easily be much better off than a "rich" man out in the wilderness.

But all these possessions, like the organic legacies of bodies and minds and souls, represent only the given conditions, the inherited setting for the living drama of today. As a spectacle, they are impressive; as a potential opportunity, they are beyond price; and I would not willingly belittle either their magnificence or their importance. But they imply no merit on the part of the generation which today happens to possess them. Nor do they, in spite of their large convenience and beauty, carry any guarantee whatever that our contemporary drama will be admirable. Right here is the crux of the whole matter. It deserves the closest scrutiny on the part of those who concern themselves with social problems, and with the large general questions of our human destiny. Broadly speaking, two points of view are possible. They are both understandable, but they are exclusive and contradict each other; consequently the social theories which grow out of them lead to opposite conclusions and programmes.

The first point of view denies, of course, what I have just said about the impotence of the world endowment to produce of itself an admirable succeeding world; and specifically asserts the contrary. It is a doctrine of necessity. Man is a puppet of fate, the product of the world endowment, the result of his environment. From this point of view, free will is an illusion, and man is logically quite devoid of responsibility. If he make himself too much of a social nuisance, he is imprisoned or hanged, just as wild beasts, when they become a menace, are summarily disposed of. But short of inconvenient extremes of misconduct, man must be looked upon in the same dispassionate natural history spirit that we feel when we watch the antics of animals, or study the growth of plants.

The major objection to this point of view is to be found in the large mass of contradictory evidence. It is too voluminous to be presented in full, but one or two pertinent facts may be indicated.

The rise and fall of nations, for example, is one of the enigmas of history; and it is particularly baffling that while their rise is so gradual, their decline is so rapid, and in so many cases follows close upon the highest wave of material civilization and power. The fortunate nations would seem to be the target for the gods of misfortune —a brilliant flowering and then disaster. Just now America is approaching the crest of the wave, exhibiting a prosperity and a material civilization never before equalled, and already some of her anxious lovers are beginning to ask whether this is but another prelude to another immense disaster. One looks back, and asks, Where is Assyria? Where is Egypt? Where is Greece? Where is Rome? Even in our own day, Where is the German Empire? Will it be asked, a moment hence, Where is America?

It has been the same with families and with individuals. The heavier the endowment of outer advantage, the more certain would seem to be their ultimate deterioration and loss of distinction. It can be seen in New England and also in the South. In the West there are signs of loss, and already on the Pacific Coast one can find, as in Florida, the less fortunate children of the fortunate. If events prove anything, they assuredly prove that growth and progress come from within, and that while they may be helped from without, they may all too easily be smothered.

The second point of view has already been indicated. It accepts most gratefully the tremendous endowment of the past, the highly organized body, the acute mind, the sensitive soul, all the wealth of structures, tools, equipment, our vast and expanding body of acquired knowledge, not as the source of further progress, but solely as substantial aid to contemporary achievement, if the will to achieve is there, and still bent upon the pursuit of perfection. But such a quest, endless in its very nature, involves genuine self-activity, genuine contemporary effort, and this is an entirely meaningless term unless we retain our old fashioned belief in the freedom of the will. If, like the animals and plants, we are the necessary and unavoidable product of our environment, if to our rich inheritance we add no power of volition, we are wholly incapable of self-activity, and are become automatons, tragic but hardly interesting.

I do not hide from myself that this doctrine of self-activity is not without difficulties. But the difficulties are at least no greater than those which dog the course of the first point of view, since both lead ultimately to the unknown, and are equally insoluble. If we were the puppets of fate, it would still be necessary to ask who plays the game and moves the puppets. One's reasonable choice depends, it seems to me, upon probabilities; and so far as I am able to read the evidence it all points in one direction. Inherited endowment, wearing the richest dress of outward civilization, has failed repeatedly, in races, families, individuals, to be the source of an enduring higher civilization; failed repeatedly to maintain even its own level; while human good will, bent upon mastery, has never failed to dominate outward circumstances and attain ultimate victory.

I state the issue between these contradictory points of view so sharply because so much depends upon one's choice. In all that follows, I assume the second view, which is whole-heartedly my own belief, that the human spirit is capable of this genuine self-activity and can control events, instead of being controlled by them,—"Gods are we,—if we will."

Self-activity, from this point of view, is synonymous with life. For each one of us, the given data are unescapable, and to that limited extent we are all fatalists,—what we now are, we are; what we now possess, we possess. But this static endowment is not life, nor is it the source of life; it is only the contemporary opportunity offered to life. The succeeding drama depends wholly upon the way in which this static endowment is handled. That is to say, the drama depends upon something added from outside itself, upon a spiritual force residing in individual human beings. As Marcus Aurelius put the matter, "Remember that this which pulls the strings is the thing which is hidden within." That this spiritual force is an admitted mystery both as to its source and its ultimate destiny does not, I think, invalidate the observed fact of its present operation. Even the dimensions of our human drama do not depend upon the magnitude of the endowment, but almost wholly upon the measure of self-activity which is brought to bear upon it. We have the familiar spectacle of strong men of good will accomplishing great things with the most meagre opportunity, even in the face of powerful opposition; while other men, given what seems to be a magnificent material endowment, make so little of it that eventually they altogether go under. The determining factor in all that happens is just this intangible, imponderable spiritual ingredient which men through their own eager self-activity add to the given data, to that vast endowment of ideas and things inherited from the past. Those who love their fellows and who regard the pursuit of perfection as the major and legitimate purpose in our puzzling earth-life, must bend every effort to conserve and heighten this priceless motive power in themselves and others; and must never under any allurement sacrifice it to the static, lifeless equipment of the outer world of either past or present. To state the case very concisely, the most important thing in every human enterprise is the spirit which gives it life and movement, which changes it from inert endowment into meritorious event.

All this is so little novel that it may properly be called obvious, but it may not on that account be impatiently dismissed. The importance of a fact does not depend upon its novelty, but upon its range, and we have here, I believe, a fact of the widest range. If we had the courage to apply it in every case, and to decline all exceptions, however plausible, the earthly pilgrimage would be a livelier and, I venture to think, a much happier and more engaging adventure. I am tempted to cite a number of instances where traditional thinking offers one interpretation and the principle of self-activity something quite different. Having touched upon natural endowments which we inherit willy-nilly, let us turn for a moment to those artificial endowments which well-meaning friends intentionally create.

The first illustration which comes to mind is in connection with the so-called "drives" undertaken by many institutions which fancy themselves in need of money. I was living, at the time, in a distinguished old town which greatly prided itself upon its culture. Among its many organized activities for the betterment of the world was an energetic association devoted to the welfare of young men. I sympathized keenly with many of its purposes. But in an evil moment (or so it seemed to me) the association decided upon a "drive," and for a rather surprisingly large sum of money. An elaborate campaign was inaugurated. Two gentlemen called at my house. They were entire strangers to me, and in their zeal did not so much solicit, as demand, a substantial contribution. If I remember rightly they had even spared me the trouble of determining its amount. I had to send them away empty-handed. Not only did I object to the insolent method of the "drive," but I found on inquiry that in spite of my large sympathy with the general purposes of the association, I disapproved *in toto* of the proposed use for the fund which they were trying in this singularly high-handed manner to raise. It was to be spent, I found, for buildings,—not buildings needed to carry on the excellent work of the association, but buildings which were to be rented out for revenue. They wished, in a word, to create a technical "endowment," an income-producing investment which would provide permanently for the salaries of the paid secretaries and for other current expenses. They explained quite frankly that it was inconvenient and somewhat precarious to have the work depend upon annual contributions. Many persons—I am bound to believe them rather unreflective persons—assented to this view and gave handsomely. I declined, because I realized that such an endowment fund was not desirable. It would kill the genuine life and self-activity of the association and induce a very speedy dry rot. I knew that so long as the association supplied a real need of the community, it would be generously supported. When it ceased to supply such a need, it no longer deserved support. Given a sufficient endowment fund, it could continue to function after a fashion, quite regardless of whether it truly ministered or not. Had the fund been asked for needed equipment,—libraries, lecture halls, class-rooms, work-shops, gymnasiums,—I should have felt quite differently about it. But to pay an agent permanently in advance for a service not yet performed, regardless of whether it is well or ill performed, whether it is wanted or not wanted, is to offer large opportunity for abuse, and to deprive the community of wholesome coöperation and control. The enterprise becomes inert, the sport of dead souls, and quite divorced from the current, palpitating life of the community. An endowed institution may, for a time, render acceptable service, but the tendency is unmistakably towards inefficiency and disservice. As it draws its sustenance from the past, so it is likely to represent the past, to represent something once wanted but no longer wanted; instead of that fine contemporary reality which a genuine self-activity alone can yield.

The same argument which I have applied to the well known association in that dignified old residence town, I would unhesitatingly apply to all those institutions which aspire to serve the spiritual needs of their day and generation,—to churches, schools, colleges, universities, boy scout organizations, girl scout camp fires, to young men's and young women's societies of all denominations, to public libraries and museums. Adequate equipment means enlarged opportunity, but endowment too often means death.

The one exception would be in the case of specific research work, yet even here there should be periodic and frequent inspection as to the chosen subjects of research, the organization of the work and the agents employed, with special inquiry into the efficiency of the efforts made to give all results suitable publicity and application. I need not recall the misuse of endowment funds in even our great universities,—courses given to suit the convenience and whimsies of old men in endowed chairs rather than to suit the obvious needs of the students themselves; professors paid six thousand a year or more to lecture to two or three young men on erudite subjects so nearly useless that they would better be left to private curiosity. The need for efficient, well equipped universities is always exigeant; but the endowed institution gets out of touch with life, and accumulates, in spite of itself, a lot of dead timber in the way of men and methods and goals.

It is commonly believed that all education must be endowed, or it will not be able to carry on. I do not myself believe this; I believe the very contrary, that all education, to be vital, must be self supporting. If education is paid for by contemporary effort, it will more nearly approximate the genuine needs of current life, and will be supplied at somewhere near cost. An institution which cannot furnish what the community wants and at a price it can afford to pay, quite deserves to go under. I do not speak theoretically. I speak from a long experience in education. I have come to believe—I have not always believed it—that all schools of whatever grade should be what our commercial friends call "going concerns," that they should in all cases pay their own way. The only endowment which they may properly and safely accept is the endowment of equipment,—land, building and apparatus, —and the small State favor of no taxation. I have found it possible to carry on very interesting educational work without even these subsidies. It has so chanced that my own field has been largely the experimental work of the pioneer, and that is notoriously expensive and precarious. To avoid three common pitfalls I formulated three guardian principles. The first was that there must be no trustees or directors; the second was that I must own the establishment myself, without debt or mortgage; and the third was that the school must be conducted so simply that I could afford to run it even if I had no students! These simple provisions gave me an immense freedom.

The first experiment, a summer camp for boys, was started nearly thirty years ago, and is, I believe, the oldest camp in existence. They are now numbered by the thousand, and may be found in practically every State. My own camp began with a capital of three hundred dollars, —in those days a dollar went much further than it does now,—and an enrollment of fifteen boys. It clearly offered something that was wanted, for it has paid its own way from the very start and is still prosperous and popular. It had last summer an enrollment of one hundred and fifty boys. The fee was made small, as it was never the purpose to attract rich boys, but rather boys from the more thoughtful professional classes, or even desirable boys who would be accounted poor. It is true that many rich boys came, for their parents found there a simple, wholesome outdoor life which they could not easily inaugurate at their own more elaborate summer homes. But they were all treated alike, and no extra privileges were purchasable. I cannot too strongly emphasize the fact that while I believe all schools should be self-supporting, I also believe that it should be the unfaltering effort of the headmaster to make the fee just as low as possible.

After seventeen very happy summers, I turned the camp over to two younger masters, and shortly after that, started another experiment, a boys' open air college preparatory school on my little plantation at Samarcand. But before leaving the subject of the summer camp, I might mention for the encouragement of other pioneers, that after a few years, as the enrollment increased, the camp became a source of adequate income. From my own limited personal experience, and much wider observation, I should say that all sound enterprises can be made, by good management, to pay their own way, and that the field for legitimate charity is much narrower than we commonly imagine.

In the case of the open air school, the initial outlay was naturally larger, but even here amounted to only twenty-five thousand dollars for everything. The equipment was by choice, as well as necessity, extremely simple, and we allowed ourselves only three luxuries,—a Steinway grand piano, the last edition of the *Encyclopædia,* and a seven-passenger high-powered car. In selecting these two experiments by way of illustration, I do not forget that they were very simple and unpretentious and not at all comparable to the huge educational establishments to which rich men give their money, and paid officials their time. But both experiments were significant. I find that the men and boys who took part in them still look back upon those early days as a unique and fortunate experience. And both camp and school became the starting points for later ventures now serving large numbers of American boys and girls.

Without subscribing too literally to Kant's famous dictum that such conduct is ethical which one would wish to see universal, it was keenly felt that as an educational experiment, neither camp nor school would fulfil its whole purpose unless it could be imitated and made the starting point for a further advance. This was an additional argument for making them self-supporting. The school was, of course, somewhat slower in reaching entire self-support. In my own mind, I gave it four years to make good. Thanks to the skill and devotion of an able colleague, and the generous help of the junior masters, the goal set for ourselves was honestly reached, and at the end of four years we planned not only to continue the school but to double its capacity. The War came, however, and brought it to an end by requiring service elsewhere.

Parents are not, as a rule, educational experts,—they are sometimes curiously ignorant about even elementary educational methods,—but they do want, with almost pathetic eagerness, the very best thing for their children, and they need only to be convinced. It is this feeling which has led me to insist all along that educational experiments, to be valid, must supply something which, after due exposition and trial, is genuinely wanted by conscientious, intelligent parents. And if genuinely wanted, such ventures will be supported. This seems to me reasonable ground, and I was the more ready to act upon it in the case of summer camp and open air school because in still earlier years I had been one of the pioneers in introducing manual-training as a culture branch in non-technical schools, and I had been deeply touched by the eagerness of parents to have their boys profit by a system of instruction which appealed, it is true, to their common sense, but which still had its spurs to win.

We may well accept the considerable endowment of the past in the way of land, playgrounds, school buildings, workshops and general equipment, and also the small contemporary favor of omitted taxation. But to make the schools vital, effective, intimate, progressive, they must be the immediate concern of those whose interests are most vividly involved, that is to say of the parents whose children are to attend the schools. Such a participation would be helpful to both parents and children. It would result in variety and in wholesome competition. We would escape the uniformity so earnestly and in my opinion so mistakenly desired by the National Educational Association when it advocates a Federal Bureau of Education with enlarged activities, and powers of standardization. In the place of this deadly sameness, this educational mill, we might so easily have a genuine self-determination, with its resulting vivacity, interest, experimentation and sincerity. The parents and children, instead of being passive material in the grip of the educational process,—the parents to pay taxes, and the children to acquiesce,—would be active agents, and through their own self-activity, their aroused spiritual participation in the educational venture, would gain an intellectual life, and an emotional and artistic delight which are not the necessary or even the common fruits of an alien administration. Education is an inner process, an unfolding and perfecting of the human spirit, and may only be realized through self-activity.

It is one of the curious anomalies in our spiritual make-up that the liberal and radical minds which fulminate most vigorously against our own control of the Philippines, and England's hand in India, and which cry out for political self-determination for everybody, everywhere, quite regardless of political development, would light-heartedly enter every American home, and prescribe under compulsion of law just what sort of education American parents shall give their own children. In Oregon they would go even further, and make all private schools impossible by the simple device of making the public school compulsory. But happily, the law was declared unconstitutional.

I much deplore the abandonment of our smaller, more

intimate district schools so near the real life of childhood, and the growing use of the motor bus to gather
the children into large remote schoolhouses which have
no educational merit easily discernible and offer a much
smaller emotional appeal to the children themselves. Big-
ness may yield greater administrative convenience, but
it does not guarantee excellence. The small school, near
the homes of the children, may be made far more effective, and for the younger children, especially, far more
convenient. In comparing the two, it is usual to offer the
very modern school palace of today in contrast with the
ancient district school of yesterday. The comparison is
not fair. The same thought and money spent on the palace
would create a series of model smaller schools where they
were needed, saving the expense and waste time of transportation; and, more important still, saving the demoral-
izing effect of crowds. At the present moment, progressive business men are working for the decentralization of
industry. Textile mills scatter themselves over the cotton
fields; automobile making moves up the River Rouge;
New York publishers send their copy out on Long Island,
or up into New Hampshire, or over to New Jersey; man-
ufacturing companies combine in order to scatter their
industrial plants over a wide territory and so bring them
near the consumer. Yet in spite of this significant experience, this growing tendency to take the work to the
worker, instead of the worker to the work, educators
continue to centralize education and to do it, curiously
enough, in the name of progress.

In the case of colleges, universities and technical
schools, the argument for self-support is even stronger
than in the case of the lower schools, for the students are
now of an age when they may properly and helpfully contribute toward their own support. At the present moment

many of us who love education and have given a substantial part of our own lives to its furtherance, have
regretfully come to the conclusion that too many boys and
girls now go to college, too many who cannot offer the
legitimate price of sound preparation and earnest purpose. Many of them go for purely frivolous reasons,—
for the social distractions and sports; for the freedom
which they gain in being away from home; for the
chance to have a hand in class politics, dances, organizations; many from simple restlessness and *ennui,* because
they do not know what else to do. Their presence in such
large numbers distinctly lowers the standard of both
scholarship and morals. It is easily possible to go to college to one's harm, gaining no substantial good, but cultivating a chronic indolence, and the fatal habit of depending upon outer excitements instead of inner resources.
The great danger of college life is that it makes boys
and girls selfish and self-indulgent. We give too much
and ask too little. We concentrate their attention upon
their own personal advantage, and during holidays and the
long vacation, upon the doubtful adventure of having a
gloriously good time; and to this end we absolve them
from all home duties and responsibilities, from all money
burdens, and too often from even the necessity of good
manners. Pour the wealth of the world into the lap of
youth, and youth is stifled and spoiled. A better gift is
that "refined poverty" which our Japanese friends strive
for in their exquisite tea ceremony. There is only one
way of becoming educated, and that is to educate oneself. And this can only be done through self-activity and
self-restraint. Emerson said truly that men are as lazy
as they dare to be. When we do for boys and girls, or for
men and women, what they can and ought to do for
themselves, we strengthen this tendency and invite de-

terioration. And I may add, as a lover of perfection, that we can hardly expect youth to escape the ugly exercise of self-indulgence, when they see their own parents and their elderly friends so habitually self-indulgent.

I am not optimistic enough to believe that the abandonment of endowment funds, here advocated, and their expenditure for legitimate purposes, will take place in the near future, or even all at once in any future. But I do believe that it will come about gradually, for already there are signs of intelligent discontent with the fruits of our present system; and intelligent discontent is ever the precursor of reform. In all the forty-eight States men are beginning to ask why we have so many schools and colleges and universities, and so few educated men and women; and they are no longer disposed to put up with the old stereotyped defense that the system is all right but that human nature is at fault. The obvious problem is to make the system work, and no excuses are valid. *Qui s'excuse, s'accuse.* Furthermore, many earnest and intelligent persons are coming to realize that the one approach to education is not alone through the self-activity of the intellect, but of the body, of the emotions, of the will, of the moral sense—that is to say, a self-activity of the whole person. When the inner life is thwarted or starved, no outward endowment, however splendid, can produce results. That ancient question is still pertinent, What shall it profit a man if he gain the whole world, and lose his own soul?

And now it may be asked, what disposition is recommended for our present large educational endowments, and for those prospective endowments which prospective millionaires, facing prospective death, may be moved to bestow? The answer is very simple. These gathered billions, no longer of any personal use to their gatherers, may all be spent to the utmost advantage instead of being hoarded. They may be made the occasion of life and achievement, instead of apathy and stagnation. There are at least four directions in which every penny of these billions could be beneficently spent, and more billions in addition. But as a necessary preface to their enumeration, let me first say that my own educational preferance will always be for small local colleges, just as for small local schools, placed near the home, within easy walking or motoring distance, so that they may serve both youth and age, and enrich immensely our whole family life. At present the college tends to disintegrate this family life by creating unfortunate lines of cleavage, without offering adequate compensations. Boys and girls are sadly stunted in normal development when they are deprived of their natural share of family duties, responsibilities, joys and burdens. These home experiences are deeply educative; dormitory life, however perfect mechanically and impressive architecturally, can offer no valid substitute. Nor is there any reason whatever why the adult world, parents and even grandparents,—a world, by the way, which pays the bills,—should not share in the intellectual life of the college, and move with their children into the ever expanding kingdom of modern thought. The unsatisfied spiritual and intellectual hunger of the older generation is now a part of the pathos and aridity of our current, prosperous American life.

With this preamble it is very easy to name four directions in which all endowment funds, past and future, however large, may profitably be spent:

1.—In building small, provincial colleges in suitable towns and centres, and in improving local institutions already established. In many cases, the county seat would be the indicated site for such a provincial college. This wholesome scattering of undergraduate students would leave the universities free to pursue their own proper work in graduate departments and in research.

2.—In setting aside adequate funds for pure research work at the universities. Even here, if the donations of the year could be wisely spent to further the research most urgently needed, instead of being put out to interest, I believe that human welfare would be vastly advanced. When millions are dying of preventable disease, it seems a cruel prudence to spend only one-twentieth of our funds in trying to save them.

3.—In supplying model industrial plants,—unless already existing in the neighborhood,—where students who so desire may healthfully earn a part or all of their expenses. The possibilities here are very large. New industries may profitably be introduced, and in addition to serving the students themselves might set up better standards for the community. Perhaps the best results would come about if the local college and the local manufacturer could work together in making industry more attractive humanly as well as more efficient. Experiments along this line are already in progress in several parts of the country and give promise of success.

4.—Last, but not least, in the service of beauty, creating parks, roads, bridges, pools, gateways, landscapes, woodlands, in the outdoor world; and indoors making more elaborate provision for the fine arts—music, drama, sculpture, painting.

In these four channels for immediate expenditure we have adequate outlet for the multitudinous securities now hidden away in our collegiate strong-box, and for as many additional billions as Time may bring to our store. It is a temptation to enlarge upon each one of these splendid possibilities, but that would take us quite too far afield.

The objection to the deadening effect of endowment funds is not limited to the case of educational enterprises, but is tragically valid as a general principle in human life. Endowments kill initiative and healthy self-activity and make for spiritual stagnation. "Paddle your own canoe" is everywhere the sounder principle. A socialistic state which does too much for its citizens and decides too many issues for them, is a left-handed giver. Even our good nature is at fault when we too readily forgive offenders before they have repented their evil deeds and attempted restitution. This failure to realize true values, this debilitating softness, we even manifest, and perhaps most disastrously, in dealing with ourselves. We want things without paying for them, we have become spiritual bargain-hunters. We want scholarship without application; we want wealth without work; we want friendship before we have proved our fidelity; we want love before we have earned the right to it,—in a word, we want something for nothing. There are few among us who do not seek residence on that delectable thoroughfare which the vulgar call "Easy Street." We are after a special private endowment fund which will relieve us from the necessity for further effort. We tell ourselves that we would work with still greater assiduity and for more disinterested ends, but the endowment once gained, we seldom do. Yet the uses of leisure are many and beneficent. Our supported men and women have every opportunity in all the sciences, arts and humanities.

Every man who wishes his life to be dignified and well-ordered, and who has a sane regard for ways and means, realizes that sickness and old age are a part of the common hazard of life, and must be provided against. But this does not require either over-provision or premature provision. Life itself is a risky business, and there are many bridges to cross, but they need not be crossed until they are reached. To make life the high adventure it may so easily be, a man must gallantly take the risk. There are many "good" reasons for saving,—in fact to many persons the mere act of saving almost takes on the quality of a Christian virtue,—but the "real" reason is generally fear. Sometimes it is personal fear; sometimes fear for one's family. A man commonly tells himself that he saves in order to keep his family from want, but what he usually means is to keep them from effort. And that, as I am here contending all along, is a grave disservice to an individual, a family, a school, a university, a church or a community.

In my own educational work, I have touched quite intimately the lives of many boys who were moderately poor, and many boys who were unavoidably rich. If reincarnation holds, and I am returned to earth, I pray to be born into a family of large talents and character, but of very moderate means. Looking out upon our American life, I have come to believe that one of the most curious and mischievous faults of a socially minded community is the almost incurable desire to do for other people what they ought to do for themselves and grow strong in the doing. The slogan of our early manual training crusade was this: *We learn by doing.* It is applicable to the whole of life.

I have come to regard endowment funds, both individual and institutional, not as the benefaction which they are commonly thought to be, but as a distinct menace to our better life. They seem to me the tribute which we pay to our indolence, our inertia, our fear—a blight which makes automatic what ought to be spontaneous; static, what ought to be dynamic; dead, what ought to be alive. If I might paraphrase the famous reply which Pinckney made to the agents of the French Revolution, "Millions for defense, but not one cent for tribute," I should be tempted to proclaim, "Millions for equipment, but not one cent for endowment." And I should mean by this, millions for present-day opportunity, but not one cent for present-day sluggishness.

THE MATING SEASON OF CO-EDUCATION *

By Frank R. Arnold

IF you happen to be a graduate of a monastic New England college and then spend twenty years teaching in a Western co-educational college your point of view on educating the sexes together does much shunting about. You first endure, then pity, but as a rule do not embrace the ambient ardor for putting young men and women through the same cultural mill. Every spring your attitude even becomes that of despair. You sympathize more than ever with Sisyphus as you fight against the triple foe of the college instructor: spring fever, co-educational calf love, and the classic indifference of the eighty-five per cent who, as Doctor Clarence Little told the Michigan alumni in Boston, attend college for reasons other than those of love of knowledge. You get a co-educational complex far different from that of ordinary citizens.

Their view-point on co-education is mainly traditional, depending largely on whether the ordinary citizen is a man or a woman, on whether he first saw the light on the Atlantic seaboard or in the middle West, and possibly also on whether he is a taxpayer. He does not recognize it as a question that will not down and never can be satisfactorily settled. He usually dismisses co-education as a universal Western college blessing and an occasional

* Reprinted from *Scribner's Magazine* by permission of the author and of the editors.

Eastern college bane, but it is not so simple as all that. It is a problem as hard to settle, with as much to be said on both sides, as that of the epigeneticists and the pre-formationists. The taxpayer says that only Ohio can expect taxpayers to support three State universities, that no State can afford to give higher education to men and women separately, that taxpayers want to see results, that the easiest result for a taxpayer to grasp is size, and that mammoth proportions in a State university are impossible without an attendance made up of both sexes. Simple and incontrovertible argument for the Babbitts and the other Main Streeters. Their point of view is worthy of all respect, but the real persons concerned are the students and teachers, and their opinions on the subject are rarely spread abroad. All the same, they are God's own appointed spies on co-education. Most young women students hold the taxpayer's opinion, but from different reasons. According to whether sex blows hot or cold, a girl student becomes an enemy or an advocate of the system. Sex in the case of normal girls is a bigger business, with more insistent demands, a far more alluring game, than careers or intellectual joys, and so there never has been a girl student who, once having tasted the joys of co-education, desires to forego them. Occasionally a girl of the bisexual college system will admit that co-education was all right for her because she knew how to handle herself, but it would never do for her sister, whose life is one constant sequence of innocent love affairs. However, most girl products of the co-educational system probably hold the same opinion as a graduate of the University of Wisconsin who remarked once that a girl couldn't have a good time in college unless she were engaged. She herself had been engaged four times, once each college year, and was an ardent advocate of co-education. She was a good student and on graduating had become a teacher of Latin in an Iowa high school. She kept up the same engaging procedure all through adolescence until she finally married a widower with two children. On a European trip a chance acquaintance asked her to wear his diamond, and she wore it all the time on shipboard but gave it back on landing at Liverpool. She didn't care anything about the man, said he was a bore, that when once you had "gone with" a college man you couldn't stand any other kind, and he was the other kind, and yet she would spend hours in his company, "playing the game." She was a girl of the type known to mothers as "thoroughly nice," and nothing in her conduct was open to criticism except possibly the fixed idea that any man's society was more interesting than a woman's. Sex with her was eternally in evidence, though never rampant, eternally calling for mild satisfaction like that of the Western student who went to Harvard to do graduate work and wrote to a chum that he should go crazy if he didn't find pretty soon some nice girl he could kiss.

The male student, however, is less concerned with sex than business. All the time in constant association with young women students, he often feels that co-education is as distracting as spring fever, as an evil conscience or as a haunting melody, and it is thus because it is so productive of what is known in modern college slang as "female trouble." When you say of a boy student that he has female trouble you mean that he is all upset and unable to work because his girl hasn't written him, or because she is walking past the house, or because she has gone to a dance or a movie with a better man than he the night before, or because she simply will not allow him, in the Shakespearian phrase, to press his suit. How prevalent this distracting female trouble is may be seen by answers to a questionnaire conducted by a Western college paper. Students were asked to send in answers to the query as to whether co-education is a blessing or a curse. It was a subject that they were all so familiar with they had never before even thought of discussing it. The girls wisely sent in no answers. Some of the men's answers were flippant but favorable. Co-education made a man shave every day. It kept him from being a brute. It broke up the adamantine monotony of classes. It made it possible to take a girl to the movies without squeamishness, because you could "stand anything" after having sat through a course in sociology with a lot of girls. Most of the answers, however, brought up the distracting side of the question. Co-education turned the college into a matrimonial bureau. No sense in wasting your time with "Janes," but you couldn't help it when you met them at every turn of the road. Ladies were always lying in wait for a student who wanted to study. What was the use of being "Anned" before you were out of college. One married student even said that co-education was a constant reminder that he had married too early. Women take too much of your time both before and after marriage, was the gist of the whole matter.

It was all the paleolithic cry that the woman tempted me and I did eat. Instead of accepting girl students as an integral part of college life, a necessary concomitant for the development of character, like strong drink and sports, to be used without abusing, the students thought they were being subjected to unnecessary and irresistible devourers of time. And though all had been developed fairly successfully under the co-education régime, the general opinion was that the Amherst or Williams man, with Smith and Mount Holyoke girls within easy reach, but fortunately not within the gates, was far more favorably situated than the middle Western student whose daily fare was flavored with the feminine at every moment of the day.

Thus the student. The professor, on the other hand, can tell you just how distracting in other ways "female trouble" can be. He uses the simple Hamlet device of looking first on this picture and then on that. Two boys, both with high school love affairs on their hands, went to a Western co-educational college. The first two years they worked well and remained faithful to their high school girls. The next year the high school girls graduated and one boy advised his beloved to go to the State university, as he was at the State agricultural college and both realized that if they were to do any college work they would have to live apart. Freed from sex obsessions, with his girl one hundred miles away and accessible only now and then, the boy made a record in his junior year that showed him to be a good human being even if he were only an average student as far as books go. He bought a Tuxedo, an act of promotion to social virility for a student. He was elected president of his Greek letter fraternity and also of his journalistic club. He wrote and sold five articles for farm papers. He was associate editor of the college paper. Most marvellous of all for a modern college student, so preoccupied with sex, movies, and sports, he had time for reading and used it to read such unrequired books as "The Plastic Age," "Martha," "The Sun Field," "Yvette," "Arrowsmith," and "The Recreations of a Psychologist," a list far from classical but a marvellous feat for a college student of to-day, who usually reads only because he has required subjects and rarely for his own pleasure. The other boy could not keep his girl from following him to his college and with her passed a purely sexual year. He dropped his fraternity life, studied only enough to get passing marks, let the French and dramatic clubs, of which he had been elected president, die of inanition, and read nothing except absolute essentials, never a book, not even a newspaper or a magazine. He had no thought in his head beyond flight to his best girl's arms, and by the end of the year he had no plans in life except to find a teaching position that would enable him to get married. The girl, who was simply marking time and was meant by nature only for a breeder, whose conversation was restricted entirely to exclamations such as "How nice!" and "That's lovely!" had no conception of her *métier de femme* that went so far as putting ambition into her future husband or even sharing any that he might have. The two children were helpless in the grip of sex, and co-education was responsible for a year that was wasted by both except as a valuable human experience from which neither had intelligence and will power enough to draw any profit. The young man's case is perhaps exceptional and is due to the opportunities of co-education, to the lack of will power on his side and of brains on the girl's side, but the case will recur constantly as long as colleges find no way of impressing on their students the elementary fact that co-educational colleges exist not as pleasure clubs with sex in the foreground, but as schools for the training of citizens and human beings. Over the doorways of every educational institution should be carved the verse: "There is a spiritual body" or else "You are human beings as well as animals," and from the first day of orientation courses to the commencement address the college should lay emphasis on the derivation and scope of the word "human."

The observing teacher will also note many false standards that spring up in co-educational institutions as upsetting in their way as the distractions of sex. An agricultural college in a far Western state sent one of its graduates to Oxford. After three years he returned to his college town, settled down as a lawyer, and while waiting for clients did much talking about Oxford before clubs of women or students. One of his most damaging statements to the cause of co-education was the fact that at Oxford he had discovered how delightful is the conversation of men.

"We used to study mornings," he said, "and devote our afternoons to outdoor sports until four, when we would gather in various rooms for afternoon tea and talk. It was then I learned for the first time in my life how extremely agreeable is men's conversation. Until then my idea of pleasure had been to take a girl to a dance, to a movie, or to ride in an automobile. All my pleasure had centred about the other sex, and as none of the girls I knew could 'talk,' as I couldn't 'talk' myself, I really discovered that sharpening one's wits against another's and juggling with ideas is more fun than associating with girls. The French, I understand, consider conversation as a national game, but you'll never get that point of view at a co-educational college. You may have to travel as far as Oxford to understand it in its finest flowering."

Of course co-educational students could not grasp this Oxford message. They just thought the speaker was queer and un-American. Their whole scheme of pleasure was built around sex, with girls for every leisure moment. Such students are, for all practical purposes, married people without first having had the mental explorations and sexless friendships which are so vastly entertaining and valuable in non-co-educational colleges. Married are they also to the point of having the financial responsibilities of matrimony. One of the chief problems that come to a man student in a co-educational college is the price of

amusements. Alone he does not mind an elevated seat in
the gallery. He enjoys it. The price is within his reach.
But he feels he has no right to go to the theatre without
taking his "girl." As he cannot afford to take her to the
best seats and no others are good enough for a man
who would rather fail in every course than run the risk
of being thought a "wet one" by a girl, he simply does
not go. Besides, he must save his money for dances. He
may belong to the dramatic club, he may be studying the
drama, he may be a student of sociology or music, but
all the same he ignores all major theatrical events such
as the coming of Mrs. Fiske, of Jane Cowl, or of the
San Carlo opera. He is happy only when second-rate companies come to town and he can "tumesce at four bits,"
to mingle familiar terms from Havelock Ellis and the
West. Once when Olga Petrova wandered into a college
town out in the Rockies she was much surprised to play
to only half a house and that half all down-stairs. She
immediately began to question local reporters and the
manager as to the cause. The town was called the Athens
of the State, was it not? Where were the Athenians?
Why were there no college men and women in the house?
Her play was of a sociological type and students ought
to see it. Were they not interested in the drama? Was the
movie menace responsible? She had hoped to play to a
houseful of students. Where were they? When the explanation finally came, she exclaimed: "You say that
neither men nor women students go to the theatre alone or
in groups? They must pair off like married people? Have
they no intellectual courage? Why, they are simply sex
automatons! They haven't even the fun of intellectual
youth. Long ago I dropped the word 'intolerant' from my
vocabulary. Now, I simply wonder at things. And I must
say your college young people drive me to wonder, amaze-

ment, awe, disgust. They almost make me intolerant. They are intolerable."

Another false standard is the inherent right which every man feels to show good-fellowship and affection toward college girls in public. It is known in country colleges as "pawing" or to animal-husbandry students by even a more technical name. A Yale student who came to teach in a Rocky Mountain college remarked that the way in which the sexes fondled each other in public was the most remarkable thing about the college. The men were always grabbing the arms or waists of girl students to help them upstairs or down, into chapel or out of lecture rooms. Students never sat demurely side by side but always tipped toward fascinating female curves or strokable necks and arms,. And all in a perfectly innocent spirit of playful *camaraderie,* though subconscious sex must have been boiling below. The Yale man asked a student why so much love-making was done in public. Hadn't good breeding decreed that love demonstrations should lighten dark corners and private homes rather than bright businesslike college halls?

The student looked at him in perplexity. Finally perception seemed to come. "Hell! That ain't love-making. That's just pawing." All the same, the Yale comment seemed to scatter a great awakening light and evolved an editorial in the college weekly from which we quote the following cogent sentences:

"There is a pernicious habit among certain love-stricken youths of our college which can most accurately be described as 'pawing.' We have all seen it; the sane denounce it; too many girls permit it. This method of courtship, while it is no doubt ridiculous, is at the same time pathetic. We have one type of infatuated young man who thinks himself in love and wishes to inform the entire world of it. He meets the feminine object of his affection as she comes through the hallway between classes or elsewhere on the campus, greets her with outstretched arms and lets his hands flutter lightly over her dimpled cheeks, fondles her silken hair, and gazes searchingly into her dark, luminous eyes.

"Another kind of girl-enamored swain proceeds in a somewhat different fashion. He sights his maiden on a walk on the campus, calls loudly for her to halt, strides up with a 'Lo, kid,' twines one of his brawny arms firmly about her neck, pinches her cheek, grabs her hand, and after a slight, noisy struggle appropriates her books or vanity case. Finally the class bell rings and the two separate. The girl goes to her next class thinking herself popular. The fellow, with the spirit of 'conquest' still high, seeks another victim.

"Sex attraction is inborn. It is something we cannot well destroy. However, it can, to a desirable extent, be controlled. This open, unleashed, mauling mode of lifting the safety valve of calf-love is entirely out of date. It is primitive, barbaric, and indecent."

Co-education is certainly distracting and full of false standards for both men and women students, and yet, if college is to be a complete preparation for life, if sex and business must be mingled early in life, there is no better school for mating than that offered by co-education. Most young men and young women are imperfectly polygamous or polyandrous before they settle down to monogamy. The young man enjoys an athletic girl for outdoor companionship, another for dancing, another for mental stimulus, and another still for steady domesticity. He has to learn, preferably before marriage, that no one woman can be all women to him. The young woman student has similar discoveries to make with regard to the young men of her generation. Her life happiness demands that she learn to hold her man with brains as well as sex, to realize that if he should ever murmur to himself with Andrea del Sarto, "Why not a brain?" her goose is cooked. In this respect co-education may be the best training ground for a pre-marital understanding of the opposite sex, but, on the other hand, it holds too constantly alert the mating instinct in woman. The crying need of the world is mental mothers. Primitive, physical, passionate mothers we have in abundance. But the mothers we need, the mothers who are to stimulate mentally the town, family, and church are all too rare and are not likely to be produced by the co-educational institutions. Such mothers need years of meditative acquisition, mental brooding as well as physical, and the fault of co-education is that it awakens the mating mother instinct too early. If a woman is to be merely a physical mother, co-education is an admirable preparation. If her main business in life is to be a mentally resourceful human being as well as a mother, then co-education is objectionable for her. Whether you look at it from the point of view of the man or woman, student co-education interferes with the main business of life of the student, which, from eighteen to twenty-two, is preparation for being a good homo rather than stimulation of the mating impulse.

This point of view was admirably brought out by a superintendent of schools in one of the "cow counties" of a far Western State. He had moved to the capital to educate his five children, the oldest a girl of sixteen. For her he demanded a private school for girls and gave the following explanation: "I want my daughter to have some girlhood. Co-education in high school or college won't let her. It eliminates normal girlhood. If I let her go to our country high school she would have to be like other girls, go to dances three times a week and get married when she is seventeen and be a worn-out married woman with four or five children by the time she is twenty-three. I want her to associate with girls whose mothers don't want them to marry until they have had an undistracted opportunity to get an education in high school and college. In our cow county we think an unmarried girl of twenty-three has every chance to be an old maid. I think she is just beginning to have sense enough to venture on marriage. I've known nothing but co-education all my life, and I'd like to try something else for my children."

FOOTBALL *

The Overgrown Darling of the Press

By Alfred S. Dashiell

If you should unfold your favorite newspaper on the morning of November 21 and find no front-page headline on the Yale-Harvard football game, and if, after a search, you found only a half-column report buried deep in the sports section, would you think the editor had suddenly gone mad? Of course, nothing of the sort will happen. The banner head will be there; the colorful story by a well-known sports writer will be there. On the inside pages you will find a play-by-play account of the game and the analysis of first downs, distance gained by rushing, and so on. But if college football were in the position of college baseball, you would have to supply your own color and make your own play-by-play record.

Suppose football were played in the spring when the major league baseball season is getting under way, with race tracks going full tilt, golf and tennis matches, crew races, and track meets being held. How much would you then know of the activities of Johnny Dooley, Dartmouth's doughty quarter back, or of Jake Slagle, Princeton's shifty triple threat?

Competition, for space at least, is not the life of football's trade. The gods of sport have so arranged it that

* Reprinted from *The Independent* by permission of the author and of the editors.

the gridiron game almost completely dominates the sporting pages of America's newspapers for the months of October and November. The entire battery of sports writers is turned loose on the colleges. None of them is detailed to tell what Babe Ruth had for breakfast. No one has to record the doings of Bobby Jones. Instead, they are scattered over the country to report the gloomy sayings of Gil Dobie, to size up the prospects of Notre Dame, to discuss the huddle system. Columns cease to herald the highest batting averages and begin to record the longest kicking distances.

The part the press plays in making football what it is today affords interesting material for speculation. The grotesque overgrowth of the game is apparent. It is much commented upon, but the doctors can't agree on who fed the fair-haired boy so much fattening candy. The papers say, "We give the public what it wants. Did not 300,000 people witness eight football games on October 16, with the season just hitting its stride?" But, asks the skeptic, how many would have gone to see New York University and Tulane play, how many would have attended the Notre Dame-Penn state contest, if newspapers all over the country had not been heralding Tulane and Notre Dame as the greatest peripatetic football teams on record? Would Tulane have traveled 4,000 miles in three weeks if the papers had not assured the gate receipts?

I do not pretend to lay all the ills of college football at the door of the press. Nor can the press be expected to do anything about it. The colleges themselves are accessories before the fact. Athletic directors courted publicity. There were deficits to be made up and stadiums to build. College presidents were not averse to it. There were endowments to be raised and students to be obtained. Everyone remembers the Four Horsemen of Notre Dame, the Praying Colonels of Centre College, even though they are now past history. Ohio State's band, its big drum, and its manœuvres on the football field are famous. Who knows anything about the academic quality of these institutions? The American nation is devoted to sport. Why not capitalize that devotion? Why not, indeed? The only reason I can think of is that the colleges are supposed to be educational institutions.

The college authorities are responsible for the disproportionate growth of football. The alumni mind keeps it from reducing. And the newspapers are the great pamperers of the alumni mind. What is more, they have taken down the fence and allowed the public at large to feed the elephant. Few metropolitan newspapers there be which do not devote at least four pages to sports. When the conservative New York *Evening Post* capitulated and put out a sports extra, that made it unanimous for New York. On a midweek day, selected at random in early season, the New York *Times* printed approximately 10,000 words on football. Special writers make tours of the colleges and write articles on the prospects of the teams. During the season, newspapers print a story a day, sometimes running nearly a column in length, on teams of important universities and near-by colleges. These reports are usually written by student correspondents who, at the same time, have difficulty in getting more than a column or so a week into print on the other activities of their colleges.

We will omit the argument about the hen and the egg. Whether the press creates or supplies the demand, it is obvious that extras, headlines, and long stories can lend undue emphasis. Even so, you can't blame the papers very much. Their job is to shout, and they are shouting louder every day. You can't blame the sports writers too much,

either, except for a lack of humor. Some of them are intelligent and love the game. All of them have to make
their jobs seem important. They can see bits of humor on
the field and in the press box. But they miss the huge
joke—the spectacle of "higher education" financing richly
paid trainers of the sound body and often hiring hacks
to attempt to develop the sound mind. Of course, the college authorities have missed the joke altogether. They
can't see it for the glitter of the gold pouring into their
coffers.

These officials are in the midst of an impossible situation. They would not shut the floodgates of publicity if
they could. They perhaps cannot help it if their institutions are judged largely by the football teams they produce. But they find themselves in the position of having
to pay coaches twice the salaries received by professors,
and of having to allow their alumni associations and
wealthy graduates to see to it that football stars are
steered their way. They have large stadiums on their
hands and must draw crowds to them during the two
months of the season. With a wry smile they see sports
pages adorned with articles by their star athletes who
may be a bit shaky in their English courses, and by their
coaches who make little pretense in the matter of grammar. They know the reports of their own activities will
be buried in two sticks of type. And, as Tex Rickard
says, the secret of success is to "get your name and your
proposition in the papers, and then sit back and take life
easy." They have the interests of their colleges at heart;
therefore, they make football their "proposition" and
rival Mr. Rickard in the promotion of monster athletic
enterprises.

The effect of their sagacity may well be judged by the
multitudes of people who asked, after Harvard's inau-

spicious opening of the football season, "Who the hell is Geneva?" Many were surprised to find that it is a small college in western Pennsylvania with fewer than five hundred students. But the mystery is made clear when it is brought out that Geneva's coach is none other than Bo McMillin, who as a player did valiant service in bringing Centre College into the limelight for a brief period. Geneva College is good for space in almost any newspaper as the first team to beat Harvard in an opening game for fifty years. And the endowment potentialities of that institution are immeasurably increased thereby.

While the money rolls in, college authorities follow the example of the strong, silent man in the White House. The real Babbitts of sport, the shouters for the *status quo,* are the alumni. Fancy the pride with which the members from Geneva walked into the university club of his home city on the Sunday morning after that game. Certainly a great section of this pride is donated by the newspapers. They give him the illusion that some remarkable quality is attached to himself by the feats of his Alma Mater's football team. Indeed, they find him a not unwilling recipient. The large majority of alumni return to their colleges only on big-game days. They talk of their colleges only in terms of the football team. But their reverence for the printed word is, in large measure, responsible for it. If they read in the papers only of the team, the rest can't be very important.

What about the attitude of the press? What is its problem? Almost 2,000,000 words on the Dempsey-Tunney fight were filed at the ring side in Philadelphia, not to mention the 60,000 words a day telegraphed from the training camps for weeks before the battle. It is apparent, now that the fight is over and all the alibis in, that something must fill the gaping columns of the sports pages.

The World's Series helped, but now there is nothing—nothing, that is, but football.

Is the emphasis going to be shifted from football to education by legislation? Well, reformation by law is not 'in particularly good standing just now. Certainly the press cannot be expected to soft-pedal the sport of its own accord. There are only two possible solutions. One is that college faculties, having got themselves into the mess, stop howling about it in reports such as that of a committee of the American Association of University Professors, and that college administrators put aside their *laissez faire* attitude and devise a curriculum as thrilling as an eighty-yard run. Vain hope. The second is that some other sport will come along to compete with football in the newspapers. The press made major league baseball possible. There are now two professional football leagues, the National and the American, each with several clubs. However, the professional game is young yet. Last year was its first of importance. Give it time and it may attract the populace and relieve the colleges of the necessity of providing shows for the mob. Then the experts will be assigned to cover the organized spectacle, and the undergraduate sport will return to the hands of student correspondents. Perhaps Red Grange did college football a service by turning professional.

AS THE PROFESSOR SEES THE GAME *

By an Assistant Professor in a Western University

GAME time!

How do I, a mere assistant professor, a joy-killer, a bird conducting a recitation on Saturday afternoon, a purveyor of mathematics, a person with a desire to shove unnatural mathematical processes down the throats of real, honest-to-goodness he-men students—how can such a grub as I tell it is game time?

I can tell by the look in their eyes.

If I, with my mouth full of figures, should suddenly topple over in a fit and pass to the Great Beyond, those students would shed no tears. That is the look in their eyes. They are disgusted, are those young men, with me, with mathematics, with the programme which has insisted that they be so engaged at such a time as this. The game begins at 2.30; until 1.20 they shall be with me, unless fits intervene. To some, persons uninspired in the presence of a great event, the day might seem singularly drab, a brooding, bitter November day. But the perpendicular face of the new stadium, which can be seen through the class room windows, is topped and aflutter with pennants, and the whole world of men and automobiles seems to swarm in its direction. Of these things my class is con-

---

* Reprinted from *Scribner's Magazine* by permission of the author and of the editors.

scious, and my class is very unhappy. Out of this general depression there stand forth two exceptions—Treadwell and Stinger.

Treadwell is big, equable in temper, likable. Treadwell is varsity end, and he must be dressed and on that field by 2.15. But is he downhearted? Not that you could notice. He and Stinger alone watch me write upon the board. Apparently they alone listen as I prattle about the hieroglyphics. Apparently, I say. For, as a matter of fact, Treadwell isn't listening at all. Determinedly and conscientiously Treadwell keeps his eyes fixed on my chalk, but it is quite impossible for Treadwell to keep his mind off that football field, where in a very short time he will be careering to the applause of the assembled thousands. There is in Treadwell a great strain of honesty, of decency. It wasn't gained at the university, nor developed on the football field. It was simply born in him. So in class Treadwell always keeps his eyes on the board. But Treadwell is no student, though he is no fool. He has no more real interest in mathematics than I have in the man in the moon. He desires to be a college graduate, preferably an engineer, and for some reason, concerning which Treadwell is not quite clear, Mathematics rears its scaly back between him and his ambition. Very well. Treadwell neither whines nor sneers. His job is to get a diploma. The diploma he will get, through his affability, his size, his good looks, and his just sufficient mental effort. Even I, classroom representative of the scaly one, profess a liking for Treadwell. I had him as a freshman in analytics, and I passed him then because of his size, affability, etc., as much as for any knowledge of the subject. I admire him now, so uncompromisingly eying the symbols of integration when the world without is so full of pennants, whisking autos, and girls.

To end the unholy farce of teaching at such a time I announce, at 1.05, that class is dismissed.

There is a large gasp of astonishment. It is promptly followed by a press at the classroom door, and then, like a cork from a champagne bottle, that class is gone.

Excepting Stinger.

"Going to see the game, Prof?" he asks.

"I think I will. Are you?"

"Nix."

Here Stinger is quite positive. Stinger is wiry rather than strong, and has a long nose and thin lips. His eyes are keen, and not at all innocent. Never does he grow familiar with me in the presence of other students, but always does he when we are alone. For Stinger has by far the best mind of that class, he knows he has the best mind, and he knows I know it.

"Where are you going?" I ask.

"I think I'll go down-town and look 'em over," he answers with a grin.

"You'd better go to the game," I advise, and I am sincere.

Stinger makes a face. I understand. In the past Stinger has given me his opinion of athletics, laughing—and slyly sneering—as he did so. So acute were his remarks then, so unbiased by sentiment or—to give the devil his due— by ill-feeling, that I was positively shocked. For, while truth is precious and I am supposed to teach it, yet I suffer, as do ninety-nine out of a hundred adults, from the haunting fear that young persons will see too much of it.

Briefly, Stinger pooh-poohed college athletics.

"Don't you think it develops college spirit?" I had asked.

"Spirit for what?" he had retorted. "Spirit for study?"

I shifted my attack.

"You ought to go to more games," I had insisted.

"Why?" he asked. He was very fond of that "Why?"

"Why, hang it, Stinger," I had exclaimed, "it's color-ful! There's plenty of action, there's the university band, and there are thousands of pretty girls!"

"But out there the girls don't look at me," he had re-torted. "And I don't get any kick out of watching Tread-well and the team run around the field."

Thinking of that remark afterward, I concluded that here Stinger struck nearer the truth than perhaps he had intended. Stinger craved applause. But imaginative he was and analytical—I have said he had an unusually fine mind—as well as young; so that the applause that came his way by reflection, that moiety of applause due every student of an institution whose teams win, that overflow of applause, if you please, which the team can not take care of, Stinger did not want. And thus this young man, who might have been a very successful football coach, but could never be a first-rate football player, went gallivant-ing down-town and out of the influence of that institution of learning which on Saturday afternoons packed itself into the stadium. I could not persuade the young man to do otherwise.

When I arrived at the stadium the beginning of the game was not far off. I obtained a modest seat, a cheap seat, at the far end of the stadium behind a goal line. The stadium seats sixty thousand; I figured there would be some vacancies here. I was right, and here throughout the game I was able to sit, to smoke, to cogitate, and to keep my hat upon my head.

An intercollegiate football game is worth seeing. What-ever may be one's opinion of the propriety of the affair, or of the game itself as a Saturday relaxation from the usual terrific intellectual strain of the student body, or of the price of tickets, the thing is worth seeing. A gathering of half a hundred thousand human beings is never negligible, and when that gathering is very largely one of youth in a bubble of anticipation, its spirit is surprisingly catching and tonic. There are to the affair noteworthy trimmings. The cheer leaders, bedizened and supple, with their vivid genuflections, able to draw from the crowd mighty cadences that sound something like "Rip, snort, zip boom ba-a-a!" The university band, a hundred strong, crashing forth frequently and harmoniously, and always with plenty of pep. And the pennants and colors and horns and megaphones and gaily dressed ladies—as the columnist of the university daily once said, "the latest styles of Paris gracing the Coliseum of Rome."

It is when the preliminaries are being staged, with the teams trotting through a few signals and the ordered blasts of the multitude booming like waves of the deep sea on a rock-bound coast, that I like to observe that shining individual, the football coach. Lucky, lucky man. Blessed with power sufficient to relegate the dubs among his pupils to fields of endeavor for which they are most eminently fitted. But, as the professor realizes, the coach's path is not all bestrewn with roses. For the coach must, with great consistency, win. A professor, if he be a man of some learning, of reasonable industry, of decent character, may retain his job even if he is no howling success as a teacher of his subject. A coach, though he work like a devil and have the character of a god, is not wanted if he cannot teach his pupils to win. The university is tolerant of a poor teacher of anything but football. It would take a bold individual to suggest that the university should be tolerant of poor teaching in football rather than in anything else.

The whistle blows, the game is on, the ball soars into the heavens, the crashing as the opposing forwards collide is very audible and significant indeed. The team which is playing ours is from a small school, said to enroll only a few hundred students, but it is a very famous team. The school has no stadium of its own, but the ability of its team to fill other stadia is universally admitted. Thus on one Saturday this team will be in New Orleans, the next week in Minneapolis, the next in New York, the next in Des Moines, and so on. For me the visitors hold something of the fascination of a theatrical troupe, one of those rare organizations that not only travel but can also be depended upon to fill the house when they care to stop. They have drawn a hundred-thousand-dollar gate to-day. What a wonderful existence is that of these young fellows! Young, athletic, continually on the wing, and playing games on Saturdays! Will they, in after life, experience times to compare with this? Will they, when the college days are over, settle down to the grind of lesser men which alone gives any assurance of later approaching to the present heights? Or will they, quite hopeless of ever again attaining to the public popularity and public prints, from college on dangle at the fringes of the athletic world, advising schoolboys at play, forever more interested in games than in life, growing thick around the neck and thighs—the perfect pictures of men who have shot their bolts? Oh, that such an existence as their present one might continue forever!

The game has settled down to an affair of exceedingly hard work and small gains. The teams are evenly matched. If one were blindfolded one could visualize the situation. From the sudden mighty silences one would know that the crowd was utterly tense upon the efforts of our eleven sweating boys, who vainly try to push the pigskin oval through the devoted vitals of their opponents; as one would know at the sudden roars, the unified exhausts of fifty thousand humans under high pressure, that our men were thrusting back the little school at least a yard or two. Treadwell is playing well. There is no particular affability about the big boy now. Football, like war, offers no particular encouragement to affability. So far Treadwell has knocked down a forward pass, has turned in several plays directed his way, has charged and blocked as well as the thing can be done. A very good end is Treadwell, a man upon whom the coach may rely to give all he has to win. I think Treadwell is determined upon two things: to get his diploma in engineering and to play his position at end in a way that will please his coach. But of course the two ambitions call for different methods of accomplishment. In football a man must be determined, always alert, concentrated upon the subject, utterly devoted.

I wonder, while I watch Treadwell and his mates fall upon these visitors who resist them, just what is the connection between this sort of thing and higher education. Does a college environment stimulate these youths to labor so? Or does football urge them on through college? Do they fulfil scholastic requirements for the sake of football, or do they play football the better to meet scholastic requirements? Has the game attained to its present proportions because it educates or because it entertains? To these fifty thousand people, which is the element predominant at this moment—the school or the circus? Is this stadium the centre of university life or an adjunct? Which is cart, which horse, here? I admit I am no less puzzled when I remember that Treadwell is down there on the field and Stinger is not, when as a matter of fact if the positions were reversed Stinger might be kept out of mischief down-town and Treadwell might be studying a bit more those subjects an engineer is supposed to know. In the crowd of fifty thousand there cannot be more than six thousand men students, for that is the maximum number in school; and I ask myself how do the six thousand benefit by what is here spread before them. Most of them seem to be dressed in their Sunday best, and all of them rise frequently to give voice to the feelings that convulse them. Is there great good in this? It is said to be good to stand in the open and roar, nor does the wearing of one's holiday apparel necessarily nullify the effect. But Tread-well's physique wasn't developed by an hour's vocal exercise once a week. Unquestionably, physical exercise is desirable for students, and all teachers believe in it, whether or not they take any themselves; but just how will the game going on below correct the deficiencies of spindle-legged spectators? Undoubtedly, the bulging calves of the athletes arouse some envy in those who view them, and even some shame among spectators whose supports are thin, but what do such unfortunate spectators do about it? At sight of the game is a languid young man, who has had trouble pulling on his shoes and walking to classes in the morning, suddenly stimulated to dumb-bells and the wrestling mat? After all, is not the correction of students' physical deficiencies, as a matter of the greatest importance, a matter for the university itself to oversee and insist upon? And if such is the case, what has the staging of an athletic contest before fifty thousand people, more than half of them utter strangers to the university, to do with it?

The first half is up, and a desperate affair it was, keeping those who beheld it very tense, and at times very uncomfortable. Score, 0 to 0. Both teams are bundled off the field in blankets, and the spectators relax and stretch and argue, and the hundred-piece band suddenly bursts into jazz. But while the spectators are being somewhat soothed by the musical hot stuff, the two rival teams, closeted with their respective coaches, are hearing sounds far from soothing. We spectators know not just what the coaches say, but we can imagine. Our young men must hear themselves described in defeat as spineless, useless, utterly repulsive cadavers. For when, fifteen minutes later, we see them reappear upon the field they come spouting flames. When the whistle blows and the ball is kicked off once more they rush at their eleven opponents, who have been similarly worked upon and worked up. Whereupon we are treated to visible proof that when irresistible force meets irresistible force dull thuds result, without much gain for any one.

Throughout the third quarter the battle rages. The visitors from the little school are demons. When we have the ball they are mountains in the way; when they have it they move forward like landslides. Yet they can no more score on us than we on them. Throughout the quarter the ball gets no nearer than thirty yards to either goal. No spectator of such a struggle could be indifferent to it, and in watching it the crowd forgets to cheer, the band to play, and the somewhat officious officials to assess penalties. So the quarter goes.

At the beginning of the fourth and final quarter three men in the jerseys of our school run upon the field. They are fresh backs to replace the two halves and the full worn out by the preceding three quarters. At the substitution the visitors look rather blank and glum. Theirs is a small school, good substitutes are scarce; they will finish the game with the men who began it. The crowd yells approval of our substitution. I ask myself—sotto voce, of course: Is this substitution of men on our part proper ethics? Is this true sportsmanship? Before I can reach any

conclusion the battle is on; and I defy any living man situated as I am to consider ethics while it is on.

The three new backs turn the tide. The game begins to
swing definitely in our favor. The ball remains in the
opponents' territory, and gradually, very gradually, approaches the goal they defend. But the visitors are far
from being defeated even now, and it is very evident that,
despite our three fresh men, the nearer the ball approaches
goal the harder the job to push it on. With only five minutes more to play, the ball is still twenty-five yards away
from the goal-line, and the outcome very doubtful, when
an unexpected play decides the issue.

The ball is put in play at about the twenty-five-yard line,
and nearer the sideline where sit our substitutes than the
other. Treadwell runs over to this sideline, and the visitors are on the watch for a forward pass to be thrown
to him. But when the ball is snapped Treadwell immediately charges the man opposite him, bowls him over, and
falls, himself. The play is very fast and brilliantly exe-
cuted, and already there is one of our men where Treadwell so recently was. The ball is shot to this man, he gets
it, and goes careering down the field.

Now occurs something which, I believe, is seen clearly
by only Treadwell and me. For some distance the man
with the ball runs along the side-line, and once, only
once, very lightly, very quickly, he steps over the side-
line—as I see it. I am in the seats at the end of the field;
if the side-line were continued it would pass between my
legs. And it happened that I had been staring with a sort
of horrible presentiment at the runner's shoes as he
danced along the side-line. And I had seen his fatal misstep. And as he continued on, my eyes remained upon
the fatal spot, as if the print of his shoe were burned in
the sod there. And of all of the fifty thousand pairs of

eyes gazing down, only one other pair besides mine, I believe, watched those shoes as I did. The other pair was Treadwell's.

The runner was between Treadwell and me. Treadwell, coming to his feet after bowling over his man, was on his hands and knees straddling the side-line when the runner stepped over. And his eyes, like mine, remained fixed upon the spot. For some moments Treadwell's mouth hung open, he remained on his hands and knees, the most undecided football player I had ever seen. And all this while the man with the ball was squirming, twisting, pirouetting, advancing. Though neither Treadwell nor I moved our eyes from a certain damned spot that would not out, we could tell from fifty thousand voices that a touchdown had been scored.

Immediately the captain of the opposing team protested that the runner had stepped out. The captain's players gathered about to protest with him. Immediately our captain contradicted any such protest, and our players gave support to our captain. The spectators took up the argument, and from that stadium rose the rumble of discontent. Yet, I am convinced that the vast mass of those shouting and insistent spectators, those protesting and contradicting players, had not seen the runner's twinkling feet. And the officials, who had not seen, yet were experienced and honest men, decided promptly and finally without having seen, because they knew that to seek impartial evidence and get it under such circumstances was an unheard-of and useless effort. Has an intercollegiate football match, outside of the literature and poetry of the game, ever been decided in such a torn and troubled moment as this by some player stepping forward and saying: "Yes, Mr. Referee, I saw our man step out of bounds. Our touchdown was illegal. Though

what I am telling will cost us the game and the championship, I can not cheat, I can not take an unfair advantage."
And did his fellow players step up to congratulate him
afterward? Perhaps so. But I have seen many football
games, and I have seen a number of disputes arise on the
field of play; and in such cases I have never seen the officials decide with other than full knowledge that they
would be damned if they did and damned if they didn't.

That touchdown being allowed, the game was ours.

I remain at my seat watching the exodus of the fifty
thousand from the stadium. For many minutes the crowd
continues to swarm out, a jubilant swarm. We have won,
a famous team is beaten, a championship is in sight. Outside, motors roar, horns toot—sweet pæans of victory.
But of it all that which remains most significant to me
is the blanketed figure of Tom Treadwell moving off the
field with his comrades to their quarters. For Treadwell
walks with bowed head, not as a victor should, but with
the dejected and thoughtful look of one who has lost.

As I walk home I ask myself if for failing to tell the
truth regarding that touchdown any one can blame Treadwell—and me. Sidestepping direct response to that query,
I then inquire why it is that we two—if Treadwell saw
as I did—failed to show true sportsmanship when the
opportunity presented itself. And the best I can say for
Treadwell and myself is this: that that in which he and
I have just been participating, he as a player, I as a spectator, was not a game. It was a battle. It was an economic
and financial struggle, and at bottom as heartless and un-
sentimental and unsportsmanlike as struggles of that sort
usually are. For this stadium will be packed next Saturday and the Saturday after. But had we not won, had
Treadwell and I told the truth, the stadium would not
have been filled on the next two occasions. Had Tread-

well and I spoken out it would have cost some one a hundred thousand dollars. We remained silent. In my estimation the train of circumstances connecting young Treadwell and poor me with that hundred thousand exists with a perfectly hellish clearness. A hundred thousand and more is at stake; to win the stake the games must be won; to win the games an intelligent, thoroughly competent, highly paid coach is obtained; to win is this coach's business, it is his bread and butter; his competency and success are measured by the degree of his own desire and determination and necessity to win that is transmitted to his pupils; and thus are the student body, the community in which the school is located, the American public, treated weekly to exhibitions and influences as glamorous, as inciting, and as ethical as bull-fights.

"Oh, yes," exclaims a small voice, "but isn't a winning football team the best advertising in the world? Don't these victories advertise the university? And you grubbing bookworms with it?" To which I, exhausted by this mental flagellation, wearily reply: "Why in the name of seven devils does higher education have to be advertised!"

This is mere spleen, of course, the exclamation of one who is rapidly losing his bearings. I admit it. I admit it the more readily, thinking of Stinger. I began by saying that Stinger might have done better at the game and Treadwell away from it. I am not now so sure. Seeing Treadwell's departing and dolorous figure, the figure of a Treadwell for once in his life intensely thinking, I am left doubtful. Had Stinger witnessed the fatal misstep over the side-line, with the game won despite it, he would have laughed. The cynicism of Stinger, already too pronounced in a man of his age, would have been in no wise lessened by the incident.

ELIOT AT HARVARD: THE MIDDLE
YEARS *

By R. M. L.

In 1889 President Eliot had been at Harvard for twenty years, and the turning point in the long road had been reached. The fruits of his policy were beginning to appear. The elective system had come to seem the natural order of things. The growth of the schools of law and medicine had shifted the emphasis from Harvard College to Harvard University, and the graduate school was beginning to count in the same direction. In spite of the success of his administration the President was not popular within college walls or without. To the great middle class public, toward which his educational policies were directed, he was a suspicious character—a Unitarian, a free trader, a Democrat, the defender of Mormonism and other unsanctified causes. He had lately uttered some very plain truths about daily journalism, and certain Boston newspapers kept on his trail night and day. Within the university and among the alumni he was still on trial. He had won the faculty to his side in the matters of voluntary religious service and free election of studies: he proceeded to divide it again by the proposal of the three-year course. The alumni felt that this would be the last blow to the old college system and morale. And Harvard teams were being beaten regularly by Yale and Princeton.

* Reprinted from *The New Republic* by permission of the author and of the editors.

When I went to Harvard in the fall of 1888, I cannot remember that I had ever heard a word in praise of President Eliot. On the contrary, I had a distinct impression that Harvard was getting along as well as could be expected under a president who could not be compared in character or ability with those sterling Christian gentlemen, Mark Hopkins of Williams, Julius H. Seelye of Amherst, or Timothy Dwight of Yale. My first view of the President was therefore an illumination. I strayed into Appleton chapel one morning to the service which we no longer had to attend, and saw him sitting in one of the side pews—and no words of mine can convey the sense of eminence and what I then and always thought of as nobility which that erect form and calm, strong face conveyed. He sat there in his place every morning. After chapel he walked, always alone, across the campus to his office in University Hall. I think such undergraduates as ever caught a glimpse of the President felt as I did. We trusted him against all the cavil of the world; but he was a figure incredibly removed from us, austere and splendid, always alone. That was before the days when Harvard men sang A Health to King Charles.

The first time I heard President Eliot speak was at a meeting of the college in Sever 11 to receive the gift of the new athletic field—the Soldiers' Field—which Major Henry L. Higginson had given in memory of six men who had died in the Civil War. His speech was of a kind of eloquence such as few of us had ever heard, literal, precise, restrained—but we knew that these men had been his friends.

I may be wrong, but I think that up to that time the President had not often addressed the college. This occasion broke the ice, and after that he seemed to enjoy meeting his constituents. The next year he proposed to end the practice of the rush on Bloody Monday Night, when sophomores and freshmen used to maul each other about the campus, by addressing the older class on its responsibilities. Eliot rarely made a verbal slip, so that when he incautiously announced that the freshmen should be taken in there was more laughter than such a mild break would usually cause. And after a second of surprise he grinned back genially at his audience, and that did still more to break the ice.

The President had his blind side and somewhere on that side were intercollegiate athletics. He had been an oarsman in college, and had rowed in the boat that first met Yale on Lake Winnepesaukee. Rowing he thought the best of team sports because it was a clear straight-away trial of strength and skill. Baseball he looked at with suspicion because of its encouragement of the reprehensible habit of stealing bases. Dean Briggs told me that the President came to him one day with the light of triumph in his eye and a newspaper in his hand. "You tell me that it is a clean sport," he exclaimed, "and here it says that he *pretended* to throw to second and caught the man off third." Football was prohibited at Harvard for a time, and when it was resumed the teams had no tradition of training and coaching and were easily beaten. At last in the fall of 1890 we beat Yale at Springfield— 12 to 6. It was an occasion for which we had no guiding precedent, and in a fumbling, self-conscious way we got the self-conscious team on top of a coach and with a dim sense that it was the proper thing to do dragged it to the front of the President's house and called him out. He came and said a few words of congratulation. "But," he added, "the finest thing about the game was the way the Yale men rallied at the end." If he had been at Springfield, and had waited through those agonizing last minutes

for the whistle to sound before Yale should have tied the
score he would scarcely have felicitated our battered war-
riors on their opponents' prowess.

Of the President's gift of saying the wrong thing in
the happiest way there used to be many tales. One such
occasion, I remember, the Phi Beta Kappa dinner when
Professor Goodwin, the president of the society, in his
magnificent Corinthian manner spoke admiringly of the
perfect Latin in which Eliot had conducted the commencement exercises the day before. The President replied
that they ought to have been in English. In this habit of
speaking his mind he met his match when Matthew
Arnold visited him. From a reading of Literature and
Dogma Doctor Eliot assumed that the Unitarian church
would be acceptable as a place of worship, but Matthew
Arnold preferred the Anglican—"the only church for a
gentleman."

Undoubtedly President Eliot's austerity of manner and
his honesty of speech gave rise to the notion current in
those days that he was hard and cold, absorbed in his own
plans, unsympathetic to others. It needed but a touch,
however, to show him as completely human. My first
meeting with him was on the occasion of the founding
of a society of undergraduates for religious discussion, in
contrast to the Y. M. C. A. which made evangelical belief
a condition of membership. We felt that so momentous
an enterprise demanded sanction in the highest quarters,
and I was deputed to see the President. Chapel was the
obvious place to find him, but I had never seen anyone
join him in his stately march across the campus, and so
I dogged his steps until he reached University, and then
put myself forward. He swept me into his office and I
began to tell him why I was there. Suddenly it came to
me that he liked to be consulted about such matters, that

he was actually pleased that I had come. He went into the subject with perfect seriousness and much detail. Even when I stated the fear that was in our young minds that we might contribute to the ill fame of Harvard as a hot-bed of infidelity he did not smile. "They say so much against us anyway that a little more won't make any difference," he said kindly. I remember another interview some years later when my budding career was to me the most important matter in the world, and with commencement on his hands I suppose the President had other things to think of. There was no sign of this, however, until I had said everything I could and he had taken everything up, thoroughly and earnestly. I was through and sat in silence, utterly in doubt. He sat, in no doubt at all, but equally silent. I have often wondered since how many precious minutes that silence continued. At last I heard a low, very gentle, very patient sigh. I jumped up and tried to thank him for his kindness, but he waved that aside. "Come in tomorrow when you've thought it over further," he said. Another interview I recall vividly. Eliot had been asked to send an instructor to a school closely connected with Princeton, and picked me for the forlorn hope. I wanted to please him and accepted, and after a night of reflection declined. I saw that he felt that I had let him down badly, both in the deed and in the manner of it, but he considered only the latter. "It was—permissible," he said at last, and I felt that he had handed me a pass mark with charity.

I always felt that a scrupulous sense of responsibility was one reason for the attitude on Eliot's part that was characterized as distant, unsympathetic. He must have been conscious of his power over men, especially over young men, to make them do what he wanted, but he honorably forbore to exercise it. He believed in individual-

ity and respected it too thoroughly to impose his own
personality on others. No one dreamed in those days
of imitating Eliot in thought or manner or speech. In any
case he was too much in the grand style to be an easy
model. There were tales about his bullying his faculty,
but I doubt them. He believed in decisions arrived at by
discussion, in letting reason have its sway. Theoretically,
he disliked authority. He would have opposed schemes
of student self-government had they been in fashion then,
because he preferred as little government as possible. This
belief in individualism was responsible for the extreme
development of the elective system under which we ex-
perimented widely in the intellectual life. It was reflected
in the undervaluing of the training involved in team
play; and it probably had something to do with the pre-
valence of a disease of which we heard much from Theodore Roosevelt and other recent graduates—that Harvard
indifference, of which the symptoms were a disposition
to go your own way and do the things you liked without
much interest in playing the game that others wanted
to win—for Harvard's sake or Christ's. Of course it was
all wrong by modern standards, yet as I see that time
through a glamorous mist of years it seems to me that
such unhappiness as we had was caught from Matthew
Arnold's poems and could be relieved by Omar Khayyam.
On the whole, men got what they went out for if they
cared enough, and I never knew a Harvard man to commit suicide because he failed to make the Porcellian or
even the Pudding.

This laissez-faire in regard to college government,
studies and activities seems old-fashioned. Indeed it was
part of the old Liberalism of the nineteenth century of
which President Eliot was a conspicuous example. The
same habit of mind can be seen in his attitude toward the

labor movement. He could not accept collective bargaining as a principle when it implied the control by an organization of the individual's right to labor. This attitude has done President Eliot as much disservice with Liberals of the present day as his advocacy of free trade and civil service reform did with the conservatives of the past. His disapproval of labor policy, however, never dulled his interest and sympathy with the worker as such. He was too clear-minded to let a difference of opinion run into a prejudice. Probably no system of government ever devised by man was more objectionable to him than Communism, but to the last he was deeply concerned in plans for helping the Russian people. I am glad to remember that my last word from him was a cordial response to an invitation to serve on a national committee for the relief of the Russian famine.

SHE LIVED TO GIVE PAIN *

By R. F. DIBBLE

PERHAPS the essential fact about Transcendentalism is
that its germinal principle, nonconformity, soon became
as conventional and stereotyped as Calvinism itself. Creed-
lessness became a creed, idiosyncrasy became normal, the
gospel of individualism damned itself by becoming a Gospel, and the glorious duty of following whim degenerated
into a codified regimen as stiff as the Thirty-nine Articles.
The self-sustaining Thoreau sustained himself by obtain-
ing generous snacks from his mother's larder; masculine
Margaret Fuller became Mrs. Ossoli; Hawthorne ceased
milking cows at Brook Farm to accept a political appoint-
ment; Emerson preached against preachers; and Fruit-
lands, the crowning absurdity of the period, perished
because its lofty-minded founders failed to raise enough
fruit to sustain themselves. But Transcendentalism, intrinsically unoriginal and unimportant in itself, accomplished what far more revolutionary movements have not
always done: it fathered a brood of enormously, ever-
lastingly interesting children. Kings, empires, and presidents might come and go, but the flaming devotees of
Newness talked forever on and on—and how resourceful
and stimulating that marvelous conversation was!

The minutest facts concerning most of them have been

* Reprinted from *The Century Magazine* by permission of the
author and of the editors.

dug up and exhibited in countless books, pamphlets, and piously accurate dissertations, yet one austere and formidable figure in the movement has never received her due. Here and there, in the febrile journals which every one of importance, and even of no importance, seems to have kept in that day, are to be found stray references to Mary Moody Emerson; but no one except her worshiping nephew has written at any length about her, and his sketch, composed shortly after her death, is—what else could it be?—fragmentary and elusive. And yet, if one may judge by the comments of her intimate associates, Aunt Mary was even more electric, more volcanic, and more unaccountable than Margaret Fuller herself. She can be defined only in the language of a paradox: she was a female Diogenes, philosophical saint, a devout skeptic, a Calvinistic rebel who revolted against everything and everybody, including herself. Thoreau called her the "wittiest and most vivacious woman" whom he knew; and years after she was food for those all-devouring worms that haunted her macabre imagination throughout her tempestuous life, Emerson continued to cherish her "monitory" diaries and her "moral inspiration." He wrote: "All the men and women whose talents challenge my admiration from time to time lack this depth of source, and are therefore comparatively shallow." Emerson, one reflects, was not invariably guiltless of hyperbole as well as of family pride, and it may be that he had momentarily forgotten, let us say, Plato, Shakespeare, Goethe, and Carlyle; yet had any one of those worthies been privileged to be inmates of the Emersonian household for some years, as Aunt Mary was, one wonders whether such a sentence would have been written of him.

For Aunt Mary, with her scrawny angular form, her peaked face, her long sharp-pointed pug-nose, and her "eye that went through and through you like a needle," acted the part of fairy godmother to Ralph Waldo from his earliest years. Born in 1775, she lost her parents when she was but a baby, and was adopted by an aunt and uncle who were so hard up that one of the child's chief duties was to watch out for the deputy sheriff who, it was feared, might thunder in at any moment to arrest the uncle for debt. When her brother William, Ralph's father, died in 1811, Aunt Mary came to live with the widow and her children. The family was very poor, and once, when Ralph paid a few pennies for the loan of a novel from a circulating library, his aunt grimly reminded him that he ought to be ashamed of himself—"How insipid is fiction to a mind touched with immortal views!" she once burst out—but the lad got some revenge by plaguing her with quotations from "Don Juan."

Her influence upon the boy's plastic mind can never be accurately known; it is possible, and even probable, that without it he might, like his forefathers, have been just another Reverend Emerson all his life. She constantly scourged and prodded him to essay higher things. "Scorn trifles, lift your aims; do what you are afraid to do," she primly admonished him over and over again. She advised him not to go to the Cambridge Divinity School because, she said, it lacked reverence. It was tainted, she firmly believed, with the aridities of German scholasticism; and the lowliest things in nature, "Mr. Horse, Mrs. Cow, and Miss Sparrow," aye, even "the whole of Calvinism," were better than it. When he earned the unbelievable sum of about two thousand dollars from teaching, she became much worried over his genius, which her acute perception had already detected; "hard fare for the belly" would be much better for him, she snorted, and she ceaselessly chided him for not *daring* more. In his ministerial days he corresponded regularly with his "Abbess of a humble Vale," seeking her "high counsels" to illumine him "upon the dark sayings and sphinx riddles of life"; and she in turn sent him multitudes of what he accurately called "moral scrawls and Sibylline scraps." Certainly no one but Emerson could have got any meaning from some of her outpourings. "How little can we recapitulate without vomiting at mortal conditions," is the opening statement in one of her paragraphs; and she doubtlessly strengthened his moral fiber by such a pronouncement as this: "Illimitable prospects can best apply euphrasy to the understanding." When Emerson's young mind was nourished upon such pap as this, who can wonder at the enigmas and obfuscations in his works? And yet . . . Aunt Mary unquestionably was, as he said, "always new, subtle, frolicsome, musical, unpredictable." When she realized that her amiable nephew had swallowed her metaphysical bait—hook, line, and sinker—she apparently became a little worried. She once wrangled with him about his "high, airy speculations" and refused to see him for a time; and once again, when he sent her his agonized questionings about the "miracle of life and the idea of God," she replied by asking him concerning the condition of his knee.

Indeed, despite her crotchety ways, her thorny mannerisms, and her incomprehensible style, she was "endowed with the fatal gift of penetration" into other people's weaknesses and vagaries. "She disgusted everybody because she knew them too well," wrote Emerson; and that seems to have been the central truth about her. This curious lady, who wrote prayers teeming with "prophetic and apocalyptic ejaculations," who believed implicitly in angels and archangels, who used her thimble less for sewing than for impressing seals upon the wax of her letters, and who deliberately chose bonnets that did not conform to contemporary tastes, sometimes manifested a hard-headed earthiness that utterly confounded her moonstruck associates. "I knew I was not destined to please," she wrote. "To live to give pain rather than pleasure (the latter so delicious) seems the spider-like necessity of my being on earth." In brief, it was her job both to inflate and ballast the flighty balloon of Transcendentalism. Nothing deterred her; she was, as Emerson remarked, "embarrassed by no Moses or Paul, no Angelo or Shakespeare." He compared the impact of her terrific personality to the ponderous influence of Dr. Johnson; like him, she "impresses her company, as she does, not only by the point of the remark, but also when the point fails, because she made it." The most devastating thing about her was that one could never be quite sure whether she was thoroughly sincere or was merely amusing herself at the expense of her auditors; her most scorching discourses might be conceived in a spirit of levity, whereas her lightest remark might be loaded with dynamite. Thus, while she naturally hankered to get into "good society," her bewildering oddities so teased and exasperated people that she was perpetually debarred; for she was too proud and crabbed to conform.

In one respect she did conform: she kept a diary into which, "night after day, year after year," she poured her dark and incommunicable emotions. In reading those cabalistic sentences, filled with gnarled and knotty solecisms and inexplorable deviations into mysticism, one is reminded of Emily Brontë, of Sir Thomas Browne, of Thoreau, and of many more. Occasionally she is perfectly clear: "Rose before light every morn; visited from necessity once, and again for books; read Butler's Analogy; commented on the Scriptures; read in a little book,— Cicero's Letters,—a few; touched Shakespeare,—washed, carded, cleaned house, and baked." She can on occasion describe her mystic moments with crystal clarity: "Alive with God is enough,—'tis rapture . . . in dead of night, nearer morning, when the eastern stars glow or appear to glow with more indescribable lustre, a lustre which penetrates the spirit with wonder and curiosity . . ." In her youth she had promised God that "to be a blot on this fair world, at His command, would be acceptable." She felt so assured of her own direct intercommunication with the Almighty, in fact, that she paid, says Emerson, a superciliously "polite and courtly homage to the name and dignity of Jesus" which patently showed her "organic dislike to any interference, any mediation between her and the Author of her being." She seems indeed to have had what amounted to a secure sense of private ownership of the Almighty. "Reading from my manuscripts to her," wrote Thoreau, "and using the word 'god' in perchance a merely heathenish sense, she inquired hastily in a tone of dignified anxiety, 'Is that god spelt with a little g?'" And he dryly adds, "Fortunately it was." This surely might be Thoreau himself speaking, though it was written ten years before his birth: "The evening is fine, but I dare not enjoy it. The moon and stars reproach me, because I had to do with mean fools." But then . . . there comes a change. "O Time. Thou loiterer. Thou, whose might has laid low the vastest and crushed the worm, restest on thy hoary throne, with like potency over thy agitations and thy graves. When will thy routines give way to higher and lasting institutions? When will thy trophies and thy name and all its wizard forms be lost in the Genius of Eternity? In Eternity, no deceitful promises, no fantastic illusions, no riddles concealed by thy shrouds, none of thy Arachnean webs, which decoy and destroy. Hasten to finish thy motley work, on which frightful Gorgons are at play, spite of holy ghosts. 'Tis already moth-eaten and its shuttles quaver, as the beams of the loom are shaken." Small wonder that Emerson, constantly poring over her diary, was irresistibly reminded of Dante's "Inferno." Perhaps that passage may at least suggest why, when she was offered marriage "by a man of talents, education, and good social position," she refused him. A woman who wrote like that would scarcely feel inclined to hitch her star to a matrimonial wagon.

Not that she despised men; they were much more endurable than women. When young people intrigued her interest, she would go to any lengths to win their confidence; and, having gained it, she made the most of the brief intimacy, for she realized only too well that they would soon tire of her queer impish grotesqueries; but if they proved to be dull—to her mind dullness was the one unpardonable sin—she was disgusted and got rid of them by asking them to run on some senseless errand. She habitually referred to the head of the family with whom she happened to be sojourning as the "clown," but she preferred even him to the lady of the house. One of the very few women whom she really admired she called "Whale-hearted." She once had a felon on her thumb and therefore decided to employ a nurse—a veritable Sairy Gamp, who immediately climbed into bed and began to snore so loud that Aunt Mary woke her "to forbid her making such a shocking noise"; and in the end she hustled the offender out of the house before morning, after having "passed the worst night she remembered." When a woman chanced to speak in mixed company, Aunt Mary would place a heavy hand on her shoulder and utter this admonishment: "Be still. I want to hear the men talk." If she heard any lady excessively praised, she would interrupt with the caustic query, "Is it a colored woman of whom you were speaking?" Once when a Mrs. Brown had waxed ecstatic over the Italian patriots, Aunt Mary broke in: "Mrs. Brown, how's your cat?" Observing Mrs. Thoreau wearing pink ribbons one day, she closed her eyes while the two chatted for a time; then she said, "Mrs. Thoreau, I don't know whether you have observed that my eyes are shut."

"Yes, madam, I have observed it."

"Perhaps you would like to know the reason?"

"Yes, I should."

"I don't like to see a person of your age guilty of such levity in dress."

Aunt Mary was assuredly guileless in that respect; her attire was far from gaudy. As old age drew on, she thoughtfully prepared for the end by making her own shroud; but the years continued to pass, she was still very much alive, and, thrifty and frugal as her Puritan ancestors, she finally wore it as a night-dress and a day-gown, and she sometimes rode about on horseback with a flaming scarlet shawl thrown over the ominous white. She wore one out, then made another—and another. Her eccentricities increased with age. In her peripatetic trips all over New England to find 'boarding-houses' within the reach of her scrimped income, she encountered some families who were likable—and some who were not. Meeting one day a couple who looked vaguely familiar, she courtesied frigidly; then, recognizing them as a pair whom she had once dwelt with but had almost forgotten, she approached and unburdened herself thus: "I didn't know who you were, or should never have bowed to you." Perhaps the reason for her aversion was that the pair had children—for Aunt Mary loathed babies of every description. "Give us peace in our boarders," she once wrote, in words that were meant to be a prayer for the nation's welfare; when the error in spelling was pointed out, she laconically commented that "it would do as it was." Hating to throw away anything useful, she treasured her precious chest of medicines; and when she had a surplus of drugs on hand, she would mix a drop of laudanum with various pills, a little antimony and quinine, and then swallow the concoction to save it. On rare occasions she would drink tea, but she immediately made haste to sip coffee to get rid of the tea-taste. Noticing an idle horse hitched to a chaise one day, she sought out the owner and asked him to let her take a ride to Dr. Ripley's while the man himself was making his purchases. When he mildly protested, she curtly informed him that she "was his own townswoman, born within a mile of him"; she then climbed into the gig, and the dumfounded fellow actually told her not to hurry but to take her time. Yet her own comment on her foibles should be noted: "My oddities were never designed—effect of an uncalculating constitution at first, then through isolation. . . . It is so universal with all classes to avoid me that I blame nobody."

She doubtless met all the notables who forgathered in Concord with Emerson, with Margaret Fuller, with Alcott and the others, but exasperatingly little information on this point has been recorded. Did she ever argue with Margaret on the position of a woman?—what would one not give for a report of an encounter between these

two dialectical giantesses! She certainly met Alcott—
that half-crazy, half-inspired visionary who fervently
believed in preëxistence, phrenology, and vegetarianism,
and who founded the first kindergarten in America—
for she wrote him a letter in which she deliberately paro-
died his spasmodic oratorical style: "While the form
dazzled,—while the speaker inspired confidence,—the
foundation of the—the—superstructure, gilded and golden
—was in depths of—I will tell you plainly what, when I
am furnished more with terms as well as principles,—
after I have seen the account of your present instruction."
Years later, however, she made amends. One night, in
Emerson's house, for the first time in his life Alcott became utterly speechless when confronted with the scath-
ing paradoxes of Henry James the elder; then of a sudden
Aunt Mary bounced up and completely squelched James,
as successfully as he had quieted Alcott, by her fiery pronouncements against his "dangerous Antinomian views
concerning the moral law." Nevertheless she did not depend on the Concord savants for her intellectual stimulus; she read avidly all the time—Plato, Plotinus, Marcus
Antoninus, Edward Young, Cousin, Jonathan Edwards,
Goethe, and Madame de Staël were her constant companions. For years she conned "Paradise Lost" in a book
without title-page or covers, and it was not until she
bought a new copy—for some one told her that she really
ought to know Milton—that she discovered she had been
reading him all these years. She even gloated over the icy
wit of Talleyrand, though she once closed his glittering
pages with the sigh, "I fear he was not organized for a
Future State."

Extreme old age drew on, bringing recurrent thoughts
of death and worms—where was the serene sense of divine
immanence, where were those youthful raptures now?

"Could I have those hours in which in fresh youth I said, To obey God is joy, though there were no hereafter, I should rejoice, though returning to dust." For years she made up her bed like a coffin, and she was elated to note that a church steeple across the way cast a shadow shaped like a coffin before her window. But death still dragged, and the worms still loitered. "I have given up, the last year or two, the hope of dying. . . . Tedious indisposition :—hoped, as it took a new form, it would open the cool, sweet grave. . . . Ill health and nerves. O dear worms,—how they will at some sure time take down this tedious tabernacle, most valuable companions, instructors in the science of mind, by gnawing away the meshes which have chained it. A very Beatrice in showing the Paradise." Even death on the gallows would be preferable to life: "If one could choose, and without crime be gibbeted,—were it not altogether better than the long drooping away by age without mentality or devotion? The vulture and the crow would *caw caw,* and, unconscious of any deformity in the mutilated body, would relish their meal, make no grimace of affected sympathy, nor suffer any real compassion." And yet, as late as 1855, Thoreau wrote that she was "the youngest person in Concord, though about eighty. . . . She says they called her old when she was young, and she has never grown any older." Her friends—such is the high privilege of friendship!— were wont to say to her in all sincerity, "I wish you joy of the worms." And when the beatific worms triumphed in her eighty-ninth year, the event had something of cosmic comedy about it, and those same friends dared not look at each other during the funeral "lest they should forget the serious proprieties of the hour."

JAMES WHITCOMB RILEY *

By Edgar Lee Masters

The County Fair of Middle Western America was not a Vanity Fair to the people themselves. The balloon ascent was thrilling enough, and no one dreamed of the aëroplane. There were side-shows of performing Chinese, fire-eaters and the like; wheels of fortune, and barkers selling razors, can-openers and glass-cutters. The event attracted the country fiddlers, some of whom played for the platform dancers. Under the big trees beyond the race-track the shadows and the grass invited the farmer people and the villagers with their lunches, and the fire blazed for the making of coffee. For a week the same people walked the grounds ruining the grass and making paths to the sheds where the live stock was exhibited, or the products of the soil.

One saw for all this time, day by day the same faces, the same roisterers, the same old notables wearing stove-pipe hats and doe-skin coats; the same couples paired for the occasion, and soon to be paired for life. Every day the merry-go-round whirled to some melodic air that the boys were soon whistling, and which, after the Fair was closed, became the memorial voice of the ended carnival. A neighborhood flavor and character was developed in that one happy week, as it does in a town, as it did in fact

* Reprinted from *The Century Magazine* by permission of the author and of the editors.

in Indiana, which became a Fair with a spirit all its own.

A few other things must be added to the allegory. The Fair draws to its side the Muse of Memory. The old are present, those who have made the county, held office and waged the wars. The young sit on the grass with them at the lunch hour, and learn the tales of an earlier day. Queer characters, rural wits, men happy in drink, move amid the throngs, or stand about regaling each other with neighborhood news. By them may be standing bright-eyed youths with aptitudes for character and humor; and one of these may be a future James Whitcomb Riley feeding his genius on idiomatic turns of speech, odd sayings, and pictorial episode. In fact this very thing happened to Riley. Indiana was a happy County Fair to him, which he saw under unusual advantages, and with eyes peculiarly gifted for gathering in what was quaint and joyous and innocent in country and village life. His State and his people had developed a culture distinctive of the first pioneer days; they had a spirit of their own of which such politicians as Voorhees was one expression, and Lew Wallace, Charles Major, Meredith Nicholson and Booth Tarkington were another; and Riley in poetry was still another. Each had his individual voice; but the overtone was this Indiana, this beautiful State carved from the old Northwest, with its admixture of southern feelings and ways of life, and its alertness to business, means of prosperity, politics, learning, books and the romantic outlook, transmuted from adventure, land hunting, the log-cabin, and the happiness of primitive living.

Riley did not wish, even if he could have done so, to go behind the happy appearances of the Fair. He might mention at times that there were fights, that some one was "stobbed"; but he did not penetrate to dramatic reasons. The old fiddler was always lovable, never trivial or clownish. The pioneers were heroic figures of the land-clearing days, of the trials of the wilderness, of the log-cabin with its happy simplicities. If they were prudent and sagacious old land traders who made good use of their chances, that was not for poetical treatment. He showed the Fair and its personages in their holiday dress, gay and amiable, laughing and feasting; if grieving or wounded, tenderly attended, and if ludicrous, still lovable. At the Fair he found the Aunt Marys, the Orphant Annies, the philosophical cobblers, the happy crippled boys. He did not probe for secrets and for causes; for to him, diagnosis was a form of cruelty. He may have learned something from Hogarth, whose life he studied with diligence as a boy and young man. If so he applied what he admired in the work of that painter to character depiction of amiable humor and tender sympathy. He did not gather stories in Vanity Fair. Aunt Mary's faults, if any, remain unveiled; the crippled boy's father is dismissed with a humorous line. When he became famous he gave his creed to the younger Cawein for him to follow too, confiding in him the secret of the great truth which the poet sees and should guard from any touch too merely human. "Give nothing to it," he wrote, "but pure joy and beauty, and compassion and tenderness: a Christ-like laying on of hands on brows that ache, and wounds that bleed, fainting from pain, and worn and weary."

What Riley did in his more than twenty books, was to give pure joy and compassion and tenderness, and very often great beauty to the Fair that he knew, to the life of Indiana of the pioneer days down to the dawn of the twentieth century. He put Indiana as a place and a people in the memory of America, more thoroughly and more permanently than has been done by any other poet before or since his day for any other locality or people. This challenging comparison will evoke the claims of other poets: Whittier and Bret Harte, for example. But Riley created many more types than Whittier did; and he did it with greater variety and charm, and truer to the atmosphere of the fair. Riley was more of the people than Whittier was, for he had a richer *wanderjahre;* but if he was not more of the people, Riley's people were more to be with than Whittier's. The stocks of Scotch-Irish and English and Germans which poured into Indiana during the first half of the nineteenth century from the Carolinas, Virginia, Pennsylvania, from Tennessee and from Kentucky, were a more vital, human and picturesque people than the New Englanders with whom Whittier dealt, and who for two centuries before his day, had lived in a state of unchanged and arrested activity. Bret Harte succeeded with a few strokes of satiric genius, the "Heathen Chinee," in chief, perhaps; but all in all, Bret Harte merely made a report of the American adventurer who absorbed a Spanish colony into the body of American life. The California of Bret Harte is a land that came and went as a camp, pitched and taken down. The Indiana of Riley was the spread of a people who founded a State and populated it before he was born. His first vision of it showed him what it was at first, and what it had grown from without greatly changing its character.

By 1870 when Riley was about twenty years of age, and had begun to appraise the part of the world into which he had been born, and who its inhabitants were, a definite and coherent culture met his active imagination, though it was in fact the culture of the County Fair

which he saw. Around him were settled counties named
for Jefferson, Jackson, Washington, and for Putnam,
Clay, Fulton and DeKalb, all notables of the great days
of struggle and beginning in America. He was born in
Greenfield, Hancock County, not far from Indianapolis,
and something more than half way across the State from
Vincennes, which was the scene of the heroic exploits of
George Rogers Clark during the year of Valley Forge
in the Revolution. As things go in America, Indiana was
old when Riley began to know it. It was thoroughly
suited to his genius, and he loved it from his boyhood to
his last days. Nothing ever allured him from it, nor so
much as tempted him to leave it, even in the days of his
fame and when his life was still in the making. He was
happiest among its people, to whom he returned, glad as
a boy to be home again; once from England, which did
not attract him, and often from travels over America
when he became the greatest platform poet that our country has produced.

In the twenties of the nineteenth century, the father
and mother of Riley came into this land of Indiana. His
father, born in Pennsylvania in 1819, was a soldier and
afterward a lawyer of fame in his locality of Greenfield,
for his eloquence both at the bar and on the stump. His
mother was born in North Carolina, but as an infant
came to Indiana, where Reuben Riley, the father of
James Whitcomb, had preceded her by a few years. It
was not into poverty that the poet was born, but into
an atmosphere of moderate resources which was found
among the rural professional and trading people of that
day in Indiana and Illinois, and known in both States
much later than Riley's youth. Riley was blessed, as
Goethe was, by a mother of happy spirituality. She was a

woman of joyous heart, a nature of pure delight, in love
with the life about her in Indiana. Her father, John Marine, was a flatboat builder, a revivalist and maker of
rhymes, and a leader in the Methodist camp-meetings.
For the faith of Wesley had largely taken Indiana by
John Marine's day, and even as late as 1900, the Methodist church led all others in Indiana in the number of
its communicants. The vision of mystical transformation of heart, with sudden purity of spirit, in which the
convert felt and knew God, was in harmony with rolling
prairies, and grassy hills and valleys around the Wabash
and its tributaries. This religion under the influence of
nature, became a form of pantheism, which influenced
its children to tender pieties and hospitable fellowships,
spiritual emotions which entered into the receptive genius
of Riley.

Elizabeth Riley was a true child of this primitive country, and as she heard from her father and mother the
story of Lafayette's visit to Henry Clay, which was being paid while they bore her as an infant down the Ohio
and into Indiana, so later when she was growing to maturity on the banks of the Mississineva in Randolph
County, she talked face to face with Johnny Appleseed,
the happy and ragged planter of orchards, as he sat like a
crow on the rail-fence, and recounted his travels. Along
the way she gathered a fund of stories upon which she
nurtured the imagination of her son, and bequeathed to
him her passion for Nature, her genius of delight with
the hills and the streams, which entranced her from the
days when she was accustomed to climb to high spots in
order to have the happiness of looking at the blue smoke
curling from cabins in the pure air of the dawn. Gardens
and fruit-trees enthralled her, and one of her friends re-

ported that when she stood amid hollyhocks, she seemed to be in a spell. She saw oranges in the evening sky and red birds and goldfinches appeared to her fancy as flying flowers.

The love between Riley and his mother is one of the most beautiful in literary annals. Her very name, Elizabeth, was music to his ears. He repeated it in awe, lingering with rapture over its cadences. He treasured her stories of the old days, her accounts of tramps about the little streams of Randolph County and her descriptions of the Beautiful River, which were her words when speaking of the Mississineva. And thinking through the years of her blue eyes and bright hair, she came to him as his dream of the Golden Girl, the Good Muse, and it dawned upon him that it was his mission to write poems of Indiana and its people, and to dedicate to memory the pictures and the music which this mother of the woodlands had given to his receptive mind. She was the love and the support, and also the divinity, who arose to bless and guide his dreams, and to inspire his hands to the portraiture of the pure beauty which he instinctively sought, when almost with the suddenness of a mystical transformation of heart, he became conscious of his genius. Before his awakening, and by the time that Riley was ending his sign-painting days, she died, leaving him to say of her, that taking "the first step with the good thought, the second, with the good word, and the third, with the good deed, she entered Paradise." So runs the Persian parable.

As Riley had everything in the influence of his mother to stimulate his vision of the goodness in women, to see the Aunt Marys, the kind Lizy Ellens, the tender Malindys who talked so "lovin'" of their men "that's dead and gone," of the Katys who grieved for sons killed in the war, of the whole gallery of simple-hearted and lovable souls; so in his boyhood in Greenfield was his life shaped for that intimate depiction of childhood which he gave to those most moving poems of little orphan girls and of little crippled boys, and to the inarticulate sorrow which comes from the loss of a child—poems stamped with deathless fame. They are truer to the current speech of a people than any poems written by an American, for not only are they truer in idiom, but they are truer in cadence and in dramatic fidelity to the language that his people spoke.

In choosing incidents and situations from common life, Riley employed a "language really used by men," to quote Wordsworth's preface to his own "Lyrical Ballads"; and if he did not actually surpass Wordsworth in the results, he used the Indiana dialect with such perfection that we in America must find his work more understandable, as it is closer to our lives. If a vernacular is to be reproduced, grammatical errors and elisions must be reproduced; but more important still the ways of thinking and feeling of the particular people must be divined and portrayed. Riley did all of this. Because he knew and loved the children of Greenfield when he was a boy there, and the children of other places too, as he went on in life; because he knew the people of his land, his poems have in them the rise and fall of living voices; the whispers of wounded affection, of patient sorrow; and they carry of their own internal inspiration, the rhythm and the music of human passion.

In addition to the influence of his mother and the happy environment of his adolescence, his schooling was adequate, and not at fault. In the common schools he found poems in the McGuffey readers. At home he had Hawthorne's "Tanglewood Tales," which gave him the Greek and Roman myths; he had the "Lives of Eminent Painters and Sculptors," over which he pored again and again. He read Irving's sketches and histories, the "Alhambra" in particular; and "Oliver Twist" and much of Dickens. Later he went to the township library where he found the life of Boone, "Don Quixote," "Robinson Crusoe," and the "Arabian Nights" which became his constant delight. He read Tennyson and then Longfellow, whose poems never cease to hold his admiration and devotion. To the last he traveled with Longfellow's poems and kept them by him. All the while in these formative years there were Greenfield and his boy chums, the walks into the country to Deer Creek, to the old swimming holes, where he stored his mind with details of color, and with sounds of animals, birds and pastoral life. In the evenings he had an instruction and a delight which have probably passed away from American boyhood, since the movie has come to amuse the youth of the land. There was the cobbler shop of Tom Snow, the Greenfield Socrates, where the boys came to sit for long hours to listen to words of wisdom and tales of wonder. The movie does not take the place of the cobbler's, or the barber shop, for it furnishes character made, not the material of character to be made by the observer.

One opportunity for gathering stories and poetical material seems to have left Riley's interest unexcited. He did not haunt the court room and listen to the trial of cases. Rather he was to be found walking with his beloved school teacher, Lee O. Harris, who diverted him from dime novels to Scott and Longfellow. These two strolled through the sugar-orchards together, making up rhymes as they went. In this happy boyhood that Riley lived, he acquired the most minute knowledge of the farmer folk, their mode of life and speech; and noting the speech of the village people, he discerned the difference between their locutions, between farmers and traders, laborers and odd characters. It was Riley's extraordinary ear, which making fine distinctions, heard and stored the idiom of the Hoosiers, so that when he made a character say, "When the army broke out," meaning when the war broke out, he was able to meet criticism out of the East and to prove that his ear and hand had not gone astray. His ear was equally sensitive to the speech of children, the brogue of the Irish, the broken words of the German, and the humorous turns and slips of the negroes. "When de Folks is Gone" is not surpassed in our American production for keen portrayal of a certain type of negro, his way of talking and feeling. It is a perfect piece of dialect verse. So it was in these days of care-free life in Greenfield that he came to know the Griggsbys, and Squire Leachman, and numberless others whose portraits adorned his gallery at last.

Something happened now after the boyhood days in Greenfield, after his failure as a clerk in a store, after working for Tom Snow in the cobbler shop. He became a roving sign-painter, writing little rhymes as well, for the stores of the villages which he visited. This led to his traveling with Dr. McCrillus, who sold patent medicines. And at last he joined the Wizard Oil Company, which in those days sent a wagon and entertainers about the country, who barked on the village streets, and sold liniment to the rheumatics. Under a flaring light some member of the troupe told stories and heralded the magical therapy of the oil, and some one else sang a topical song and played the banjo or guitar. Riley was a rich acquisition to such an enterprise. He could not only sing songs, but he could compose them; he could not only tell stories, he could mimic character. In fact, so unusual were his histrionic gifts, that years later when Coquelin and Sir Henry Irving heard Riley recite character poems, they expressed the opinion that the stage had lost a star. And at last while strolling with these medicine-wagons, he learned to play the guitar, and he played and sang to the crowds, not in monotonous chords, but with variety out of his excellent musical ear. He was not destined, however, to be a musician, even though Ole Bull came into the field of his various inspirations. He heard the great violinist, then took up the violin, but having jammed his thumb in a door one day, he could not afterward manipulate the strings. One employment after another for his talents dropped away. He had failed miserably in mathematics at school. His father wanted him to be a lawyer, and put him to reading Blackstone, but his mind stumbled over dates, and over the tangle of feudal tenures. Meanwhile his signs in rhyme, his verses were going about from mouth to mouth, giving him a local fame, while he had been dreaming of being a musician, an actor, and at last an editor. And then, when twenty-six years of age, he sold a poem to "Hearth and Home," edited at the time by Ik Marvel. This fixed his ambition to be a poet, and to join a newspaper for a livelihood.

Launched now upon his career as a country editor, first on the "Greenfield News," later on the "Anderson Democrat," and later still on the "Indianapolis Journal," he poured forth an amazing quantity of verse in conventional English and in dialect. These early verses show a competent command of form and rhyme, of swinging meters harmoniously constructed. And in spite of alliterations like "glamour and glory," and of sentiment run to excess at times, some of his first lyrics have merit, but they

did not have marked individuality. They were not subtle—
their music was commonplace; but they were well turned.
Considering what his contemporaries were producing then,
and the susceptibility of a beginning poet to the fashions
of the hour, either to follow them successfully, or to vary
from them consciously, and in doing so to betray the line
of departure, it is easy to make allowance for these first
verses. One might say they were better in Riley's case,
than "Hours of Idleness" were in Byron's, while they
may be compared to each other in respect to conforming
skill and music. But on the other hand his purely topical
or newspaper verse which he was turning out as fast as a
reporter writes copy, is better than much of the newspaper
verse of this day. Indeed when he resorted to dialect, he
was highly successful from the first, for dialect always
gave him the most authentic command of his genius for
telling a story or drawing a character. In addition to these
more serious productions, he abandoned himself to quips
and cranks, to parodies and to literary pranks out of an
abounding vitality among which was the hoax of "Leon-
anie," palmed off on the Indiana public and the country
at large as a poem of Edgar Allan Poe, and which deceived both for a time. As a parodist Riley has never had
an equal in America.

He was now in the middle twenties and past, a youthful wonder, perhaps, to his intimates; certainly a writer
of fast growing reputation; but he was a talent of late
and slow growth. He was thirty-four when he published
his first book, "The Old Swimmin' Hole and 'Leven
More Poems"; but it contained "When the Frost Is on
the Punkin," first given to the world in 1882; besides
"Thoughts of the Discouraged Farmer," and "On the
Death of Little Mahala Ashcraft." The last, though included by Stedman in his American anthology of 1900, is

less successful than many of Riley's other poems in the same manner. The writing of verse is like the playing of the violin or the piano, in the particular that the same instrument and same piece of music in the hands of different virtuosos, yield entirely different results in point of manner, emphasis, everything that makes an interpretation. The physical and psychical organization of the player make the difference. And similarly iambics or anapests reduced to the same meter in the hands of different poets make a different music. Iambic pentameter when used by Tennyson does not sound like the iambic pentameter of Swinburne or Bryant; any more than their voices resembled each other's. It is the way the stops are played, the pauses made, the stresses employed; it is the manner of varying the use of other kinds of feet that produce the total result. All of these things are to be accounted for on the basis of the spiritual diaphragm of the poet; and that is his genius. The characteristic voice of the poet, in consequence, will sound in everything he writes, no matter what rhythm or what meter he uses. His inner ear will inevitably select the time and the tone best suited to it; and these will adapt themselves to the landscape he loves and the spiritual flavor of the people he understands, so subtle is the penetration of musical words. Now Riley wrote quatrains and sonnets, even in dialect; he used in fact a good many verse schemes; but the most characteristic expression of his spiritual timber was in this rhythm, and the modifications which he made of it:

"When the frost is on the punkin and the fodder's in the shock."

This is ascending rhythm, suited to narrative; and with its anapestic feet, and four stresses, remains fast, even under the colloquial drawl with which it must be spoken.

It was a measure peculiarly adapted to Riley's emotional pulsations, and therefore to the ends of his lyrical and dramatic genius. Whenever he drew portraits of horse-traders, rural philosophers, returned wanderers, beloved neighbors, old men and farmer folk, he used it. The fact that he employed it in his first poem of note is in itself, significant, and shows how his spirit guided his hand. It was also adapted in its exact beat, or in modification, to his idealization of the "airly days," to that emotional reverie through which he saw color and light, shadows and forms, and the descriptive details of his beloved Indiana.

Before Riley published his first book he had opened a correspondence with Trowbridge, who was not so gracious to him as Longfellow was, to whom he sent some poems for criticism as early as 1876. Longfellow wrote him that his poems showed "the true poetic faculty and insight," but that he could not enter into a minute discussion of their merits. Yet Longfellow was particular enough to say that Riley had used the word "prone" when he meant "supine." When Riley published "The Old Swimmin' Hole and 'Leven More Poems" Longfellow was dead, the year being 1883 in which Browning gave to the world "Jocoseria," which contained "Wanting is—what?" "Never the Time and the Place," and "Ferishtah's Fancies"; and to Browning in Italy, among other celebrities of the day, Riley sent his book. What Browning thought of these dramatis personæ of Indiana, we are denied the pleasure of knowing. He seems not to have acknowledged the receipt of the book, if in fact it reached him. But perhaps the impassable gulf lying between *Evelyn Hope* and little *Mahala Ashcraft* put it beyond Browning to greet the new bard.

Now Riley's name began to rise in the world, and soon

the lecture platform called to him. He had the problem of
making a livelihood, and at first his books did not bring
a great deal of money. But there was prosperity ahead in
reciting poems, and at first there was the delight of delighted audiences, and he knew his mimetic gifts from the
old days of the medicine wagon. He quickly won great
favor as a lecture star, and later money too, after he had
extricated himself from an improvident contract, made at
the beginning when he was oblivious of business considerations, and was thinking of the unusual career that was
opening for him. Finally when he associated himself with
Nye, with whom his friendship was intimate and affectionate to the last, America saw a combination of platform talent better than anything that had preceded it, and
which has not been duplicated to this day. He had wonderful mastery over such poems as "The Happy Little
Cripple," "Griggsby's Station," and "Little Orphant Annie." It was an unforgettable experience to hear him render them. Audiences sat spellbound, and then gave themselves to laughter and the drying of eyes. And with his
recitations over the country, and many books successively
appearing, and with his name very much in the magazines
of New York, many honors and friends came to him. Degrees were bestowed upon him; he was elected to membership in learned societies. Lowell hailed him as a true
poet; Howells and Mark Twain, Joel Chandler Harris and
Charles A. Dana acclaimed him; many of the great of that
day became his devoted admirers and correspondents. He
bore his honors with dignity approaching humility; for he
could scarcely see himself, once the sign-painter and roving medicine vender and maker of little rhymes, as the
celebrity now deserving such attention. But he did not get
the idea that his success entitled him to leave Indiana, and
to try for something more in keeping with his new life in

Boston or New York. He never lost perspective upon himself. After all the applause of the country, the great dinners where he sat with other notables, the tributes paid him in oratory and in verse and prose, his greatest honor, as he deemed it, was when the governor of Indiana appointed Riley's birthday anniversary a State holiday, and he rode through the streets of Indianapolis, hailed by the school children whom he loved with such perfect integrity of heart.

This is a hurried outline of his career. He lived a busy and intense life, and as a poet and a reciter of poems his days were crowded. In his fame he was much sought, and often had to steal away to secluded and unknown places, to write.

At about sixty years of age, ill health came to him, due as much or more to the exhaustion of the lecture platform as anything else. Any one who reads of Riley's tours of the country, particularly if he has ever gone through the ordeal of catching trains, greeting people, being dined and keeping irregular hours, will believe that these labors more than anything else took away his strength, and shortened his life to something less than the allotted three score years and ten.

In classifying Riley's total output, making allowance first for the fact that many of his poems belong in two or more columns, for example that many of his child-poems are also dialect poems, it will be found that he wrote 223 poems about or for children; 141 poems of nature; 139 love poems; 136 humorous poems in dialect; 119 poems of tribute or for occasions; 77 poems of reflection; 74 narrative or dramatic poems; 70 poems of bereavement; 60 poems of backward turning fancy to old days; 40 poems on the various holidays; 25 on friendship and 22 on patriotism. The love poems have tenderness; a few ap-

proach to a certain passion, but they are not really passionate. They belong to the chivalric days of America
when it was believed that women were better than men—
to the days of the angelic woman. At the first he wrote a
good many poems to inamoratas, but they are romantically
mild. In 1875 he published "An Old Sweetheart of Mine":

> As one who cons at evening o'er an album all alone,
> And muses on the faces of the friends that he has known;
> So I turn the leaves of fancy, till in shadowy design,
> I find the smiling features of an old sweetheart of mine.

To quote this and drop the subject would be unfair to
Riley. He did vastly better than this over and over again.
In 1885, for example, he wrote a sonnet entitled "When
She Comes Home," a beautiful celebration of domestic
reunion after absence. In the same key of intensity is "The
Wife Blessed," a lyric of exquisite refinement which sings
marital happiness. But of passion that overwhelms with
disaster and suffering, but with ecstasy too, he wrote no
line. Men and women separated by tragic circumstances,
trusting souls reduced by faithlessness to misery, could
not have escaped his observation. And for dramatizing
such souls he had before him Byron and Browning; yet
Riley held to his creed of "laying Christlike hands on
brows that ache and wounds that bleed." That creed belonged to the nature of the man who was enraptured of
hollyhocks and old-fashioned roses, but whom the beauty
of woman led neither to memorable romance nor to matrimony.

His mild and chivalrous treatment of romantic love
might be analyzed until its causes were traced to their
source; but it suffices here to mention the fact alone.
Neither Longfellow nor the poetical fashions of his day

would have held him to the course he pursued if it had been in him to follow another. And similarly Hogarth, whom he read about so diligently in youth, left him uninfluenced for the contemplation and report of Hogarthian types, men or women, who were so much before his eyes in Indiana, look where he would to avoid seeing them. He took note of raggedy men, rural loafers at the country store, tramps, and such types, but he depicted them lightly and humorously; their deeper tragedies he never touched. He had vivid powers of character-drawing; but had he had capacity for more searching drama, which he did not have, the brake which he really put on his genius, and the blinders which he fastened over his eyes, kept him from portraying other than the rural mirth and the innocent sorrows of the Fair.

Looked at another way, his work divides itself between poems written in conventional English and in a variety of measures; and poems written in dialect, but chiefly in the Hoosier dialect. When he wrote sonnets and lyrics in the traditional manner of the great English poetry he spoke for himself. When he wrote in dialect his characters spoke. They were a more authentic voice of his genius than his own voice was. Though his sonnets at their best were as effectual as those his American contemporaries produced, they lacked the unified condensation, the crystal summation which makes a sonnet a thing of memorable perfection. To enforce this point comparison may be made between his sonnet on a cricket and Keats's. Keats was a great master of the sonnet, to be sure; but the fact that Riley was not can be proved by placing their sonnets side by side. Stepping to a lower level of comparison, Riley's lyrics at their best are not inferior, and perhaps they are not equalled by those of any American poet of his day; and this is true in spite of the fact that sometimes only

Riley's childlike sincerity saves them from over tenderness, from the unrestraint which blinds sympathy to reality.

At times he attempted work that in no way belonged to him, such as "The Flying Islands of the Night." Indeed many of his poems in standard English give the impression of Aunt Mary dressed for some great occasion, and who looks odd to us in her silk gown, too fine and yet not fine enough. It may have been that the critical attacks made upon him for the use of dialect caused him to show the world what he could do in the Keats, Longfellow or Swinburne manner. But he was sustained in many ways for his use of dialect, by the example of Burns for one thing, and Tennyson for that matter. And certainly when Lowell and Howells called his successes in dialect indisputable poetry, he was justified in heeding them more than his critics, who were nothing but poetical scribes at best. Lastly he must have known that in this field of poetry he was a master, and one of the few conspicuous masters of the world. "Out to Old Aunt Mary's," "Griggsby's Station," and "Little Orphant Annie," "Jim," and "The Happy Little Cripple," are not surpassed for pathos in the English language; and they have great beauty—the beauty of the Indiana hills and fields, of hollyhocks and yellow roses, and the song of the robin, in no wise impugned by a preference for the majesty of mountains or the ecstasy of the skylark.

But his work of incomparable merit, of unmatched excellence, was in the field of childhood delineation. Here he has no equal, and no one to be mentioned in the same breath with him. Here he was pure genius. The work of other poets in this domain is artificial compared to Riley's. It is but tin toys prettily made and brightly painted and varnished when placed by the side of Riley's flesh and blood creations, native to a spot and a life of America—

now vanished! His success with poems of children was largely due to the fact that he really loved them, and by reason of his child-like heart entered into their secrets. For humor one will look far to find anything in verse to excel "A Liz Town Humorist," "Joney," "Doc Sifers," "An Idiot," "Jap Miller," "Thoughts on the Late War," "The Raggedy Man," "Our Hired Girl," "Some Scattering Remarks of Bub," "Rubáiyat of Doc Sifers," "His Pa's Romance," and many besides these. They make a whole gallery of American types, too priceless ever to be lost. They are distinctively our own.

Satire and irony do not conduce to "pure joy and beauty and compassion"; but they were not among Riley's gifts. Neither did the experiences of his life, his early conditioning prepare him to use them. Saving a romantic pining for the "airly days," America suited and pleased him. The religious atmosphere around him gave him no disturbance; the course of the country politically met his approval. He venerated such figures as McKinley and Harrison who was one of the poet's friends and admirers. His man with the hoe owned a farm; there was no emptiness of the ages in his face, but it was lighted with smiles, and the jaw was not let down and not brutal; it was square and strong and told of the forests which had been felled, and the fields which had been cultivated. Riley's fallen in the Philippines had served the country patriotically, and they had joined the son of Katy, with whom Riley could sympathize "as she reads all his letters over, writ from the war,"—from the camp at Gettysburg. The liberty that Whitman chanted did not interest Riley; and if he may be classed with Burns as a singer of the wildwoods and of simple hearts, he has no part with the saturnine Scotchman when he flamed forth with such searing satire upon hypocrisy, privilege and cant. Riley lived

and wrought in what might be termed the Old Gold Age
of American life; and his best work was done when he
was about fifty, and the twentieth century dawned. When
he was thirty-seven he sang:

> Tell me a tale of the timberlands,
> And the old time pioneers—
> Somepin a pore man understands
> With his feelin's well as ears.

To the last he looked back wistfully at a halcyon past, as
if, after all, his present was not everything he made himself believe it was. Well for him that he did not see much
of the Age of Steel, which had begun to build factories
and blasts, at the very gates of the County Fair!

SHERIDAN—WHOM THE GODS LOVED *

By J. Brooks Atkinson

I

Upon Richard Brinsley Sheridan the gods let themselves go with a jaunty, ironic flourish. They made him fascinating; they made him a study in superlatives. What other figure in all English literature can match him for sheer volatility? For a few maddening seconds Sheridan danced on the icy pinnacle of Cosmopolis. Of face and figure he was so beautiful that his eldest sister was never unmindful of "the glow of health, his eyes,—the finest in the world, —and soft as a tender and affectionate heart could render them." Of personality he was so attractive, at once so brilliant and charming, that even men could feel melancholy when he went away. "After you had been gone an hour," wrote his friend J. Richardson, "I got moped damnably." Before his twenty-second birthday he had fought two duels with a middle-aged scoundrel over a captivating young singer, the most beautiful of her day, and married her while his closest friend and a hundred others were wooing her with ardent verses. At twenty-six he had written two of the only three comedies that have survived on our stage since the time of Shakespeare. Ten years later he delivered in Parliament a speech epochal in English statesmanship. Yet when he was dying at the age of

* Reprinted from *The North American Review* by permission of the author and of the editors.

363

sixty-five, alienated from some of his friends and un-
sought by most others, only the stubborn persistence of his
physician prevented the bailiff from arresting him in his
sick-bed and carrying him off in the blankets to the spunging-house. Nor was this all the ignominy of his declining
days. When he was to be buried his wife was so fearful
(perhaps needlessly) lest he might be snubbed at his funeral that she wrote personal letters to many of the most
distinguished, beseeching them to come. Byron wrote in
his diary: "He has written the best comedy (*School for
Scandal*), the best opera (*The Duenna*—in my mind far
before that St. Giles's lampoon, *The Beggar's Opera*),
the best farce (*The Critic*—it is only too good for an
after-piece), and the best address (*Monologue on Garrick*),—and, to crown all, delivered the very best oration
(the famous Begum speech) ever conceived or heard in
this country." At the moment when Byron was writing
this panegyric, Sheridan was, as the result of his own indolence, profligacy and helplessness, afflicted by distresses
from which he never recovered. One of his most lurid
biographers, many of whom sprang gratuitously to the
maw of the press the instant Thomas Moore's faithful
study had appeared, asserts that on the day of the funeral
procession a stranger squirmed into the house of mourning on the pretext of viewing Sheridan's corpse, touched
the face with his bailiff's wand when the coffin was
opened, and arrested the corpse "in the king's name" for
a debt of £500! Well, perhaps and perhaps.

II

Although the Sheridan claquers were busy soon after
his death, puffing their hero into a superman, they did not
succeed. That nimble hack Earle, who wrote a colorful
and sometimes specious book on Sheridan and signed him-

self "Octogenarian," hotly resisted the assertion that
Sheridan was no scholar. Alas! his learning seemed all too
feeble beyond the polite equipment of fashionable chaps of
the day. He who wrote *The Rivals* at twenty-two was
pronounced an "impenetrable dunce" by his Dublin schoolmaster. At Harrow, Dr. Parr, famous in his day and
long after as a schoolmaster, found Sheridan indolent,
shiftless and much too idle for learning. Such scholarship
as he had, Sichel avows in an excellent biography, was
"stealthy." Doubtless it was not family penury alone
which kept this wit from essaying the university. He was
disgusted by the spectacle of ponderous learning, such as
that of Dr. Johnson, whom he called "a monster with a
leaden eye and lumbered brain of Greek and Latin lore."
A man of learning or profound respect for learning would
not have been duped, even on the recommendation of Por-
son and Malone, into buying a Shakesperean forgery
(Ireland's *Vortigern and Rowena*) and setting it on the
stage of his theatre as genuine Elizabethan tragedy. Although Boswell obsequiously kissed the sacred pages of
this hoax and declared he could now die happy, the skeptical audience detected the false ring of such base metal on
the first night. Would Garrick have been so obtuse? Especially in youth and even down to the last of his life Sheridan seemed ignorant of the literary grace of spelling; he
wrote *whether* as *wether*, *where* as *were*, *which* as *wich*,
and *thing* as *think*, and the double *s* and *m* were too frequently single. For him the gods had not emptied their
chest marked "Scholarship."

But whom the gods love need not be learned. Of what
avail is heavy-eyed scholarship against the insinuating,
mordant subtleties of Lady Sneerwell and Sir Benjamin
Backbite? Even at the moment when he was bemoaning
Sheridan's impatience with his studies, Dr. Parr glowed

over the youth's attractive personality. And so, indeed, it
was. "I admired—I almost adored him," wrote his sister:
"I would most willingly have sacrificed my life for him."
A stripling of twenty-one, he captured the heart of Elizabeth Linly, "Maid of Bath," as the enthusiastic called her,
when she was enjoying with the naïveté of a girl of seventeen the hot suits of Nathaniel Halhed, Charles Sheridan,
Mr. Long, and Captain Matthews, villain of her youth,
and the admiration of half of all England's young men.
It was said that when this paragon of loveliness gave concerts at Oxford the students could scarcely breathe, such
was the effect upon them of her charm of face and manner,
and sweetness of voice. "I am petrified," said Halhed in
describing her concert. Once she had refused Sheridan;
once he had given her up and begged only that he might
be forever her friend, as the others had not. Yet it was he,
unknown in Bath save for a clever skit or two and as the
son of a maundering, pedantic actor and elocution teacher,
who skilfully uncovered the foul object of Captain Matthews's suit, whisked Miss Linly off to a French convent
more secretly and expeditiously than he did anything else
as long as he lived, challenged Captain Matthews in a
London coffee-house (after the party had been scared
away from Hyde Park), broke though the captain's guard
and broke his sword; and fought him again in a desperate
duel at Kingsdown where the impetuous youth nearly lost
his life. "My husband, my husband!" cried "Lizzy" instinctively when the startling news reached her ears as she
was returning to Bath in a coach; and thus at the moment
which a Scott or a Bulwer-Lytton would have chosen, she
betrayed the secret of her marriage to him in France.

Not learning but youth succeeds in the writing of artificial comedy. Congreve wrote his best before he was
twenty-five. Farquhar wrote *The Constant Couple* at

twenty-two, and everything else before he was thirty. And Sheridan was no sooner settled down in London as the fortunate and nearly famous youth upon whom Miss Linly had smiled than he, too, succeeded with comedy. Necessity drove him to the task. Lucky for them that the doddering old Mr. Long, rejected by "Lizzy" some time previous, had endowed her with £3000, half of which she still retained; for Sheridan had no money of his own, and despite the protest of musical London he would not let her sing again in public. "He resolved wisely and nobly, to be sure," declared Dr. Johnson when Boswell plied him on that subject which was then the tittle-tattle of London. "He is a brave man. Would not a gentleman be disgraced by having his wife sing publicly for hire? No, Sir, there can be no doubt here. I know not if I should not *prepare* myself for a public singer, as readily as let my wife be one." Their dwindling fortunes Sheridan reëstablished within a year by the production of *The Rivals* at Covent Garden, which soon set the town agog and was played by other companies in Bath and Liverpool. The celebrity which surrounded the marriage of so well-loved a singer as Miss Linly (celebrated by the irrepressible Foote in *A Trip to Calais* and *The Maid of Bath*) was now augmented by the fulgurant genius of her husband. They were invited to the great houses—even by so snobbish a woman as the Duchess of Richmond—and their life became one of unending gaiety. Great people came to their snug abode; the young people were rare entertainers; Charles Fox said some years later, "An evening at Sheridan's is worth a week's waiting for." Yet Sheridan did not fritter away his time; he got up at sunrise, or worked with light and a glass of port after the guests had departed towards midnight. Within the next four years he squeezed into this glamorous life the writing of a rough-and-ready

farce, a comic opera which ran twelve nights longer than
the formidable (and much more substantial) *Beggar's
Opera,* a stop-gap and fairly emasculate version of Vanbrugh's licentious *Relapse,* and crowned his career in the
theatre with *The School for Scandal,* which filled the
empty coffers of his Drury Lane Theatre. Once again two
years later his wit was keen enough for *The Critic,* which
had a long showing in the theatre, although a contemporary critic observed it was "a species of dramatic entertainment entirely critical, and very little relished or understood by the British public in general." But all the
jests and sardonic gibes of that merry farce he had forgotten when he essayed the phlegmatic and swollen *Pizarro* twenty years afterwards. An anonymous critique of
this play printed at Manchester in 1799 described it as

> Five *ling'ring* acts stuff'd full of stage *devices,*
> Five acts of pantomime—at *playhouse prices!!!*

His day in the theatre was resplendent with the wit which
the gods had given him. It soon ran out. Lamb termed *Pizarro* a "procession of verbiage stalking on the stage."
Lamb had seen *The School for Scandal* (on complimen-
tary tickets) when Palmer was acting Joseph Surface.

III

Wit never ran so high in England as it did in Sheridan's society. Wit was highly esteemed and assiduously
cultivated in the days of Addison, of Vanbrugh and the
writers of the drama of sensibility, of Lady Mary Wort-
ley Montague and Mrs. Aphra Behn; but at best it was
categorical, and at worst obscene. In Sheridan it was
spontaneous, nimble and irrepressible. It was, moreover,
spotlessly pure; doubtful stories which were not so coarse
as to offend the ears of women were sometimes disagree-

able to him, and at his wife's request were not repeated in
his presence. His *bon mots* fill an ample volume compiled
by an enthusiastic defender and hack. His house was a
whirl of gaiety and high spirits where the most brilliant
English society came with high expectations that were
well gratified in the give-and-take of jest and rebounding
humor. Nor was Sheridan always eclectic in the quality
of his humor; on occasion he descended to the obvious-
ness of practical jokes or horseplay. Bacchus had a hand in
his creation; the slapstick buffoonery of Scarron and Rabelais was there. At one time, having covered the floor of
a dark passage with plates and dishes packed close together, Sheridan provoked his friend Tickell into giving
chase. Having left a path for his own escape he ran
through easily, but Tickell crashed on the china and was
cut in several places. Again, during a house party near
Osterly (General Burgoyne was among the guests) Sheridan proposed that a certain divine who was visiting them
should deliver the sermon next Sunday in the local parish. The clergyman's objection that he had no sermon
Sheridan met by writing one himself on the *Abuse of
Riches*. The clergyman delivered it in his best pulpit
style; but several months later to his undying chagrin he
discovered that it was throughout a personal attack upon
a rich member of the parish, and a friend, who was just
then unpopular for his treatment of the poor. Riding
through the streets of London one day in a coach for
which he could not pay the hire, Sheridan saw his argu-
mentative friend Richardson on the street and invited him
inside. Whereupon Sheridan lost no time in engaging him
in conversation on a subject which easily piqued Richardson. At the proper moment Sheridan declared he could
not think of staying in the coach with a person who could
use such vile language, got down into the street and, while

Richardson shouted heated last words through the glass,
left him responsible for the heavy fare. In the heyday of
his membership in Parliament Sheridan spent reckless and
hilarious evenings at Brookes's famous club in St. James
Street, at the "Bedford" in Covent Garden, and was a
member of a sportive, informal club which met at the Sal-
utation Tavern kept by Dame Butler in an alley off Covent Garden. There he revelled none too delicately with
the Prince of Wales, Charles Howard, Earl of Surrey and
later Duke of Norfolk, Selwyn, Hare and Charles Fox;
and there the flowing bowl, upon which Sheridan ever
depended as writer and speaker, bubbled merrily all the
night through. Even when he was too old for such frisk-
ing he accompanied the Prince and the Earl incognito in
the darkness of early morning on several mad quests
through the pitch-black streets; and once engaged in a
battle with thugs and ruffians in the Brown Bear Tavern,
when all three were arrested by the watch.

IV

It suited Sheridan's whim, as it suited Hugo's vanity,
to give out that his rarest works were tossed off rapidly
from a surcharged brain. A touch of youthful bravado
made his personality sprightly. "How comes it to pass that
you are ever in appearance indolent without being really
so?" asked Ker. In actual fact he sweated at his tasks, perhaps less earnestly than Goldsmith and less hypercritically
than Flaubert. He did not pitch his gibes into the air, as
Gautier pitched his sentences, trusting that like cats they
would come down on all four feet. With the actual writing of *The School for Scandal* he was characteristically
indolent. The comedy went into rehearsal before he had
finished writing it. He had, so the story runs, one rough
draft of the last five scenes scribbled on detached pieces of

paper. Of all the preceding scenes there were numerous transcriptions, interlined and revised. On the last sheet of all, which still exists as no doubt Sheridan despatched it to the copyists, are the words: "Finished at last, thank God! R. B. SHERIDAN"; to which a relieved prompter appended: "Amen! W. HOPKINS." One of his contemporaries asserted that when Sheridan was writing *The Critic* and the last scenes of the piece did not come, he was tricked into a room in the theatre one evening by King and Ford, and locked there with wine and sandwiches until he finished the farce. Another declares that the last act of *Pizarro* was written on the evening of the first performance while the first four were being given behind the footlights. No doubt that stretches the truth; one so brilliant as Sheridan lends credence to the most colorful stories. Sheridan was as a rule a far-seeing workman. Apparently he had *The School for Scandal* in mind many years before he wrote it. Four years or so earlier he had worked at a comedy entitled *The Slanderers,* in which Lady Sneerwell appears, as well as much of the dialogue to be found in *The School for Scandal.* Subsequently he sketched another comedy to revolve about Sir Peter and Lady Teazle. Where and how he joined the two preliminary comedies into *The School for Scandal* is quite apparent now in the change of tone between the second and third acts. He labored over his most glittering remarks and jests. The paradoxical statement of Lady Teazle to Joseph Surface: "So you would have me sin in my own defence, and part with my own virtue to preserve my reputation," exists in several of Sheridan's papers as if he had been whipping it into form for use at the right moment. He watched his moments; he would wait through most of a social evening to drop a brilliant joke at the most effective instant. In preparing his speeches, often in

bed when it was supposed that he was sleeping, he made
note of the places for appropriate gestures, had the whole
speech in mind before he began it, and worked up the decorative passages to a fine polish. On the famous Begum
speech, which Burke characterized as "the most astonishing piece of eloquence, argument and wit united of which
there is any record or tradition," Sheridan, his wife, and
most of his family labored feverishly for several days.

V

But that cruel perversion of divine prerogatives by
which he was deprived of a balance wheel became at
length his undoing. Sheridan touched life in many places;
simultaneously he wrote plays, managed a theatre, debated
in Parliament, trafficked with statesmen and agreeable fellows most of the night, enlivened the ballroom. But over
the mundane affairs of life he had no vestige of control.
William Smyth, tutor to Sheridan's son and later a poet
of some distinction, has reported Sheridan's total absence
of self-control "a torment" to those around him. While
"Lizzy" was still alive, conscious alike of his genius and
its limitations, and matching his ardent affection for her
with an unvarying affection for him, he was kept in some
sort of order. If he had not already planted deep the seeds
of his final ruin, one might count her untimely death as
the cause. His second marriage was not stimulating; at
times it irritated them both. It is said that for thirty years
Sheridan earned an average of £15,000, and spent £10,000
of it on interest, lawsuits costs and judgments. To him,
and to chaps like him, a debt delayed was a debt half-paid.
To this fellow wrestling reluctantly with the mechanics of
living belongs the distinction of offering a promissory
note to a highwayman. "Thank God, that's settled!" he

once exclaimed, handing over an I. O. U. for £200 to a
friend from whom he had just borrowed that sum. He
was perennially "money-bound." And when his pockets
were filled they soon became flat again. So little order did
he have in his debts and credits that a committee of
friends, whom he once persuaded to run through his affairs to discover just how much he owed, soon gave up
the task in despair; and when he died he fancied he owed
four times as much as he did. He found it more convenient to pay a debt twice rather than produce proof that he
had already paid it. While traveling on the highways in
a coach he frequently found himself penniless, and obliged
to summon a usurer to pay his tavern fees. His servants
were irregularly paid, and often had no money at their
disposal for household expenses. He gave generously to
friends and relatives when they could find him. Being in a
thousand places during the course of the day, he could
never be found by those who wanted him. He took his
breakfast in bed while he composed his speeches, dressed
hastily, and then with a mad rush shot from his room and
the house at noon-time; he was not to be found again until midnight. Those who required his attention lined up
at the door; if they did not catch him as he left he was
free for the day—and by so much the richer. He main-
tained three expensive establishments at one time—one
at Wanstead, where his son resided with his tutor; another
at Isleworth; and the third, his town-house, in Jermyn
Street. He raised enormous sums of money from mysterious sources, and seldom at advantageous rates. Befuddled by wine he made reckless bets at the clubs:

25th March, 1793.—Mr. S. bet Mr. Hardy one hundred
guineas, that the 3 per cent. consols are as high this day twelve-
month as at the date thereof.

Mr. S. bets Gen. Tarleton one hundred guineas to fifty guineas, that Mr. Pitt is first Lord of the Treasury on the 28th of May, 1795,—Mr. S. bets Mr. St. A. St. John fifteen guineas to five guineas, ditto.

On his inability to pay a bet of 500 guineas he once wrote the following confession: "At the same time that I regret your being put to any inconvenience by this delay, I cannot help reverting to the circumstance which perhaps misled me into the expectation that you would not unwillingly allow me any reasonable time I might want for the payment of the bet. The circumstance I mean, however discreditable the plea, is the total inebriety of some of the party, particularly of myself, when I made this preposterous bet."

VI

Yet his misfortunes were not always the result of his helplessness in the world. It was no fault of his that the Drury Lane Theatre, antiquated and decayed, had to be torn down in 1792, that the new one was long delayed by various negotiations and obstacles, cost £75,000 more than the architect estimated, and all that while the company was playing at enormous expense first at the Opera House and later at the Haymarket. Surely it was no fault of his that seventeen years later this theatre, still encumbered with notes and mortgages, burned to the ground. Sheridan was at the House of Commons that evening, listening to the talk of the conduct of the war in Spain, when the house was suddenly illuminated by a blaze of light as the flames leaped from the roof of his theatre. When a motion was made to adjourn, Sheridan said "Whatever might be the extent of the private calamity, he hoped it would not interfere with the public business of the country." Later he was discovered at the "Bedford," watching the flames and sipping a glass of wine. To a friend's ob-

servation that he received so vast a calamity with equa-
nimity, he replied: "Surely a man may be allowed to take
a glass of wine at his own fireside." Perhaps he did not
grasp the full importance of this disaster. Little could he
foretell exactly what it meant. For when a committee was
formed at his suggestion to raise money for the sale of
public shares for a new theater, Sheridan, who had main-
tained the Drury Lane at the standard set by Garrick and
made its walls echo again and again with salvos of unmatched wit, was gradually crowded out by a turncoat
manager. To Samuel Whitbred, M. P. (who inherited the
Thrales' brewery), he entrusted the business of a new theatre. For his moiety of the property Sheridan eventually
received the generous sum of £28,000. But while he was
hard pressed on every side, and begged for an advance of
£2,000 to conduct an election, Whitbread stubbornly invoked one technicality after another and delayed. With
merciless fidelity to the facts he reminded Sheridan that
he was to have "no concern or connection, of any kind
whatever, with the new undertaking." "You are in no
way answerable if a bad Theatre is built," he wrote; "it is
not you who built it; and if we come to the *strict right* of
the thing, you have *no business to interfere.* . . . Will
you but *stand aloof,* and everything will go smooth."

VII

Forced out of the theatre and Parliament, the remaining
few months of Sheridan's life were black melancholy. Distresses increased. Executions followed close on the heels of
writs. He once sobbed out a night in a spunging-house.
He sold the books from his library, the silver cup once
presented to him by his constituency; and like Charles
Surface parted with his pictures—four Gainsboroughs and
a Morland; and the Reynolds portrait of "Lizzy" Linly

went out of his possession. He fell a victim to disease. "I am absolutely undone and broken-hearted," he wrote to a friend less than two months before he died. The usurers no longer flocked around him. For some time his wife had been reduced to beseeching the treasurer of the Drury Lane for petty sums—"four pounds for washing house linen," and the like. When the bitterness of his distress got about town, somewhat belatedly, Vaughan, Rogers and Lord Holland came willingly to his assistance. An anonymous contributor to *The Morning Post* called for immediate aid: "Prefer ministering in the chamber of sickness to mustering at 'The splendid sorrows that adorn the hearse'; I say, *Life* and *Succor* against Westminster Abbey and a Funeral!" That nearly became the case. Sheridan died soon afterwards. Nobility attended his splendid funeral and solemnly, almost ironically, buried him in the Abbey. Contrasting Sheridan's dying penury and the magnificence of his funeral, a French journal said: "France is the place for a man of letters to live in, and England the place for him to die in." Thus the gods received back the tarnished spirit of the man whom they had so generously endowed. Other English men of letters have died as miserably. But none such had drunk so deep of the intoxicating draft of fame; in the ears of none had rung such deafening applause; none had played on many instruments so resourcefully. That platitudinous epitaph, "He touched nothing that he did not adorn," may be applied with full truth to Sheridan. He did many things, and brilliantly. Yet where the world touched him it did not adorn.

SHAKESPEARE'S QUEEN *

By Tucker Brooke

THE Mayor of London and his brethren of the corporation and forty of the chief citizens were commanded to be at the christening, on the tenth of September, 1533. "Upon which day"—so the old chronicler Holinshed informs us in one of his most picturesque accounts—"the Mayor, Sir Stephen Peacock, in a gown of crimson velvet with his collar of S's, and all the aldermen in scarlet with collars and chains, and all the council of the city with them, took their barge at one of the clock; and the citizens had another barge; and so rowed to Greenwich, where were many lords, knights, and gentlemen assembled. All the walls between the King's palace and the Friars' were hanged with arras, and all the way strewed with green rushes. The Friars' church was also hanged with rich arras: the font was of silver, and stood in the midst of the church three steps high, which was covered with a fine cloth; and divers gentlemen, *with aprons and towels around their necks,* gave attendance about it, that no filth should come to the font. . . . Between the choir and body of the church was a close place with a pan of fire, to make the Child ready in. When all these things were ordered, the Child was brought to the hall, and then every man set forward: first the citizens, two and two; then gentlemen, esquires, and chaplains; next after them the

* Reprinted from *The Yale Review* by permission of the author and of the editors.

377

aldermen, and the Mayor alone; and next the King's
Council; then the King's Chapel in copes; then barons,
bishops, earls, the Earl of Essex bearing the covered ba-
sins, gilt; after him the Marquess of Exeter with a taper
of virgin wax; next him the Marquess Dorset, bearing the
salt; behind him the Lady Mary of Norfolk, bearing the
chrism, which was very rich of pearl and stone.

"The old Duchess of Norfolk bare the Child in a mantle
of purple velvet, with a long train furred with ermine.
The Duke of Norfolk with his marshal's rod went on the
right hand of the said Duchess, and the Duke of Suffolk
on the left hand. . . . When the Child was come to the
church door, the Bishop of London met it, with divers
bishops and abbots mitred, and began the observances of
the sacrament. The godfather was Lord Thomas [Cran-
mer], Archbishop of Canterbury; the godmothers were
the old Duchess of Norfolk and old Marchioness of Dorset, widows: and the Child was named ELIZABETH.
And after that all things were done at the church door,
the Child was brought to the font and christened; and
that done, Garter, chief king of arms, cried aloud: 'God
of his infinite goodness send prosperous life and long to
the high and mighty Princess of England, ELIZA-
BETH!'

"And then the trumpets blew. Then the Child was
brought up to the altar, and gospel said over it. After
that immediately the Archbishop of Canterbury confirmed
it, the Marchioness of Exeter being godmother. . . .Then
was brought in wafers, confects, and ipocras in such
plenty that every man had as much as he would desire:
then they set forward"—but somewhat less steadily, it
may be, than before.

By this time, we learn with relief, the child had been

restored to the seemlier precincts of the nursery, where she grew apace through all the stirring years, while her redoubtable father (of whom she was always inordinately proud) was sending to the beheading block the bulk of the distinguished company that had officiated at her baptismal orgy.

When death removed Henry the Eighth, Elizabeth had passed her thirteenth birthday. A gentleman of the court writes approvingly of her: "The Lady Elizabeth, which is at this time of the age of fourteen years, or thereabouts, is a very witty and gentle young lady." Gentle she did indeed show herself to be as long as her brother Edward ruled the land: the succeeding reign of her sister Mary called into play every atom of her superabundant wit. The reign of Edward the Sixth, which lasted from Elizabeth's fourteenth till her twentieth year, was the most charming part of her life. There was a tender affection between her and her young half-brother, both of whom lived like babes in the wood amid a flock of rascally, ambitious nobles. The boy king called her "his sweet sister Temperance"; she wrote him some of the nicest letters that a little princess ever composed, and she scribbled the name "Edward" lovingly over her exercise books.

The Tudors were a gifted lot; and Elizabeth had the best brain of them all, with a physique quite worthy of her father. "She was of admirable beauty," says Camden, "and well deserving a crown: of modest gravity, excellent wit, royal soul, happy memory, and indefatigably given to the study of learning; insomuch as before she was seventeen years of age, she understood well the Latin, French, and Italian tongues, and had an indifferent knowledge of the Greek. Neither did she neglect music so far as it became a princess, being able to sing sweetly and play handsomely on the lute." Her hair was "inclining to pale yellow" (she was "whiter" than the red-haired Queen of Scots); her eyes were black, and her nose "somewhat rising in the midst." As Bacon tells us: "She was tall of stature, of comely limbs, and excellent feature in her countenance. Majesty sat under the veil of sweetness, and her health was sound and prosperous."

Elizabeth's proficiency in languages was no joke or courtly fiction. Roger Ascham used it as a cudgel for the idle wits of the young gentlemen of the day: "It is your shame (I speak to you all, you young gentlemen of England) that one maid should go beyond you all in excellency of learning and knowledge of divers tongues. Point forth six of the best given gentlemen of this court, and all they together show not so much good will, spend not so much time, bestow not so many hours, daily, orderly, and constantly, for the increase of learning and knowledge as doth the Queen's majesty herself. Yea, I believe that, beside her perfect readiness in Latin, Italian, French, and Spanish, she readeth here now at Windsor more Greek every day than some prebendary of this church doth Latin in a whole week."

When her brother Edward died, in 1553, Elizabeth had fifty years more to live. The first five of these, during the reign of Mary, were spent in the acquirement of tenacity, tact, and worldly wisdom; and then—for over forty-four years—she ruled. Hardly was Mary seated on the throne, when Elizabeth was implicated in the Wyat rebellion, cross-examined and bullied, carried a prisoner to the Tower of London, and "ignominiously conducted through the Traitor's Gate." They got nothing out of her, and finally sent her to prison at Woodstock. Thence they dragged her back to court—at the suggestion of King Philip, it is said—and plagued her with demands that she change her religion. Elizabeth dissimulated, conciliated, and remained firm. One of the scenes reads like "Hamlet":

"One night, when it was late, the Princess was unexpectedly summoned and conducted by torchlight to the Queen's bedchamber; where she kneeled down before the Queen, declaring herself to be a most faithful and true subject. She even went so far as to request the Queen to send her some Catholic treatises, which might confirm her faith and inculcate doctrines different from those which she had been taught in the writings of the Reformers. The Queen seemed still to suspect her sincerity, but they parted on good terms. During this critical interview Philip had concealed himself behind the tapestry, that he might have seasonably interposed to prevent the violence of the Queen's passionate temper from proceeding to any extremities."

There were gentlemen behind the arras before Polonius. A week later Elizabeth was freed from most of her guards and permitted to retire to Hatfield, where she was astutely living when Queen Mary died. They who would learn to rule must first learn to obey. Imperious as Queen Elizabeth often showed herself to her subjects, the obedience she demanded was but child's play in comparison with that which she had herself rendered, with imperturbable tact and good-humor, during the three arbitrary and inconsistent reigns in which she grew up and acquired the lessons of discipline.

She was crowned in London, at the age of twenty-five, on January 14, 1559. Since her predecessor's death a month had been passed at Hatfield and in a leisurely progress to Westminster, and another month in preparation there. On the twelfth of January she crossed the Rubicon, or, in the language of the day, "shot London Bridge"

—that is, negotiated the dangerous arches. Holinshed brings this scene also to life:

"On Thursday, the twelfth of January, the Queen's majesty removed from her palace of Westminster by water unto the Tower of London. The Lord Mayor and aldermen in their barge, and all the citizens with their barges decked and trimmed with targets and banners of their mysteries, accordingly attend on her Grace. The bachelors' barge of the Lord Mayor's company—to wit, the mercers—had their barge with a foist [light galley] trimmed with three tops, and artillery aboard, gallantly appointed to wait upon them, shooting off lustily as they went with great and pleasant melody of instruments, which played in most sweet and heavenly manner. Her Grace shot the Bridge about two of the clock in the afternoon, at the still of the ebb, the Lord Mayor and the rest following after her barge, attending the same, till her Majesty took land at the privy stairs at the Tower Wharf."

Magnificent pageantry and every indication of genuine popular enthusiasm accompanied her coronation journey through London. Nor did her subjects omit the opportunity to point out to her allegorically the way in which they wished her to walk. "In a pageant erected near the Little Conduit in the upper end of Cheapside, an old man with a scythe and wings, representing Time, appeared, coming out of a hollow place or cave, leading another person all clad in white silk, gracefully apparelled, who represented Truth (the daughter of Time); which lady had a book in her hand, on which was written *Verbum Veritatis,* i.e., The Word of Truth. It was the Bible in English: which, after a speech made to the queen, Truth reached down towards her, which was taken and brought by a gentleman attending to her hands. As soon as she received it, she kissed it, and with both her hands held it up, and then laid it upon her breast, greatly thanking the City for that present, and said, *She would often read over that Book.*"

At this point she received also a purse containing a thousand marks in gold; in which case the intervention of the attending gentleman appears to have been unnecessary, for, we are told, "The Queen's majesty with both her hands took the purse," and answered the giver "marvelous pithily, and so pithily that the standers by, as they embraced entirely her gracious answer, so they marveled at the couching thereof, which was in words truly reported these:

" 'I thank my Lord Mayor, his brethren, and you all. And whereas your request is that I should continue your good Lady and Queen, be ye ensured that I will be as good unto you as ever Queen was to her people. No will in me can lack, neither do I trust shall there lack any power. And persuade yourselves that for the safety and quietness of you all I will not spare, if need be, to spend my blood. God thank you all!' "

Meantime she gave herself up to showy public entertainments, which after the gloom of Mary's reign pleased the Londoners as much as they satisfied the queen's renaissance tastes. On the following St. George's Day, April 23, she supped at the residence of the Earl of Pembroke; "and after supper she took a boat and was rowed up and down in the River Thames." For a time the staid metropolis became a second Venice, "hundreds of boats and barges rowing about her, and thousands of people thronging at the waterside to look upon her Majesty: rejoicing to see her, and partaking of the music and sights on the Thames; for the trumpets blew, drums beat, flutes played, guns were discharged, squibs hurled up into the air, as the Queen moved from place to place. And this continued till ten of the clock at night, when the Queen departed home. By these means, showing herself so freely and condescendingly unto her people, she made herself dear and acceptable unto them."

It was a merry England while she reigned. Plays flourished, as we know, and music was more native to the soil than ever since. One of her Puritanical subjects, writing in Latin, ventured to speak of her in 1563 as consuming days and nights in flirtations, hunting, hawking, choral shows, and ludicrous entertainments ("choreis et rebus ludicris"). A Spanish report, nearly forty years later, contains one sardonic sentence which may well have raised a wonder in Castilian minds beyond even what the Armada had instilled: "The head of the church of England and Ireland was to be seen in her old age dancing three or four galliards."

Deerslaying, with crossbow and arrow, was a major passion; and those whom she delighted to honor profited by the fruits of her marksmanship—though often (as was usual when she condescended) not without embarrassment. Her loyal henchman, Robin of Leicester, was rather put to it when commanded to deliver to Archbishop Parker of Canterbury a stag she had killed at Windsor on a hot September second. The ingenious Dudley met the situation like a statesman, and thus he writes to Parker:

"My Lord: The Queen's Majesty being abroad hunting yesterday in the forest, and having had very good hap besides great sport, she hath thought good to remember your Grace with part of her prey, and so commanded me to send you from her Highness a great and fat stag killed with her own hand; which, because the weather was hot, and the deer somewhat chafed and dangerous to be carried so far without some help, I caused him to be *parboiled* in this sort for the better preservation of him —which I doubt not but shall cause him to come unto you as I would be glad he should."—If no longer handsome, we may hope that the queen's gift was still worthy the digestion of an archbishop when he arrived.

Elizabeth's bashfulness was famous and unique. Young Gilbert Talbot, son of the Earl of Shrewsbury, wrote to his father of an episode that occurred on the May Day when the queen was forty-four and Gilbert twenty-four: "In the morning, about eight of the clock, I happened to walk in the tilt-yard, under the gallery where her Majesty useth to stand to see the running at tilt; where by chance she was, and looking out of the window; my eye was full towards her, and she showed to be greatly ashamed thereof, for that she was unready and in her night-stuff. So when she saw me at after dinner, as she went to walk, she gave me a great fillip on the forehead and told my Lord Chamberlain, who was the next to her, how I had seen her that morning, and how much ashamed thereof she was."

There can be no question that Gilbert loved the old lady ever after, nor doubted that she was every inch a queen. The mottoes that Spenser places around the walls of Busirane's castle were what Elizabeth taught all Englishmen to see about her presence: "Be bold!" "Be bold!" *"Be not too bold!"* The one certain thing is that her subjects loved her, and that, indeed, to love her was a liberal education.

Temptingly formidable at home, Elizabeth was doubly so when she travelled—and she travelled, of course, incessantly, though she was never off English soil. Her "progresses" were not the least ingenious development of her statesmanship. They amounted to a super-tax, by which the wealthy contributed to the expenses of the

court; for regular taxes under Elizabeth were moderate
and by no means rigorously collected. What more was
needed for governmental purposes was largely defrayed
by the remarkable succession of public-spirited men to
whom she entrusted the direction of the various departments. The excess cost of maintaining the royal court
itself came from the well-filled purses of the nobles and
gentry among whom she "progressed" some six months
in the year. It was hard work for the queen, this gypsy
life, though she did it *con amore;* but it taught her to
know England from Dover to Berwick, and it inevitably
brought culture and a sense of public affairs into the
citadels of Bourbon insularity.

Of course, the country magnates, whose hospitality the
queen and her multitudinous court elected to enjoy, were
beset by many emotions. There was pride over the distinction conferred, anxiety over the success of the visit,
inward ruefulness at thought of what the entertainment
would cost, and loud exclamations over the difficulties of
assembling enough food for the throng. When Lord Buckhurst, author of "Gorboduc," a considerable favorite of
Elizabeth and one of the wealthiest men in England, ap-
prehended a visit in 1577, he was moved to write in terms
like these to the Lord Chamberlain, who arranged the details of the progresses: "That he beseeched his Lordship
to pardon him that he became troublesome unto him, to
know some certainty of the Progress, if it might possibly be; the time of provision was so short and the desire
he had to do all things in such sort as appertained so great,
as he could not but thus importune his Lordship to procure her Highness to grow to some resolution, both of the
time when her Majesty would be at Lewes, and how long
her Highness would stay there. For that, he having already sent into Kent, Surrey, and Sussex for provision,

he assured his Lordship he found all places possessed by
my Lord of Arundel, my Lord Montagu, and others
[that is, other expectant and foresighted hosts] ; so as of
force he was to send into Flanders, which he would speed-
ily do, if the time of her Majesty's coming and tarriance
with him were certain."

Nichols, the guileless Georgian laureate of Elizabeth's
progresses, introduces this with the statement: "The Lord
Buckhurst in particular was very desirous to entertain
her at his house in Sussex." Was he? Henry Goring, Esq.,
of Burton in Sussex, writes in unconcealed apprehension
to his old friend, Sir William More of Loseley, that,
"hearing the Queen has lain two nights at Loseley, and intended to lie two nights at his house in Sussex," he wishes
to know how he is to entertain her; "whether she brings
her own stuff, beer, and other provisions, or whether Sir
William provided every part." The answer doubtless was
that ordinarily the queen provided very little, though she
did show, on the whole, a judicious discrimination in her
demands and knew how to temper the wind of her favor
to the shorn host.

It is said that when Queen Victoria visited her subjects
—far more rarely, and less numerously attended—a chief
object of anxiety was the quality of the royal rice pudding. With Elizabeth it was the beer that made most
trouble. When she visited Cambridge in 1564, she was so
much pleased by the academic entertainment that she
stayed a day longer than had been intended; "and a saying was, if provision of beer and ale could have been
made, her Grace would have remained till Friday." On
another occasion the beer was found unsatisfactory, and
the resulting displeasure excited her *fidus Achates,* Leicester, out of all care for his h's. "Hit," as he reported to
Burghley, "did put her very far out of temper and almost

all the company beside." However, a better brew had been discovered, and "God be thanked, she is now perfectly well and merry."

The "Sayings of Queen Elizabeth," lately collected by Mr. Chamberlain, are in part as apocryphal, doubtless, as the once famous "Sayings of King Alfred"; but there are some which are authentically documented and have the authentic ring. Thus she admonished her judges: "Have a care over my people. You have my people: do you that which I ought to do. They are my people. Every man oppresseth and spoileth them without mercy: they cannot revenge their quarrel nor help themselves. See unto them; see unto them, for they are my charge. I charge you, even as God hath charged me. I care not for myself: my life is not dear to me; my care is for my people. I pray God, whosoever succeedeth me be as careful of them as I am."

To Philip the Second she is reported to have written concerning his rebellious Dutch subjects: "What does it matter to your Majesty, if they go to the devil in their own way?" Her vanity, intellectuality, and heroism are all illustrated by the words she is said to have spoken to the Archbishop of St. Andrew's, when the Scots were threatening her: "I am more afraid of making a fault in my Latin than of the Kings of Spain, France, Scotland, the whole House of Guise, and all of their confederates."

And so she passes down the ages, not perhaps the imperial votaress that Shakespeare saw "in maiden meditation fancy-free," but surely as fascinating and inscrutable as Mona Lisa. She has been charged with all the moral and political vices—with nearly all the frailties of her sex and species. All her good qualities, except her courage and her love of the English people, can be plausibly impugned; but nothing can yet be proved against her.

A woman who for seventy years stood on as slippery footing as mortals have often trod, at the most perilous post in one of the most perilous ages of the world, exposed to the scandal, intrigues, and prying, not of a nation, but of a continent—the ambiguous queen continues to smile down the truth of Antony's saying,

> The evil that men do lives after them,
> The good is oft interred with their bones.

The good that Elizabeth did has not yet been interred with her bones: the unexampled achievements of her reign are still the heritage of her nation and one of the truisms of history. Ten years after she was dead and buried, when an alien dynasty was settled on her throne, John Fletcher (in the play called Shakespeare's "Henry VIII") dramatized the scene of her baptism, with which I began this essay, and he put into the mouth of the officiating Archbishop a prophetic recapitulation of the queen's achievements:

> . . . Let me speak, sir,
> For Heaven now bids me; and the words I utter
> Let none think flattery, for they'll find 'em truth.
> This royal infant—Heaven still move about her!—
> Though in her cradle, yet now promises
> Upon this land a thousand thousand blessings,
> Which time shall bring to ripeness. . . .
> She shall be lov'd and fear'd: her own shall bless her;
> Her foes shake like a field of beaten corn,
> And hang their heads with sorrow. Good grows with her.
> In her days every man shall eat in safety,
> Under his own vine, what he plants, and sing
> The merry songs of peace to all his neighbours.

If Elizabeth did evil, it is so far from living after her that to this day the suspicion of it has not crept beyond the twilit limbo of discredited gossip. Froude employed volumes in an effort to disprove her greatness as a sovereign, to present her as a meddling and inconstant marplot, hindering the schemes of her great agents, Burghley, Walsingham, and Drake. And for this, most of all his sins, the brilliant and captivating Froude is to-day rejected of historians. If Elizabeth lacked political wisdom, one may well ask, by what unparalleled luck did she keep herself surrounded by such a succession of able ministers, so arduously and self-sacrificingly zealous in working out her policies? To explain why none who knew her doubted her fitness for her throne, one need but quote a couple more of her sayings. When Parliament was eager to force its policies upon her, she answered: "I am your anointed Queen. I will never be by violence constrained to do *anything*. I thank God, I am endued with such qualities that if I were turned out of the Realm in my petticoat, I were able to live in any place in Christendom." And to one of the sanest and truest of her servants, the Lord Keeper Bacon, she remarked in the difficult middle years of her reign: "I have followed your advice, these two years past, in all the affairs of my kingdom, and I have seen nothing but trouble, expense, and danger. From this hour, for the same length of time, I am going to follow my own opinion, and see if I find I do any better." It hardly matters whether or not we can to-day prove that these were indeed the great queen's *ipsissima verba:* it is enough that they were the words which the age that knew her best thought it characteristic of her to utter.

Elizabeth's love affairs and flirtations were always notorious, and were meant to be so. They were part of her nature and part of her diplomacy. There was the strange girlhood affair with Admiral Seymour, and the succeeding affairs with Leicester, Alençon, Ralegh, Essex, and Hatton. One would like to believe her unchaste, in order to believe her human, in order to lessen the oppressiveness of her mystery. In logic, she must have been. How singular that all the public inquiry she was perpetually challenging, all the private papers of foreign ambassadors and spies, and all the research of historians have left the hypothesis of her virginity still unrefuted! Mr. Frederick Chamberlin, whose examination into the "Private Character of Queen Elizabeth" has recently aroused some interest, admits that he began his studies with extraordinarily liberal assumptions of guilt. "I had never doubted," he says, "that Elizabeth was the mistress of Leicester, of Essex, of Ralegh, of Hatton, &c." His investigations, however, forced him to a surprising change of front, resulting in the conclusion that Elizabeth had been virtuous because of lifelong debility. Debility, indeed! Another biologic endorsement of the queen's purity, more credible in character, figures in the gossip with which Ben Jonson entertained Drummond of Hawthornden in 1618; but the merest gossip it remains, unfounded and unlikely, though natural enough to be invented out of the circumstance of her celibacy. The opinion of good historians, which was voiced over twenty years ago at the conclusion of Mr. Martin Hume's book on "The Courtships of Queen Elizabeth," still stands: "All the love affairs that we have glanced at in their non-political aspect were but the solace of a great governing genius, who was supremely vain. Though they were accompanied by circumstances which were reprehensible, undignified and indelicate for any virtuous woman, much less a Queen, the arguments and evidence that I have been able to adduce should lead, in my opinion, to the delivery of a verdict of non-proven on the generally believed main charge against the Queen of actual immorality."

And so again she eludes us. The Virgin Queen! The

despair of skeptics, the shame of the historical mud-slinger. After three centuries, and despite some of the worst atrocities of modern historiography, her queenliness remains, and her virginity is still—where it was. With whom are we to match her? With whom but with the man of Stratford, the greatest of all her subjects, her mightiest colleague in building the age we know alternatively by both their names? Shakespeare, too, stands garbed in dubiety, fretted and pursued by modern Guildensterns, who would fain uncrown him, "would seem to know" his "stops," "would pluck out the heart of" his "mystery." At the end there are no better words to apply to Elizabeth than those Arnold addressed to her poet:

> Others abide our question. Thou art free.
> We ask and ask: Thou smilest and art still,
> Out-topping knowledge.